THE NIGHT IS FAR SPENT

'THE NIGHT IS FAR SPENT,

A TREASURY OF
THOMAS HOWARD

Selected by Vivian W. Dudro

IGNATIUS PRESS   SAN FRANCISCO

All Scripture quotations are from the
King James Version of the Bible
unless otherwise noted.

Cover photograph by Richard Livingston

Cover design by John Herreid

© 2007 Ignatius Press, San Francisco
All rights reserved
ISBN 978-1-58617-132-2
ISBN 1-58617-132-1
Library of Congress Control Number 2005929141
Printed in the United States of America ♾

CONTENTS

THINGS LITERARY AND LITERARY MEN

On Fictions and Gospel   3

Beowulf and Company   13

Of Towers and Wardrobes   25

C. S. Lewis and the Sanctified Imagination   39

The Life and Legacy of C. S. Lewis   56

The Wages of Reading   74

Brideshead Revisited Revisited   82

Ave, Muggeridge   96

A Portrait of Dietrich von Hildebrand   108

Light on Charles Williams   125

Perplexity in the Edgeware Road: A Note on T. S.
   Eliot   134

Let Us Purify the Dialect of the Tribe   145

The Catholic Angler   154

THINGS SACRED

The Power of Wise Custom   175

The Image of the Cross   184

What Is a Sacrament? Part I   196

What Is a Sacrament? Part II   208

Saint Joseph   221

Catholic Spirituality   226

On Brazen Heavens   239

Ascension   246

Recognizing the Church: A Personal Pilgrimage and
    the Discovery of Five Marks of the Church   250

The Touchstone of Orthodoxy   268

EXISTING THINGS: SELF, SOCIETY, GOD

Who Am I? Who Am I?   281

Ballet and Gender   292

To Bear My Father's Name: An Awesome Honor   296

The Yoke of Fatherhood   306

Family Worship   319

Notes Upon Hearing Handel's *Coronation Anthems*   325

Christian Studies: Anachronism or Salvation?   332

Being Forgotten   349

THINGS LITERARY AND
LITERARY MEN

ON FICTIONS AND GOSPEL

When I was a small boy my mother used to sing a certain song to me as she had done for all of my older brothers and sisters. It went this way:

> Hush my baby, do not cry,
> Five brave knights go riding by.
> One is dressed in bonny blue,
> He's the leader strong and true.
> One in crimson bright is dressed,
> With a star upon his breast . . .

That song represents my own earliest experience of the power of narrative. To this day some chord is struck in the depths of my being by those words. The picture conjured in my imagination is of a very dark forest of conifers at twilight, and of the knights approaching across a green meadow toward a castle where I watch them from an open casement window of leaded glass and stone mullions.

Something was awakened in me by those words—some capacity to yearn, I think, for purity, and for courtesy, and for fidelity and valor and gentility, and also, perhaps, some notion that mystery arches over our little life like the crepuscular light suffusing that scene.

Lecture given in a slightly different form on January 9, 2004.

There is a strange power in words to call to us mortals, and to summon us, as it were. Anyone who has ever himself been a child to whom stories were read or sung knows that the whole point of stories, from *Peter Rabbit* to *War and Peace*, is to summon us.

Summon us to what? The answer here would lie along some such line as this, surely, that all words, spoken or written, have as their task to call us from mere silence and solitude to some sort of participation in the real world. The first words spoken to us by our mothers and fathers when we are mere burbling infants, have everything to do with introducing us into this world of other selves, and of food and drink and play and love and relationships, as over against the solitude and tranquility and repose and safety and silence of the only world we have ever known up until then, namely, the womb. And the first words we attempt, even our shrieks in the delivery room, acknowledge that we are not alone. There is something out there.

But do not *Peter Rabbit* and *War and Peace* summon us away from reality and off into an imaginary world? To be sure, Tolstoy's vast work is about the real world, if by that we mean Russia in the time of Napoleon, but for us now, that world is not much closer to our ordinary circumstances than is Peter Rabbit's. We do not often find ourselves at glittering cotillions in cavernous ballrooms lighted by thousands of candles and waited upon by liveried footmen and studded with grand duchesses and field marshals. Actually, Peter's humdrum circumstances are probably closer to our own world of errands and gardens and small disobediences than are the circumstances of Tolstoy's characters.

But the objection could be raised against both of these tales, and against all fiction, that they siphon us away from present actuality and tempt us to dawdle in merely imaginary byways.

It may be nice to turn from the hurly-burly of the market-place, or from the interstate, or the office, and to relax in a bit of once-upon-a-time, but no one will argue, surely, that this represents anything more than an escape from reality—perhaps even an indulgence we permit ourselves briefly before we return to our knitting, so to speak.

All of this is true. But there is also a sense in which story lies close to the center of the mystery of our existence. Mortal life is a mystery of course. What is it all *about*, we wonder. What are we to make of our odd situation, we who share flesh and blood with the animals, but who are hag-ridden with notions of immortality and grandeur, and who cannot ever quite accede to the sentence of certain death that hangs over us? All of us are beleaguered from time to time, especially when things are not going well, with the bald fact that, in spite of all the excellences that seem to crown our human life—our intellect, our will, our imagination, our capacity for laughter and generosity, and our enormous achievements—in spite of all of that, our life hangs by the merest gossamer filament. Anything can snip it without a moment's warning. King Lear found himself bemused by the irony that all of this grace and beauty and dignity that we call humanness should be snuffed out while mere beasts go on living. "Why should a dog, a horse, a rat, have life, / And thou no breath at all?" (IV, iii, 307), he asks, addressing the dead body of his beloved daughter Cordelia, which he carries in his arms. Who of us has not asked some such question?

But returning to the notion that storytelling may lie close to the center, we might wonder. The serious business of life has always entailed things like earning our bread and raising our families and fighting for our country and generally attending to the business of simply keeping going.

Storytelling, surely, would be out on the margin somewhere, along with dancing and playing the flute and painting pretty pictures.

But this is where we need to think twice. If we do (think
twice), we will come upon an interesting thing, namely,
that from the beginning of history—nay, from before the
centuries chronicled in what we call historical records: from
the times lost in the mists of mythology—we mortals have
been telling stories, and dancing, and carving, and painting, and singing. No matter what woolly mammoths and
saber-toothed tigers prowled outside the cave, no matter
what Huns or what Norsemen harried our gates, no matter
what Black Plagues decimated our cities and what famines
emptied our granaries—in spite of all, we kept at it. What
sort of creature are we, that, when we can scarcely keep
body and soul together and find food for our children's
mouths, we have nevertheless lived our lives in the midst of
song and dance, as it were?

From the Christian point of view, this oddity, observable
in all tribes, cultures, societies, and civilizations from the
beginning, may hint that we are aware of ourselves living
in a story. The formula "Once upon a time" is as good a
formula for our own story as it is for a fairy tale. There
probably has never been found a better way to begin a narrative. When you hear these words your imagination poises
itself. Aha—what will we encounter now? Will we find
ourselves drawn into the affairs of a family of rabbits who
lived in a wood not far from the garden of one McGregor?
Or will it be an ancient king whose knights pledged themselves to defend purity and virtue, some of whom saw the
Holy Grail and some of whom blundered into concupiscence? Or will it be young Copperfield whose life was made
miserable by the tyranny of Mr. and Miss Murdstone?

Perhaps it will be Scrooge who had so much to learn about generosity. Or Huckleberry Finn floating down the Mississippi on his raft, apparently detached in his soul as well as in his circumstances from the ordinary suppositions of life along the banks of that river.

The odd thing about all of these stories is that we cannot seem to get very far in them without finding our sleeves being plucked by the hint that we are reading about ourselves. Oh, we are not rabbits, to be sure, but who of us has not at some point tried disobedience as a way of getting some goody or other that did not seem promised to those who stayed in the well-trodden and lawful ruts? And we are not David Copperfield, but who of us has not known the forlornness that can overwhelm one when circumstances seem grimly marshaled against one? And we certainly are not King Arthur, but which of us has not wished that we could organize things so that greed and perfidy and treachery were banished, and purity and charity and rectitude guarded?

Somehow or other these tales ring bells for us. What is the genius of westerns? Is it not at least partly that we can see the struggle between good and evil dramatized in clear and exciting terms, with the Good Guys and the Bad Guys unmistakably identifiable, and the pounding of horses' hooves up and down those rocky gulches and mesas beating out a brisk tattoo as an accompaniment to our aroused anxiety that the Good Guys will win?

For most of us the conflict with evil does not commonly come down to our being obliged to stalk alone down a sandy main street between store fronts with the locals lounging on the stoops lining the street and the Bad Guy sauntering toward us with his hand hovering near the butt of the pistol just visible from the holster dangling from a wide, loose leather belt. It is much more likely to present itself to me in the form of a choice between letting a slightly derogatory remark about someone slip from my lips or refraining from saying it. My struggle is never as colorful and heroic as John Wayne's always seems to be. It's very humdrum, this business of moving along through life, trying to make a thousand small choices every day in behalf of charity, and at the same time fending off all the cleverly veiled impulses activating themselves in behalf of my ego at the expense of my neighbor. And yet there is no mistaking it: there is a recognizable echo of my own paltry efforts at goodness in the figure of John Wayne so bravely and crustily championing the good in the Wild West.

Do we not see in all good narrative the drama in which nothing finally matters but that the protagonist become such and such a kind of person? By the choices he makes, and the habits I form (let us shift to the first person), and the attitudes I permit to preside in my inner man, and the words I permit my lips to utter—by all of these things—I am, day in and day out, opting either for generosity, courtesy, peaceableness, humility, and good cheer, or for parsimony and sullenness and boorishness and cynicism. In a word, for good or for evil.

That seems to be raising the stakes quite high quite suddenly. Surely we cannot be reaching for all of this moral vocabulary every time we put up our feet to read a story?

No. The point of stories is enjoyment—even *Oedipus* and *War and Peace*. But stories do, in fact, echo our real-life situations. One way or another, everything does come down, in the end, to a very few issues: humility versus pride; peaceableness versus strife; generosity versus parsimony; fidelity versus perfidiousness; good cheer versus wrath; purity versus squalor in the inner man. And of course even that list can be boiled down to one contrast: love versus unlove. Heaven versus hell.

Once again it would seem that this is to raise the stakes too high. Heaven and hell? How did we arrive at this alarming juncture?

We got there not by setting out on a journey for some remote place, but by opening our eyes to where we are. This is the paradox about stories: they seem to lead us away into imaginary regions, but they have an unsettling way of discovering for us the immediate place where we are.

It is this way with the truest Story of all, the narrative that begins so hauntingly with the words, "In the beginning God created the heavens and the earth. And the earth was without form, and void; and darkness was upon the face of the deep. And the Spirit of God moved upon the face of the waters. And God said, Let there be light: and there was light" (Gen 1:1ff.).

Nothing could be more remote from our daily circumstances than that. But what is that Story about? Presently we find two characters on stage. All is well. No mortgage payments. No medical insurance complexities. No investment portfolio. No gold cards and GREs and IRAs and migraines and cat-scans and cavities. All is well in Eden. But then a choice presents itself. Why not try this fruit here? Why not try writing our own script just for a change? Why not add a small salting of *risk* to the recipe?

And we find that we cannot read very far in the Story without admitting that it is indeed the story of our life. On page after page we find that we are deprived of the luxury of thinking, "Aha! Look at the trouble Adam and Eve, or Cain, got themselves into. I would never do that."

Alack. It is not a matter of whether or not I would: I have. A thousand times I have murdered my brother.

Perhaps not with a rock in a field. But by a small remark in someone's ear, or the lift of an eyebrow, that has for its effect some diminishing of my brother in someone's estimation. Or by a snide or cutting or discourteous remark to my brother himself.

Somehow, oddly, the Story seems to be piercing right to the marrow; and then I remember a memory verse from my childhood in a Fundamentalist Sunday school: "For the Word of God is quick, and powerful, and sharper than any two-edged sword, piercing even to the dividing asunder . . . of the joints and marrow, and is a discerner of the thoughts and intents of the heart" (Heb 4:12).

I read about the Tower of Babel and find myself facing my own efforts to replace God with something of my own constructing. I read about Noah and wish I could identify myself with his fidelity and courage and faith, but I find I am more like the people in his world: busy, busy, busy, with this and that, and not at all disposed to offer the pure obedience of my heart to the Most High. I read about Abraham and Isaac and Jacob, and I find that all those cross-currents of obedience versus disobedience eddying back and forth across the pages of their story seem disquietingly familiar. Or Moses. I wish I could identify more easily with that man. But it is easier to see myself in the other characters—the grumbling, perfidious, recalcitrant, querulous, idolatrous Israelites with whom Moses had to cope year after bone-wearying year.

Those stories are true. But they are true on a level deeper than the merely moral or symbolic. In the Bible we have the Story of stories, so to speak—the Story that was played out on the light-of-day stage of actual history, not in a never-never land such as you find in your Greek myths, your Norse myths, and your fairy tales. The God of the Bible Story is the God who made this earth that we live on, and that all men have lived on, and up and down whose hills and valleys the feet of all men have been obliged to tread since the beginning, including the feet of the One who came to us when we had left the path laid out for us by the Most High, and who summoned us back with, "I am the Way, the Truth, and the Life" (Jn 14:6).

At Mass we recite the Nicene Creed. That Creed, in an old translation, speaks of this One who came to us:

... Who for us men, and for our salvation, came down
  from heaven,
And was incarnate by the Holy Ghost of the Virgin Mary,
And was made man.
And was crucified also for us under Pontius Pilate.

Sub Pontio Pilato. Why that? How odd, that in the middle of the mightiest mysteries of all, we find the name of a bureaucrat. But the Church was wise to put that bit of information in there. It says to us all that this Story is not a fairy tale. It was played out on the real stage of our own history. There was a Roman governor in Judea named Pontius Pilate. It was he who made the decision to hand Jesus Christ over to those who crucified him.

How can it be that the will of God is so tangled up with petty details like this? Injustice piled upon petty injustice. Is it not that the Savior who appears in that Story, complete with stable and manger, angels and shepherds, kings from the East, and wine at Cana, a boat in a storm on the lake and the house at Bethany, and Jerusalem and Pilate and Annas and Caiaphas and John the Baptist and Peter—is it not that that Savior is the protagonist in this Story of all stories, which is our story?

It may be that the formula "once upon a time", so enchanting to small children, and to us insofar as we have

not become besotted and jaded, touches with great delicacy and accuracy upon something that is of the essence of
our mortal existence, namely, that it is played out as story.
And, as the early Fathers will have it of the biblical narrative, this story of ours may be understood on the literal
level (I must travel in connection with my work), the alle-
gorical (my journey takes me further and further into Christ),
the tropological (my soul is being configured to Christ),
and the anagogical (the denouement of my story is the
Beatific Vision, which, God grant, I may approach one day).

Beowulf and Company

What with Frodo and Gandalf, not to mention Sauron, Shelob, and the Balrog, we are all in an excellent frame of mind to reread *Beowulf*. A few readers may blanch here, their schooling having somehow, oddly, omitted the reading of this epic, but that is easily remedied. There are lots of modern English versions of this poem, which was written down in Anglo-Saxon, or, as the scholars prefer to say, Old English.

The mention of *Beowulf*, of course, raises two questions: first, what has that long poem got to do with us? and second, when was it written? It is possible that one or two readers may find that their grasp of early British history has slackened a bit since their schooldays and might need to be tightened.

Beowulf may serve as a sort of eponymous title for the whole mass of literature that arose in Britain during the millennium following Julius Caesar's foray there in B.C. 55. And before any beady-eyed reader shouts, "But *Beowulf* has nothing to do with British, or English, lore!" let us agree, and continue.

But first, a dash through the centuries leading us into the era of the literature that constitutes our topic here (and yes, it is of great interest to Catholic readers). Ordinarily, English history, or, for more exacting readers, British history

This was an unpublished article originally written for *The St. Austin Review*.

(they weren't *English* until A.D. 449) gets going with Caesar's landing in B.C. 55. He didn't stay, but in A.D. 43, Claudius sent a Roman expedition, and stayed. The Romans found things a bit sticky from time to time, most notably from Queen Boudicca (she is our friend Boadicea, but that is a wrong rendering of her name) who in A.D. 61 roused the Iceni to oust the Romans—unsuccessfully, it may be pointed out. The great Roman general Agricola confirmed Roman rule in A.D. 78, and Hadrian built his famous wall from the Solway to the Tyne in A.D. 120 in order to keep out the ungovernable Picts from the north.

But, as seems to be the fate of all empires, things eventually crumbled. The Visigoths, Ostrogoths, Alans, Sueves, and Burgundians made themselves obstreperous over on the continent, and Rome had to withdraw her legions from Britain in the fifth century in order to defend Rome itself (they failed, as it turned out). Back up in Britain, which unbeknownst to itself was about to become England, Hengist and Horsa scoured across the North Sea with fire and sword in A.D. 449, drove the poor Celts up and back into Scotland, Wales, Ireland, Cornwall, and Brittany (or Armorica), and thus was born Angle-land, thanks to the two H's.

This is all most interesting, of course, but it does not bring us particularly close to the question with which I began. There were a few Catholic Romans sprinkled amongst the legions, most notably Saint Alban, the *protomartyr Anglorum* (who wasn't an Angle). He "shed [his] life-blood for Christ at this time" (A.D. 301), says the Venerable Bede (and more on *him* anon) because he gave shelter to a Christian priest who was harried by pagan marauders. Alban was impressed by this priest's prayers and courage, and converted to the Faith. When the pursuing soldiers arrived, Alban hid the priest and gave himself up in his place and was martyred. Bede says, "And although he had not received the purification of baptism, there was no doubt that he was cleansed by the shedding of his own blood, and rendered fit to enter the kingdom of heaven."

Quickly to finish off this dash through the history that surrounds the writings we are about to consider, we may point out that in A.D. 597, Pope Gregory the Great sent Augustine (the *other* Augustine, that is) up to Kent at the invitation of the Christian Queen Bertha, whose husband Ethelbert was a most redoubtable heathen. Augustine managed to convert the king, and the king saw to it that the whole of Kent, more or less, was baptized. Before long England began to send missionaries abroad: Paulinus from Northumbria went to the continent; and, from Ireland, Columban went to Brittany and Columba to Iona; and Oswald, a Northumbrian prince, asked for a bishop in the seventh century, which resulted in Saint Aidan's being sent from Iona to the isle of Lindisfarne, which community had an incalculable influence on English, and, a fortiori, Western, Christendom. Incidentally, the justly famous Lindisfarne Gospels were written there, in Latin, in the lovely uncial script that Tolkien copied to some extent as the script for at least one of his mythic languages. Bishop Eadfrid was responsible for this, and it was copied in honor of Saint Cuthbert. In A.D. 664, the Council of Whitby settled the business of the date of Easter, which might, at a cursory glance, seem to be a bit pettifogging, but it was this decision that ended the tug-of-war in England between the authority of the Celtic Church and the Roman Church. Rome won.

Now. What about all the writings arising from this epoch, and wherein lies their interest for modern Catholic readers?

The writings tell their own story. The most famous of them all is, of course, *Beowulf*. I predict that we will have a movie on this admirable man before long. His story is "the English epic", but as is the case with everything English, it is all shot through with ironies that bother no Englishman. For a start,

Beowulf wasn't English and never went to England. He was a "Geat"—one of the Danish tribes. The whole story takes place somewhere over in those parts. But England's claim to Beowulf rests on the fact that the oral tale was finally written down in eighth-century Northumbrian, and the only surviving manuscript we have is in tenth-century West Saxon. (There were seven little kingdoms back then, including Wessex, of which Prince Edward is earl now, and where Alfred ruled, and where even Arthur [maybe] was king, or at least *dux bellorum*, if we may trust an old manuscript.)

Scholars argue, not very hotly, over the "Christian" elements in *Beowulf*. The whole story of this bearlike hero's fight with the devilish monster Grendel, and with Grendel's even more frightening "dam" (which is another way to say his mother—this attractive duo lived at the bottom of a mere), and finally with your archetypal dragon who sat on a pile of gold and jewels and killed Beowulf—the whole story has the flavor of pagan Nordic legend. Fate (or *wyrd* as they called it) seems to control things, but, sprinkled through the manuscript are references to "the All-Father" and to sin, judgment, hell, and providence, which make you wonder if the *scop* (the poet who started it all by singing the lines to some king in his mead hall) had overheard some Christian missionary-monk preaching the Gospel somewhere. Somehow or other the Old Testament got into it, since Grendel turns out to be of the race of Cain, who was certainly *not* a Nordic figure. Some of the curses thrown out end with "until doomsday", an expression with biblical origins. Some scholars even speak of a "softer" (i.e., Christian) flavor suffusing the whole thing, since altruism, gratitude, moderation, and a certain refinement seem to be operative. These could all be Greek, except there were no Greek missionaries about up there, whereas there *were* Christians.

Then there was a monk called Gildas, a Briton not a
Saxon, who in the sixth century wrote a treatise entitled
De Excidio et Conquestu Brittanniae (On the destruction and
conquest of Britain), in which he excoriates his country-
men for their idolatry and pusillanimity. He draws on Scripture, Eusebius of Caesarea's history, Saint Jerome, and the
fifth-century, Spanish priest-historian Orosius. He sounds
like John the Baptist, belaboring "this island, stiff-necked
and stubborn-minded . . . ungrateful rebels, sometimes against
God", refusing "to show fear to God. . . . Nor shall I enu-
merate those diabolical idols of my country, which almost
surpassed in number those of Egypt." [1] And all of this in
spite of the fact that "these islands, stiff with cold and
frost, [had] received the beams of light, that is, the holy
precepts of Christ, the true Sun. . . . These rays of light
were received with lukewarm minds by the inhabitants"
(ibid.). But, because of the Diocletian persecution, "all
Christ's young disciples, after so long and wintry a night,
began to behold the genial light of heaven. They rebuild
the churches . . . festivals are celebrated and sacraments
received with clean hearts and lips, and all the church's sons
rejoice as it were in the fostering bosom of a mother" (ibid.).
Gildas is a bit of a theologian, taking a swipe at the Arian
heresy: "fatal as a serpent, and vomiting its poison from
beyond the sea" (ibid., 65). Like Israel, Gildas' Britons were
fickle and incorrigible. They *would* keep reverting to idolatry, "and with it grew up every kind of luxury and
licentiousness . . . and in particular that hatred of truth [and]
the love of darkness instead of the sun, the admission of
Satan as an angel of light" (ibid., 67). The laity were not

<hr>

[1] Gildas, *De excidio et conquestu Brittanniae*, in *The Literature of Medieval
England*, ed. D. W. Robertson (New York: McGraw Hill Book Co., 1970),
62.

the only guilty ones: "Our Lord's own flock and its shepherds, who ought to have been an example to the people, slumbered away their time in drunkenness" (ibid.). He deplores the disastrous error of the Celtic king Vortigern who "sealed its [Britain's] doom by inviting in among them (like wolves into the sheepfold), the fierce and impious Saxons, a race hateful both to God and men. . . . Nothing was ever so pernicious to our country, nothing was ever so unlucky" (ibid.).

Well, perhaps enough of Gildas (who wrote in Latin, by the way, but he is cited as being among the early English writers).

There is a lovely vignette, scarcely to be included in our "literature", but nevertheless a poignant fragment of prose. Edwin, king of Northumbria, in the early seventh century, had a Christian wife who, when she married Edwin, brought with her from Kent one Paulinus who had been sent from Rome to succeed our friend Augustine, the first archbishop of Canterbury. Paulinus, a bishop, tried hard to convert Edwin. During one of the sessions where the king would listen, one of the chieftains present, clearly impressed by Paulinus' message, volunteered this:

> The present life of Man, O King, seems to me, in comparison of that time which is unknown to us, like to the swift flight of a sparrow through the room wherein you sit at supper in winter . . . whilst the storms of rain and snow prevail abroad. The sparrow, I say, flying in at one door, and immediately out at another, whilst he is within is safe from the wintry storm; but after a short space of fair weather, he immediately vanishes out of your sight, from one winter to another. So this life of Man appears for a short space, but of what went before, or what is to follow, we are utterly ignorant.[2]

[2] See Bede, *A History of the English Church and People*, ed. and trans. Leo Sherly-Price (Harmondsworth, Sussex, England: Penguin Books, 1968), 127.

Edwin's subjects responded eagerly to Paulinus' preaching, and thousands of them were baptized, including (presumably) Edwin, since henceforth in his kingdom, "a woman with her new-born babe might walk through the island, from sea to sea, without receiving any harm" (ibid., 132). The Pope made Paulinus the first archbishop of York.

We come now to by far the best-known writer in these islands from those centuries, namely, the Venerable Bede. He lived across the divide between the seventh and eighth centuries and was a monk at Wearmouth under the famous Benedict Biscop (not to be confused with Benedict of Nursia, the father of Western monasticism). Again, he wrote his monumental *History of the English Church and People* in Latin, but no one grudges England's claim to Bede. D. W. Robertson, a great scholar of this period, designates this category of England's writings as "Anglo-Latin literature".

Bede covers everything, from the days of the Brythonic Celts long before Julius Caesar, right up to his own day (he died in 735 or thereabouts). His book, easily available in a Penguin paperback, is so glorious and so engaging that it deserves to be widely read. Let us just say here that Catholic readers will find themselves dancing with joy at nearly every paragraph Bede writes. For him, as for any good Catholic, there is a very low threshold between the "historical" and the "miraculous". That is a modern, secularist distinction. He just plows along like the Gospel writers, telling all and never flinching.

To mention just four more Anglo-Latin writers, we may touch, with the most extreme exiguity, on Boniface, Alcuin, John the Scot, and Asser. One may only hope that the very brevity of our treatment here might whet some reader's appetite and turn him to pursue some readings in the works of these gentlemen.

Saint Boniface was the great English missionary to what we now call Germany, taking up residence at Fulda. His

pastoral letters make splendid reading. "To my dear friend . . .
Wynfrith. . . . Walk whilst you have the light lest the darkness of death come upon you. Temporal things pass swiftly
away, but the eternal that never fades will soon be upon us.
All the treasures of this world . . . melt away like shadows, van-
ish like smoke, dissolve like foam on the sea. . . . Put aside all
harmful obstacles; strive with unflagging zest to pursue your
study of the scriptures and thereby acquire that nobility of mind
which is divine wisdom."[3] Let us have many more bishops
like old Boniface, please God.

   Alcuin. He came from York and ended up at Charlemagne's court as head of the palace school and then of the
Abbey of Saint Martin at Tours. He is generally viewed as
the one responsible for the late eighth-century "Carolingian Renaissance". He was a great theologian and educator,
but it is in some of his little poems that we have a glimpse
of his piety. He wrote a dirge for a lost nightingale:

> May all the birds from everywhere now join with me
> To sing a dirge for you, O Nightingale!
> Your color was but dull, not dull your harmony,
> A great voice from a tiny throat.
> Your varied melodies had but a single theme
> The praise of your Creator from your heart (in ibid., 97).

And, in a farewell to his cell he muses:

> Birds of all kinds sing matins there,
> Praising their Creator. . . .
> Flee! Let us love Christ.
> May God sway our hearts.
> He will defend His own from foes,
> Snatching our hearts to Heaven.

[3] In *Literature of Medieval England*, ed. Robertson, Jr., 92–93.

> Let our hearts love and praise Him—
> Our Fame, our Life, our Haven (in ibid.).

John the Scot, better known to us as Johannes Scotus
Erigena, was Irish (which still qualified as "British" in those
days before the troubles), and he, too, ended up as master
of the Carolingian palace school, this time under Charles
the Bald, in the middle of the ninth century. He is, of course,
a major theologian, with works on Saint John's Gospel and
a translation of Dionysius the Areopagite's *Celestial Hierarchy*. His own great original work is *On the Division of Nature*,
which, alas, was later condemned as heretical. He is, surely,
in heaven nonetheless, we may hope. He draws parallels
between Eden and the nature of man as created by God.
"The fertile earth of this Paradise was the essential body of
man, potentially immortal. . . . The water of this garden represents the senses. . . . The air was the Divine Wisdom illu-
minated with the rays of reason. . . . Its aether was the soul. . . .
And *pan xylon*, or *omne lignum* [i.e., the 'all tree'] is the
Word, the Wisdom of the Father, Our Lord Jesus Christ"
(in ibid., 99–100). Readers familiar with the medieval habit
of drawing out allegory as far as it can possibly be drawn,
will find rich samples of this sort of thing in this Scot (not
to be confused with Duns Scotus).

And Asser. His *Life of King Alfred* is a pure delight. The
burnt cakes are here, of course, and also the tale of Alfred's
being healed in answer to prayer. At a remote chapel where
the bodies of Saint Guerir [sic] and Saint Neot rested, "he
prostrated himself [and] entreated of God's mercy, that in
his boundless clemency he would exchange the torments
of the malady which then afflicted him for some other lighter
disease. . . . And not long after he felt within him that by
the hand of the Almighty he was healed" (in ibid., 109). As
it turned out, he asked God to allow him some affliction

for his sanctification, but not one that would prevent his carrying out his kingly duties. God obliged him, and Alfred suffered greatly for many years. He became anxious that he knew little of Scripture, so, "inspired by God, [he] began to study the rudiments of divine Scripture ... and he continued to learn the flowers collected by certain masters, and to reduce them into the form of one book [which] he called his Enchiridion or Manual, because he carefully kept it at hand day and night, and found, as he told me, [Asser] no small consolation therein" (ibid., 111).

We may now turn to the literature written in Old English. We have already touched upon *Beowulf* by far the best known of these works. But the first English poet with a name (*if* it was his name) is Caedmon. He was a simple brother at the monastery of Streanaeshalch, according to Bede, and was given the gift of verse by God himself. His "hymn" often appears as the earliest fragment of Saxon verse.

> Praise we the Fashioner now of Heaven's fabric,
> The majesty of his might and his mind's wisdom ...
> How he the Lord of Glory everlasting,
> Wrought first for the race of men Heaven as a rooftree,
> Then made he Middle Earth to be their mansion.[4]

C. L. Wrenn speaks of a "Caedmonian revolution" in Old English poetry, meaning thereby the dragooning of Germanic heroic diction into the service of Christian topics. In this little hymn, for example, God is the *metod* (Creator), and glory is *wuldor*, and men appear as *aelda*. These are all words drawn from the heroic.

There are some "Caedmonian" poems, probably *not* written by our little monk, all to be found in the Junius Manuscript, and all concerned with biblical topics. In the so-called

---

[4] See Bede, *History of the English Church and People*, 251.

"Genesis A" manuscript, we find God as the high Lord, Satan and his minions as unfaithful retainers, kings as ring-givers (this is all very Nordic), and Abraham as an "eorl". In the "Exodus", we have speeches, and the description of battles that echo the vocabulary and tone of *Beowulf*. In "Christ and Satan", we find a whole treasury of scriptural topics, including the fall of Satan, the harrowing of hell, the Resurrection, Ascension, Pentecost, and the Last Judgment.

There is another shadowy figure usually called "Cynewulf", who has no biography, alas. Actually, whoever he was (possibly a bishop of Lindisfarne), he did, in fact, sign the name "Cynewulf" to his work. "The Fates of the Apostles", "Christ", "Juliana", and "Elene" (about Constantine's mother and the finding of the True Cross) all appear as his work. He contrived to smuggle in the name Cynewulf as a runic acrostic in some penultimate lines of his poetry, very possibly as a hint to readers to pray for him.

But my own favorite of the lot is the anonymous *Dream of the Rood*. It is very difficult here to refrain from quoting the entire thing. In C. W. Kennedy's modern English rendering, it starts out this way:

> Lo! I will tell   the dearest of dreams
> That I dreamed in the midnight   when mortal men
> Were sunk in slumber.   Me-seemed I saw
> A wondrous Tree   towering in air,
> Most shining of crosses   compassed with light.[5]

If readers suppose that the typesetter of the above lines put too many spaces between some of the words, the explanation is that in Old English poetry, the chief characteristics are alliteration and this caesura in the middle of the line, rather

---

[5] *An Anthology of Old English Poetry*, trans. Charles W. Kennedy (New York: Oxford University Press, 1960), 144.

than rhyme and regular meter. You have a series of emphases rather than anything like iambic pentameter, say.

The poet here tells, in profoundly moving terms, of his own vision of the Cross, and of how the Cross speaks directly to him of its own dread privilege of sustaining the Savior as he hung there for our salvation. Christ is pictured, typically, as the young hero who hastens into the battle for us sinners against our Enemy, and who "mounts" the Cross, almost eagerly, as a knight would dash into the fray. One of the great Christian paradoxes shows up in the lines asking: Shall we think of the Cross as rugged, splintery wood? or as made of gold and studded with jewels? Well, obviously the former would win in the verisimilitude sweepstakes; but, as is the case with the Annunciation and the Nativity, artists have reached for gold and gems and gothic arches, not because they thought that that was how things looked, but because we mortals try our utmost to bring our most precious materials to bear on this rich mystery.

The poem is packed with gloriously orthodox doctrine, all appearing under the species of true poetry. The poet takes his leave of us with this:

May the Lord be gracious   who on earth of old
Once suffered on the Cross   for the sins of men.
He redeemed us, endowed us with life   and a heavenly
   home.
Therein was hope renewed   with blessing and bliss
For those who endured the burning.   In that great deed
God's Son was triumphant,   possessing power and strength!
Almighty, Sole-Ruling   He came to the kingdom of God
Bringing a host of souls   to angelic bliss,
To join the saints   who abode in the splendor of glory,
When the Lord, Almighty God,   came again to His throne.[6]

---

[6] Ibid., 148.

OF TOWERS AND WARDROBES

When my wife and I lived in New York in the 1960s, as it happened, there were several art museums within very easy walking distance from our flat. The Metropolitan Museum of Art was the closest; the Guggenheim was just a few blocks up Fifth Avenue; the Whitney was on Madison Avenue just a few blocks south; and the Frick was a few blocks farther south, also on Fifth Avenue. Hence, one found oneself popping into any of these emporia at odd moments, since no travel or parking arrangements needed to be made.

The Frick was my favorite (cf. The Wallace Collection). This was the private collection, housed in his own mansion, of one of the famous "robber barons" of the early twentieth century, Henry Clay Frick. It was Lord Duveen, that *impresario di tutti impresarii*, who created Frick's collection. As one walked from room to splendid room, one was regaled with Bellini's *St. Francis in the Desert*, El Greco's *St. Jerome* (although I have always liked El Greco's real name: Theotokópoulos), Vermeer's *Mistress and Maid*, plus endless treasures from Rembrandt van Rijn, Frans Hals, Jan Steen, van Ruysdael, Romney, and Sir Joshua Reynolds.

On the other hand, there was the Whitney. This was a building in raw concrete. There were very few windows,

Lecture given in a slightly different form at the University of Oxford, August 2004.

but what there were, were trapezoidal. It had been built to house contemporary (American?) works of art. I am obliged to avoid the word "paintings" here, since it was often very far from clear just what one was looking at. One day I came upon a pile of parti-colored sand on the floor, with a shovel lying next to it. "Yes", said the guard. "You may use the shovel to rearrange these colored sands in any mixture your fancy dictates." Or again, coming up the stairs from the ground floor to the first floor, I noted what seemed to me to be unhappy evidence of some charwoman's slapdash methods of cleaning the place. Little chunks of polystyrene foam lurked in the corners of the stairway, and, when I reached the first floor, I found that more of them lay at random about the floor there, not unlike the little puff-balls of dust that collect under your bed if you never vacuum your bedroom. I suppose I looked nonplussed; so a nice guard came to my assistance: "Those are one of the exhibits: there are a hundred of these bits, scattered from the cellar to the attic." I suppose the artist took pains to assure himself that none of the bits would be kicked about, since of course that would spoil the integrity, harmony, and wholeness of the piece (do we call it a "piece" or "pieces"?).

Clearly something had occurred during the lapse of time between our Bellinis and Vermeers, on the one hand, and these items in the Whitney. But what?

This conference suspects that what had happened warrants the word "crisis", the idea being that you can't follow the trajectory from Vermeer to the Whitney without finding yourself in the abyss. *Rien. Gar nicht. Nada.* But this abyss is not the darkness of God spoken of by Saint Teresa, Saint John of the Cross, and T. S. Eliot in his *Four Quartets.* It would be, rather, the abyss of vacuity, hailed by Eliot as "Dark, dark, dark". Hell, in other words, where *the* Word

is not heard, and hence where *no* words are heard and meaning has collapsed. Discourse, reason, truth, beauty, wholeness, integrity, harmony, solidity, and substantiality have
vanished.

I adduce all of this at the start of my remarks since I
think that what I found in those museums in the 1960s was
a bellwether—or perhaps a knell. A tocsin. Something calamitous had happened to the imagery by which the fifteenth,
sixteenth, seventeenth, and eighteenth centuries articulated
their vision of things and the imagery for which the art-
ists(?) of the twentieth reached.

I say "imagery". That is what we have, of course, in all
of the arts, one way or another. *Images* created through
some visible or audible medium give *shape* to the human
experience of the world. The word "dry", for example,
can refer to many things. By itself it is not much of an
image. But "dry as a bone" is. "Exhausted" is not itself an
image, but "I felt like a wrung-out dishcloth" is. In both
cases, the speaker has reached for some concrete thing in
order to vivify abstract language. Dryness or exhaustion
are states of affairs, and something in us mortals forever
urges us to give *shape—concrete shape*—to these and other
realities we experience.

We are coming up here to the word *imagination*, which is
the image-making faculty with which we mortals are
crowned. We have reason and will and affection and
appetite—and imagination. We can scarcely open our mouths
without reaching for some image. "Reaching" I just said.
But I didn't stretch out my arm here to grasp anything. It
was "just" an image that presented itself naturally to my
imagination in the course of typing out that sentence. A
few lines ago I said that the word "dry" is not, by itself, an
image. But if I were to say, "Professor So-and-so's lectures

are almost insupportably dry", the adjective would conjure an image. An interesting question that comes trotting along ("trotting along", he says) at this point is the question of the literal versus the fanciful. There is nothing *literally* "dry" about the good professor's lectures, in the sense that the sand of the Sahara is dry. On the other hand, however, the image somehow not only does not attenuate the literal statement: rather it clarifies it, or fortifies it, or vivifies it. The statement becomes *tru-er* when it is assisted by an image. I myself have always distrusted the—to me—cavalier remark, "Oh, that's *just* an image. It's not literally the case."

No. Perhaps not. But the word "just" is a perilous one there. It implies that an image is "merely" this or that, and that it draws us away from the literal, which is the locale of the real, we would say. But does it? My own guess is that, on the contrary, a well-chosen image draws us further *into* truth than, say, the syllogism, or the equation.

And suddenly we are head over heels in the mystery of the Incarnation. *The Word of God*, the truest thing there is, tended toward concretion. "In the beginning was the Word ... *et verbum caro factum est*" (Jn 1:1, 14; KJV & Douay-Rheims). That event was very far from being a detour, or a mere charade, on the part of God. Nor was it a *pis aller*, as though God said to himself, "Hum. What strategy will answer to the collapse of things in that universe that I made? We've almost run out of ideas." No. Any Catholic, I should think, would rather phrase it this way: "It is of the very nature of the Word that it *tends toward Incarnation*." Or put it this way: we, who find ourselves in this species called man, seem to have an incorrigible wish to approach reality via the concrete (as opposed, say, to the seraphim and all the thrones, dominations, princedoms, powers, and so forth who see reality unmediated, they tell us). The next word we need here, of course, is *sacrament*. What is a sacrament? Well, it is at the very least a *physical point* at which eternity touches time, or the unconditioned touches the conditioned, or the Uncreated touches the created: water; bread; wine; oil; two bodies, male and female; the eardrum and the larynx of the priest who hears what I am saying, and who, via his larynx, touches me with "*et ego te absolvo*". The sacrament won't work by telepathy, or private meditation, or even over the telephone. There has got to be a physical situation. The mystery—the Word, the Truth—must take concrete form.

And of course, long before the Incarnation, we have this: "In the beginning God created . . ." (Gen 1:1, KJV). Created *what*? Well, seraphim, cherubim, thrones, etc., but all of that is out of our ken. We are the species who must have things concrete. So we find that the story, as it is told to us mortals, has God *making:* making light (which, the physicists seem to be telling us, is, in fact, something physical), and earth, air, fire, and water, and elm trees and alders and aardvarks and jellyfish and kiwis and man.

And this creature man is, alone of all the creations of God, said to be made in his image. His image. We are made in the image of the Maker. We mortals somehow enact this mystery of our creation when we *make* things.

Need I say that we have been on no wild-goose chase over the course of the last couple of pages, which has taken us from the Whitney Museum to God. I did not need to drag theology into my speech in order to make it fit this conference. We are speaking of bald actuality ("bald"!) here. If Catholics wish to talk about the profound cultural crisis looming upon us, they will sooner or later have to talk about God, because the only way of assessing a given culture is to study its artifacts—the things it has made. Or

perhaps I should say the most revealing way of scrutiniz-
ing a culture is to look at its artifacts, since of course we
have the speeches of Pericles and the thought of Chairman Mao (although that took form in a Little Red Book,
they tell me). And those artifacts are the index of our
having been made in the image of the Maker. We make
things—not by way of escape from reality, but rather by
way of struggling toward reality. Our image-making faculty—
i.e., our imagination—bespeaks the truth about us.

If you are over forty, you may recall a British television
series called *Civilisation*. It was narrated by Lord Clark. He
led us all through century after century of the history of
mankind, not by reading to us a list of battles, nor of the
rise and fall of statesmen, nor even a summary of the ideas
of a given epoch. We looked at crumbled pillars and arches
and forums and aqueducts, and at towers and churches, and
the palazzi of the dukes of Montefeltro at Urbino, and at
lots of sculptures and paintings. The point was, of course,
that you can tell a great deal about us mortals by looking
at how we make these things. And this might be the place
to draw a distinction that would seem apposite: I myself
would see the word "culture" as being prior to, and bigger
than, the word "civilization". You can have cultures (who
were the Paleolithic men who drew those buffaloes on the
walls of their cave at Lascaux? and who put up Stonehenge
and how and why? And who started the Hottentots painting their shields that way?)—you can have cultures before
you have civilizations. Where does culture cross the line
and become civilization? I would have to leave it to you
anthropologists, sociologists, and historians to give us the
final answer, but certainly we would all suppose that you
get a civilization arising from a culture when you get a
written language, and edifices that are built to last, and some

judiciary system, and complex government, and certain pro-
visions for getting from one place to another—highways,
that is, rather than footpaths—and even sanitary engineer-
ing. Thus, the word "culture" subsumes the word "civilization". The crisis of which we are speaking at this
conference is indeed a crisis of culture, since more is at
stake than whether the tarmac on our motorways will last,
or whether the euro will work at the end of the day, and
so forth. The crisis raises the most fundamental questions
as to just what we *are*—we who belong to the species *homo
sapiens*.

A brief canvass of the artifacts that have arisen from our
(Western) culture over the last 150 years may throw light on
our topic. I say 150 years, but of course if we are speaking of
the West, we need to go back about four thousand years. In
that connection, let me limit myself to a single phenomenon: the image of man. Not long after the beginning of
things, you get great, statuesque, majestic figures: Nimrod, Gil-
gamesh, Agamemnon, Hector. And this impressive stature is
visible in figures as late as Arthur, Beowulf, Siegfried, Roland,
and even Henry V, I suppose. Man as hero. And these heroes
did not all have to be warriors, although that certainly was
thought to be the archetypal image of us men. I would think
that we must call Oedipus a hero, too, because of his titanic
capacity to suffer. And certainly Lear is heroic—also in his
titanic capacity to suffer. By the time we get to Hamlet, where
are we? Good question.

But, rising from the landscape and overlapping with the
heroes I have just named, we have another image of the
hero appearing in our Western itinerary. I mean the saint.
The Christian heroes tend to be martyrs, none of whom
put up a fight (one thinks of Saints Boris and Gleb here),
or else men of prayer, contemplation, or of great derring-do

in carrying the Christian Gospel to all sorts of unlikely places: Brendan, Martin of Tours, Boniface, Augustine of Kent, Dominic, Ignatius, Francis Xavier, and the rest of them. I suppose that we could descry an analogy between these two sorts of hero—the warrior as such, and the warrior of the spirit—in that both Roland (the warrior) and Francis (the friar) are *noble*.

What happens to the Western image of man then? *Il cortegiano* of Castiglione, Sir Philip Sidney, Sir Walter Raleigh, and then the seventeenth, eighteenth, and nineteenth centuries. We find the courtier, and then the gentleman. Not quite such stormy figures as your Hectors and Beowulfs.

I should, of course, have included women in this list: your Penthesilias and Boadiceas and Hildegards and Teresas and Catherines—of Siena or Genoa, whichever you like.

But then what? Some time in the nineteenth century, people found themselves troubled by a painting of a Dutch boy by Gustave Courbet. Close observers began to suspect that what they were looking at was not a three-dimensional boy at all, but a paper-doll. Or worse, paint on canvas. And then we are off and running with the Impressionists and Post-Impressionists. Cezanne would not have been happy if you had said that Mont Sainte-Victoire "doesn't *look* like that. You've got too many little bits of paint here. Can't you tidy it all up and make it look like a mountain?"

"But I am not photographing a mountain, dear sir: I am recording light on the retina of my eye."

And so on with Renoir's young man in a rowboat, and Monet's lilies. Somehow there is a recoil from the external world (even though I myself would have to confess to finding that genre of painting very beautiful).

But this "recoil"—why did they recoil? Because the modern philosophers had pulled the rug from under any confidence we all may have had as to whether what is *out there* is anything other than an illusion. You may lay this loss of confidence at the feet of Descartes, or David Hume, or even Freud, depending on how you parse the history of ideas. Very well then, we will retreat into our retinas and our psyches and subconsciousness and take that region as the locale of our work. *Les Demoiselles d'Avignon*, or *Nude Descending a Staircase*: "I've never seen a woman who looked like those ladies!" we protest.

"Well then, you'd better open your eyes", comes the retort from Picasso and Georges Braque. They knew jolly well what they were doing.

We cannot, of course, canvass the whole story of painting in the last 150 years, but I think we are obliged to see in the whole panoply a massive retreat from *the other*. That is, first of all from the external world, which had always been supposed to be *other than* ourselves; and then from other selves, who lie in the precincts of *caritas*; and finally the retreat from *The* Other, namely God.

A thousand times I have pointed out to my students the *irony* that when you get rid of God, you get rid of us. It was the ages that thought the gods were *there*, and presiding over us, and calling us to account—it was those ages that produced the gigantic heroes: Hector, Agamemnon, Beowulf, and company. What do we find as God recedes, first into the Deist distance, then into the pantheist murk, and finally into the atheist and post-atheist vacuity? We find ourselves dwindling, until our heroes are named Willie Loman and Estragon and Vladimir (as you can see, I have shifted here from painting to fiction and drama, but all the arts testify to the point I am making).

In a sense, the painters and playwrights are accurate. The stature of man *does* dwindle, and *has* dwindled, as the gods, or God, have vanished. It is an uncomfortable paradox for your nonreligious artists and authors, since one would suppose that if we could only get *God* off our backs, we would be able to stand tall and make our own decisions without fear and hence grow to our true and splendid stature. But it hasn't worked like that. We have shriveled. I found myself greatly bothered when I read Ionesco's *Rhinocéros*. It was not so much the fact that everybody in Paris seemed to be gradually turning into rhinoceroses: much worse, for me, was the ghastly fact that *nobody among the characters even noticed it*. It was not news. Obviously if we men are nothing particular to begin with, then it is neither here nor there if we show up as beasts.

The figure of James Joyce towers (very wrongly, in my opinion) over almost all other writers in English during the last century. And who was his hero? Leopold Bloom. And where did his field of action lie? Inside his psyche. And how did he acquit himself? Drearily, we would have to say.

If we wish to follow this itinerary all the way to the brink of what we are calling a crisis, we should also note the figure of Mr. Andy Warhol. In his work, we (man, that is) disappear altogether. He hailed us in the 1960s with his soup tins and scouring pads. What's this? we demanded. Why—just the icon of our epoch, Warhol could have replied. I am doing nothing other than what artists have always done. You get the figure of Hector in an epoch that perceives man in that image; or you get the Madonna and Bambino in an epoch that sees that sort of thing to be central, or you get the countess of Huntingdon or Charles I in an epoch that sees these figures as icons. But I can't do that now, says Mr. Warhol. We—we mortals—have vanished from the map. I'm left with soup tins and have no warrant to paint what Fra Angelico or Giotto took for their icons.

But there was something Warhol didn't know. He had not heard about hobbits nor of the Men of Westernesse. All of a sudden, in the late 1950s, a few people began to come across a peculiar character named Frodo and another named Aragorn. Frodo belonged to a somewhat diminutive species called hobbit, and what he liked was pipe tobacco, good beer, and bucolic tranquility. Aragorn was a man belonging to a race unheard of in our West for centuries. He was a hero. Frodo for his part finds himself haled into an adventure quite at odds with all of his hobbit's pipes and beer and tranquility.

I suspect that it is to this tale that the reference to "towers" in my title attaches. (I can't claim credit for my title. I wish I could. I only hope that what I am saying here addresses itself to what the founders of this conference intimated by giving me this title for my remarks.) We all know the tale of Frodo and Aragorn and their friends—and their enemies, one should add. Towers loom large in that tale: the towering monoliths guarding the banks of the lower Anduin River, and Isengard, and finally, of course, Minas Tirith and Minas Morgul. Towers somehow spring up from the very sources of our own story, most notably, Babel, of course.

If we use this word "towers" as a synecdoche for Tolkien's whole achievement, what can we say that achievement was, vis-à-vis this crisis in culture that occupies us here?

Almost single-handedly, Tolkien reintroduced into Western imagination the figure of the hero—and of the saint, we might add. I think both Frodo and Aragorn, not to mention Sam Gamgee, Eomer, Eowyn, Gandalf, Galadriel, and a dozen others, qualify for both categories. Perhaps the word "noble" comprises these two elements of heroism and sanctity. Let us use it that way, in any event.

I did my own graduate studies during the 1960s in English literature. I am fairly sure that the word "noble" never once showed up in any lecture or discussion we had. It was a category quite otiose by that time. Oh, to be sure we read about Chaucer's knight, and all of Shakespeare's heroes. But by the time Byron and Shelley come along, it seems to me, something frantic, or even febrile, attaches to the word. It no longer rises naturally in the poets' vocabulary.

I say that Tolkien "reintroduced" this category into serious narrative, after a century of Demoiselles d'Avignon, Willie Lomans, Leopold Blooms, and, say, Giacometti's pinheaded figures of us men or Moore's nightmarish figures with great bulbous, tumescent, and, ironically, hollow loins. That century was nothing short of brilliant, if we are speaking of its skill in conjuring images that testify to the crumpling of the figure of man. But you can't go on forever either extolling this collapse, or at least dwelling on it. That would be to conclude that hell has indeed arrived. But no Catholic is prepared to say this. The question then arises: Well, what images can we conjure that will once more speak to us of the true nobility that crowns us mortals? Everything is so sodden with irony that any such image will immediately be dismissed, with loud coughing and catcalls, as trifling, infantile, and schmaltzy.

And then along comes Professor Tolkien. He and his friend Lewis simply ignored altogether the tradition of the English novel as it was born and grew, from Fielding and Smollett, through Jane Austen, Trollope, George Eliot, and Henry James. That was a tradition of *manners*, which is all very well in itself (I happen to revel in Jane Austen's stories), but manners are a superficial thing when you juxtapose them with qualities such as heroism and sanctity. Tolkien draws us into *Midgard* (Middle Earth), where we find characters, drawn without the smallest suggestion of irony, who exhibit valor and fidelity and purity of heart and the capacity for awe and nobility and grace—exhibit all of these under a thousand variations. We need only pass from Sam Gamgee to Farmer Maggot to Tom Bombadil to Elrond to Galadriel to Gimli to Boromir to Treebeard and the Riders of Rohan to find ourselves agog at the possibilities and varieties of true nobility—again, with no smallest trace of irony. Tolkien *believed* in this world. I would repeat to my students over and over, "This is a *true story*. It is true in a sense unimaginable to Arthur Miller, Willie Loman, or a single one of the audience in the stalls." But with the materials of modernity, you can no more make a hero or saint than you can make a rope of sand. (Someone will leap up and call out "Mother Teresa of Calcutta!" But the point about her—and about Solzhenitsyn too—is that the modern world didn't know what to do with them. They weren't made with "the materials of modernity". Harvard University found itself bemused, and then irritated, by both of them, and, at least in the case of Solzhenitsyn, the intelligentsia of the West pronounced him a nonperson. He no longer exists, and he never existed.)

But we must get to our wardrobes, since my time is long since up. We push past the fur coats in that wardrobe and find ourselves in a landscape where there is real evil, not only in the witches (I am including here the White and Green Witches and Jadis), but, alas, in Edmund and Eustace Clarence Scrubb, which is to say, in *me*. Not guilt *feelings*, which is the only category our epoch knows, but real, objective guilt before an absolute standard. And there is real good, which is at the same time omnipotent. Our epoch can think of power only as repressive or tyrannical. The notion of absolute power that is also absolutely good is unimaginable. So Lewis, like his friend Tolkien, had to ignore quite unapologetically all the categories of "serious" narrative that determine what is "important" in this epoch, and whisk us, again quite unapologetically, into a land where there is external, objective truth and falsehood, and good and evil, and beauty and the ghastly travesty thereof.

Towers and wardrobes. Juvenile stuff, really. Or are they? From the Catholic point of view, the loss of the notions of valor, pellucid goodness, majesty, nobility, sacrifice, the pure capacity for awe in the face of what is truly awesome—all of this as opposed to the pusillanimity, venality, cravenness, duplicity, squalor, cynicism, travesty, and the febrile that have ruled the arts, and hence the morals and manners, of the West for a very long time now—the loss of those goods, and the hegemony of those evils, can only be said to have brought us to the brink of the abyss. A few lonely figures stand at the edge with pennants blazoned with the arms of Midgard or Narnia, waving us back.

C. S. LEWIS AND THE
SANCTIFIED IMAGINATION

We have a bit of a conundrum on our hands before we even embark here. Or at least an apparent conundrum—or, to use a phrase that seems to find its way into nearly every symposium nowadays, a *perceived* conundrum. (Parenthetically, this word gives me the philosophical vapors, since it seems to have as its point of reference, not reality, but perceived reality—that flimsy web that floats, diaphonously, through people's interior consciousness, rather than the titanic edifice called creation by which I, at least, believe a Christian finds himself addressed. Furthermore—we're still in my parenthesis here—perceived reality, or that notion at any rate, seems to smooth the seductive way across into what they now call virtual reality, which is being dumped in our laps by the computers, and which may turn out to be a euphemism for hell, because it lacks substance.)

You will be murmuring to your neighbor that the man has either brought the wrong speech with him, or he has very quickly lost the thread. Aren't we speaking of C. S. Lewis and Sanctified Imagination?

Yes. That parenthesis was just me lobbing Molotov cocktails into the argot of contemporaneity in a forlorn attempt

Lecture given in a slightly different form at the C. S. Lewis Conference, Seattle Pacific University, June 1998.

to arrest our pell-mell race through the black hole of modern discourse into hell.

But the conundrum with which I began: What do I mean? It arises from the juxtaposition of the two words *sanctified* and *imagination*. It is very easy to tuck these two words into two categories, sealed hermetically from each other. *Sanctified* is a sober theological adjective that describes that state of affairs in which we, after much tribulation, discipline, and suffering, will have been so configured to Christ—that is to say, so perfected in charity—that we will be able to survive in the precincts of holiness and to bear up under the sheer weight of the Beatific Vision.

On the other hand, we have *imagination*. Toward what precincts does *this* word bid us? Well now—we'd have Robinson Crusoe, and Gulliver, and Robin Hood, and Winnie the Pooh and Mrs. Tiggy-Winkle, and all the cloud-capped towers of our own castles in the air, and, for many of the people sitting in this audience, Puddleglum and Mr. Tumnus and Shift the Ape, and Sam Gamgee and Treebeard the Ent and Lothlorien. And of course, the particular quality all of these characters and places share is their unreality. They exist only in fancy.

Hum. Fancy, is it? Are we marching into quicksand here?

There may be a few of you in this audience who join Hobbit clubs and put on little silvery capes and sit around talking elvish and eating mushrooms. You might not be altogether beyond turning over the odd skunk cabbage leaf in hopes of startling an elf. You would wish to urge upon us all the notion that reality is very queer, and who's to say what creatures *aren't* in the cards somewhere. After all, to assert that Rumpelstiltskin exists, you have to know only one person in the whole universe: Rumpelstiltskin. To insist that he does NOT exist, you must, of course, know everyone, from the seraphim on down to the frost giants. So it is much easier to take the cagey view that there might be sylphs and gnomes than it is to rule them out categorically.

I myself have never been drawn to Hobbit societies (and I don't think our friend Clive Staples would have been caught dead at one). If for no other reason than that I am hag-ridden with bad luck, I would never turn over a cabbage leaf, since I would know ahead of time that whatever elves had been lurking there will have capered off straightaway upon any report that I was in the neighborhood.

If any of you has read Lewis' *The Discarded Image*, you will recall his statement that the old model—the one with elves and gnomes and archangelic tutelary intelligences running the planets—delighted him as he believed it delighted our ancestors. "Few constructions of the imagination seem to me to have combined splendour, sobriety, and coherence in the same degree. It is possible that some readers have long been itching to remind me that it had a serious defect; it was not true. I agree. It was not true." [1]

He then pointed out that various models of the universe are like contour lines on a map: such lines are not the landscape itself, but are nonetheless true indicators of what the real landscape is like. You might have a man who supposed that the lines themselves are the reality. This seems to be the case with many a modern man who is so sure that "mathematics are now the nearest to the reality we can get. Anything imaginable ... is a mere analogy, a concession to our weakness" (ibid., 218).

Now we begin to see where this lands us. It is naïve—quaint, even—to speak of reality in the unabashedly

[1] C. S. Lewis, *The Discarded Image* (Cambridge: Cambridge University Press, 1970), 216.

picturesque terms that served for ten thousand years in myth *and* narrative and even cosmology. If you are serious, assumes the modern man, then of course you must abandon all that vocabulary, so appealing but so misleading, and speak in mathematical, that is to say, abstract, terms.

But there is a joker in the pack. We would *rather* suppose that the rocks and moss and linden leaves and little highland burns the color of stout were real in some real sense. We find it a melancholy business to suppose that insofar as you loiter in such purlieus, you are—well, loitering, like the poor knight-at-arms in Keats' "La Belle Dame sans Merci", to be drawn farther and farther into the sweet languor that lulls the soul to dusty death.

But supposing there were a sense in which all these beguiling metaphors like moss and sparkling brooks and venerable elms were, after their own fashion, faithful metaphors? What if reality is such that, far from approaching it via more and more abstract formulae, we were to take seriously T. S. Eliot's "hints and guesses" and venture to imagine that the moss and elms are accurate—or, to return to an earlier notion, that they are better than contour lines when it comes to suggesting what things are really like.

What if, for example, the bearded patriarch with a papal tiara on his head and his robes billowing about on some baroque ceiling in Bavaria—what if it could be said, *mutatis mutandis*, that this figure is "more like" God the Father than, say, Paul Tillich's chilling effort to skirt anthropomorphism by offering "the Ground of Being" as a sturdier notion upon which to drive in the tent pegs of faith? What then? Or suppose we all decided that streets of gold are not really a very helpful hint about final reality, and that "the triumph of life" or "ongoing personality" will serve us better? Naturally we would jettison the golden streets—they are too vulgar, for one thing—and speak of the triumph of life. If you think I am indulging myself in absurd projections here, you have never heard a Modernist Protestant sermon. Most of such efforts regale us with the spectacle of a man—or a woman, forsooth—up there in the pulpit teetering along a highwire, trying desperately to avoid falling from his metallic peril into the waiting arms of a blissful reality. The trickiest point in the liturgical year for such unhappy preachers is Easter. All that about a corpse emerging from the cerements of the grave, napkin and all, and about shining young men sitting there on the ledge with the news that the dead man has risen—really, it is all too, too embarrassing. But such lovely metaphors for ongoing life! So let us keep the story, not as though it referred to an event on the flinty soil of our planet here, but rather as it expresses an abstraction we are pleased to call "the Easter faith".

Lewis' horse Bree, in *The Horse and His Boy*, was a Modernist. All that about a tawny lion with a real mane and claws and so forth—that is all very well for foals and fillies perhaps, but we grown-up horses know that it is an insult to the Great Lion actually to postulate such anatomical details about anything so ineffable, and—Hoo! Ha! Help! What ho! I say!—and poor Modernist Bree finds himself tickled by the whiskers, forsooth, of the Lion whom he had so safely caged in his sophisticated nonsense.

Where does this bring us in our remarks here this afternoon? It brings us very near our topic of sanctified imagination. And we begin to descry how the two words may be juxtaposed without absurdity. For obviously, from the Christian point of view, you cannot speak of reality for very long without finding yourself having to reach for the vocabulary of the sacred. The holy. And these are the precincts toward which the adjective *sanctified* nudges us. At the heart of reality, we find, not "The Force", as *Star Wars* will have it, nor a great monolith as *2001* has it, nor any of the cloudy vistas of that ilk, but rather the Sapphire Throne.

Come. Sapphire? That's the name of a stone found on our planet. And throne? How quaint. A great gilded and brocaded chair in the sky is it? Well, *chacun à son goût*. If you resonate to that, then, resonate away, old buddy.

What sort of a rejoinder that has any rag of seriousness to it can be mounted to this amused and avuncular attitude?

That is to say, what do *we* say to the almost universal notion of our epoch that real reality (like Francis Schaeffer's "true truth") frays out into equations when all's said and done, and that the inclination of us mortals to picture and populate the world (by which I mean what the medievals meant by it, what Lewis called "the whole show")—that this pictorial inclination is very nice, to be sure, but that it is seriously misleading. It keeps us all in a sort of kindergarten, or a Child's Garden of Illusion, so to speak. Poetry may speak of the "castled crag of Drachenfels", or of "the great, gray, green greasy Limpopo River", or of "the silken, sad, uncertain rustling of each purple curtain", or "morning in russet mantle clad" (how do you stop, once you start casting about for nice lines from poetry?), but poetry throws silver dust into our eyes. The cold view through the electron microscope, or through the lenses of that Hubble machine that's out there somewhere—this cold view will bring us no castled crags or russet mantles. You get closer to the thing on your computer screen, where the data sent out from Hubble is translated into equations.

The irony here is that this tendency toward abstraction poising itself against our native inclination to populate and picture things seeps even into religious discourse. Or perhaps we should say, seeps especially into religious discourse.

How many good Christian folk picture heaven as a region where everything is somewhat attenuated—that is, thinned out? Pray don't for a moment imagine that the streets of gold are paved with the same stuff your wedding ring is made of. Gold is "only" a metaphor there for glory, and glory is something cloudy. Dazzling, to be sure, but cloudy, somehow.

Is that so? If you think that, then Lewis would suspect (correctly, as it happens) that you are a Gnostic. A Manichean. A heretic, to put it baldly. What? Because as over against the embarrassing solidity of Christianity, with all of its bread and wine and blood and flesh and stone altars and baptismal water and great pots of wine at Cana of Galilee and splinters and nails and whips and thorns—over against all of that, Gnosticism, and its heretical Christian step-child Manicheanism, has for its whole agenda an escape from this clay we call flesh, off into a vacuous religious ether that is much more flattering to our "spiritual" nature. High-minded Bostonians like Ralph Waldo Emerson and William Ellery Channing liked this sort of thing. They probably welcomed the notion that we will neither marry nor be given in marriage in heaven: that way we'll all be free to float about, discoursing in lofty terms about ideas. But my own guess is that many's the Christian young man especially, who has heard that text with a certain melancholy. Oh pshaw: no marriage in heaven. That means no sex. Ah well, I guess I'll just have to get a lot more spiritual before I'm ready for that cerebral realm.

But what if things are exactly the other way around? What if we don't marry in heaven because we will have won through, via the kindergarten lessons of marital fidelity, or of consecrated chastity, here in this realm, to that unimaginably blissful state of affairs where we will know all other selves with an ecstasy far, far outstripping the pale, diluted earthly metaphor of sex? What if sex is the hint—the metaphor—and its fulfillment in paradise, far from being an attenuation, is a great raising of the stakes, so that our elementary experiences down here in marital union will turn out to be just that: elementary?

And suppose the honey-colored stone we see in Cotswold manor houses is only a sketchy hint of the real, solid thing awaiting us in the new heavens and the new earth. Or suppose the sweet tang of wild raspberries is itself the thinned-down, subdued hint, given to us here temporarily, until we reach the state of being known as sanctity, where we will be able to sustain the hitherto insupportable bliss of real raspberries. (I myself hope there will be double cream from Jersey cows to flood our raspberries with, and I must say, I do not want spiritual cream.)

This could all get very amusing and fanciful if we pursued the line of thought on and on. But perhaps these cases in point will have suggested the idea. Imagination, far from being an unfortunate inclination in us mortals that leads us down the garden path toward illusion and a region that is nothing but wish fulfillment, may, rather, be the faculty in us corresponding in a unique way to reality. We cannot pit it over against intellect and will and affection. All of these properties rightly crown our humanness, and each, after its own mode, enables us to respond to reality. But poor imagination is often treated as the country cousin, frolicking about in a flowered chicken-feedbag jumper, gathering dandelions and ragwort and supposing them to be orchids and bird-of-paradise flowers. When you want a recess from wearisome reality, you summon the foxfire of imagination. There you will find your elfin glades, summoned for us with such agonizing delicacy by T. S. Eliot in "East Coker":

> In that open field
> If you do not come too close, if you do not come too close,
> On a summer midnight, you can hear the music
> Of the weak pipe and the little drum
> And see them dancing around the bonfire . . .[2]

And so forth. But Eliot is not speaking of illusion here. He is not tootling us along, like the Pied Piper, into the crack in the mountain from which there is no return. He is trying his utmost to prod us with his "hints and guesses".

Lewis has a poem entitled "On Being Human", in which he draws piquant contrast between angels and us mortals: angels know what a tree *means* but have never felt

> the knife-edged severance
> Of sun from shadow where the trees begin,
> The blessed cool at every pore caressing us—
> An angel has no skin.[3]

Or again, they know what air *is*, or *means*, but they don't know the ecstasies we know of the smell of new-mown hay, the ravishing sea smells, the woodsmoke: an angel has no nose. Here we are, poor mortal clods that we are, all stuffed into a sack of skin, with embarrassing features like noses—these usually ill-shaped cartilaginous protuberances bang in the middle of our faces—and little swirls of skin flapping out from the sides of our heads in such a buffoonish way. Alas. All Gnostics and Manicheans await eagerly the day when we will have shucked off all of this nonsense and will have stepped into our true dignity as ghosts.

---

[2] T. S. Eliot, *The Complete Poems & Plays, 1909–1950* (New York: Harcourt, Brace, & World, 1971), 123–24.

[3] C. S. Lewis, "On Being Human", in *Poems* (London: Geoffrey Bles, 1964), 34.

Lewis' imagination was a sanctified imagination. He called it "baptized", paying tribute to the effect that George Mac-Donald's work had had on him as a boy. That is, he noted this peculiar faculty we have, to make something solid in order to rouse ourselves from our usual torpor—the *Pietà* for example, or Chartres Cathedral, or Jan van Eyck's great altarpiece in Ghent, *The Adoration of the Mystic Lamb*, from Saint John's Revelation. In each case here—and in every artifact of art, including poetry and drama and dance and music—we have a sensual, and in some sense solid (even music depends on airwaves and eardrums, and catgut and horsehair), attempt to launch a raid on the inarticulate, as T. S. Eliot called his enterprise of poetry. There is no such thing as an abstract poem. It doesn't matter how far into the ether or the psyche we may wish to penetrate: our poem depends entirely on the success with which we evoke the concrete (and that, by the way, is most of the definition of imagination: it is the image-making faculty in us). We can't live with sheer abstractions. Keats may start out, "My heart aches, and a drowsy numbness pains ..." and we seem en route to the ether of vacuous interiority. But what do we find? Suddenly we are head over heels in hemlock, the river Lethe, dryads, beech groves, and a singing nightingale. It's no use, says Keats the poet, trying to come at moods of the heart, difficult to depict as they may be, via the vocabulary of abstraction. I've got to stuff my poem with birds, trees, and dryads. Somehow, with all of that never-never land of imagery, we'll be assisted along toward the real truth, which is my topic here. We get toward truth, or reality, in other words, via the apparently circuitous route of images.

We all know this anyway. You have a birth. Nothing noteworthy here. Just another crying voice to be added to the billions of voices already sending up cries of "*Kyrie, eleison!*" from this sad planet. What could be less auspicious than a birth?

And yet, and yet—you know and I know, and every tribe and culture and civilization since the year dot has known— the birth is not a statistic on the hospital clipboard. We've got to *do* something about it—something useless, as it happens. Champagne, cigars, blue or pink or yellow layette, stuffed teddy bears, and so forth. Images, all of them, of the mystery that eludes quite utterly the data on the clipboards. The same is true of weddings. Why is plain Jane tricked out like that now, pray? I saw her half an hour ago in jeans and a sweatshirt. Well, she was Jane then. Now she is womanhood incarnate, with all the mystery and majesty and dignity and holiness that crowns womanhood. Her groom there in his penguin suit—he is no longer Bubba: he is the mystery of the man calling to his spouse to come and be one.

I will repeat a sentence from two paragraphs back: the poet (the image-maker, that is, according to Aristotle) knows that, oddly, we get toward truth via the apparently circuitous route of images—even images of fancy: fauns and talking beavers and one thing and another.

It all raises the question: What is truth? (I'm not trying to sound like our friend Pontius Pilate here.) As a matter of fact, let me shift over to the word *reality* here, since that is the more fundamental word. What is reality, that it should invite from us mortals this ceaseless effort to mount a raid on it via fancy—via images, that is, of places we've never been able to find and of beings who have eluded us altogether?

Does the very question give us our hint? Might reality not be such that it is most exactly suggested by these images? I will avoid here the question as to the nature of mathematical truth. I simply do not know what the precise relationship might be between reality and what you see on the blackboard in an astrophysicist's classroom. I daresay such a man could galvanize us all at this conference if he could somehow lead us into the precincts mapped out in his equations. And I also suspect that, when the chips are all the way down, we would discover that Jewel the Unicorn and the great archangelic queen, Perelandra, are to be found, entirely at home, in that landscape thus mapped out. There can't be two realities. Everything that rises must converge (thank you, Flannery).

But sanctified imagination? That is our real topic here. You've got Shelley and Keats and Byron, not to mention Yeats and company, all of whom are image-makers of the first water. For them, reality is odd, or elusive, or transcendent, or teasing, or mysterious, or heartbreaking. But holy?

With this word we find ourselves in a region quite distinct from the region of the merely ineffable. It is ineffable, to be sure, and also mysterious and elusive and odd. But what shall we call this unmistakable quality that suffuses the whole thing? There is no synonym for holiness. Purity? Light? Glory? The dreadful? All of these, yes, but none does the whole job. The set apart? Yes, but of course things can be set apart for Moloch and Baal as well as for Aslan, or, shall we say, for the God and Father of our Lord Jesus Christ.

And now, as I draw toward the end of my speech (I think twelve or thirteen pages is long enough by far for any speech in the world, and I'm on page ten, if that will bolster your sagging spirits)—as I draw toward my close, I can haul out many treasures from the work of Mr. Clive S. Lewis that will demonstrate to us all what is suggested in our title, "Lewis and the Sanctified Imagination".

In a word, Lewis, like his mentor George MacDonald and his friend Tolkien, draws us toward the realm of reality, *as* that realm is suggested for us in Sacred Scripture and in the liturgy of the Church, by means of images that, on the surface, may appear frivolous. Certainly they are fanciful, and certainly they brought down on Lewis' head all the vitriol that his Oxford literary contemporaries were able to bottle up and pour over him.

We could start almost anywhere in his fiction. What about the old priest in Glome? There he is, with his beak and feathers and bladders and amulets and blood-drenched hands, all pungent and acrid—but, says the narrator, the smell about him was the smell of holiness. Whatever that quality might be, it makes the priest entirely impervious to the blusterings and pusillanimous ravings of Trom, the odious old king. The priest is at home in a world that is quite untouched by such humbug. He dwells near the god—or the goddess, as it happens. And she is an unnerving black lump. In Glome, holiness and beauty have little to do with each other. But in this figure of the priest, we find ourselves hailed with an intractable quality—a quality not to be gainsaid. We know that, whatever it is, it is "more real" than the squalid world inhabited by the mountebank Trom. (An interesting footnote to the figure of the old priest is his successor, Arnom. Arnom is a Modernist. He tidies up the shrine and fumigates it and replaces the bloody old goddess with a rather pleasing silver figure. But the old crones in their babushkas aren't fooled. They know which one to approach with their heartbreak. The silver goddess is too plausible.)

Upon our having read of this, you and I are in a stronger position than when we began the story, to imagine ("imagine" is what I said) something about the God whom we worship, in whose presence the great seraphim cry "Holy". I like the Latin of the *Te Deum: "Tibi cherubim et seraphim incessabili voce proclamant, 'Sanctus!'"*

Or Ramandu. He was the retired star, if you have forgotten *The Voyage of the Dawn Treader*. There is that about
him that excludes altogether any notion of our approaching him with chitchat and bonhomie. He has a great,
gray beard, and well-mannered people don't tweak such
beards. But his beard scarcely exhausts what we notice
about Ramandu. He walks caparisoned in solemnity. Not
severity: solemnity. This solemnity does not dampen our
spirits—quite the contrary. But it excludes frivolity and
self-advertisement among us. Another image, hinting in
its own way, of a quality true of our God but excessively
difficult to pin down with discursive prose.

Or what about the atmosphere as the Dawn Treader
nears the utter East? You will recall that the air becomes
almost unbearably clear: there is virtually a weight of clarity about it all that causes one to forget hunger and fatigue
and even the need to talk. The sea water becomes sweet,
and a sweet smell is abroad in the silence. The children
feel almost burdened with bliss. A weight of glory, in other
words, which suddenly wakes us up to Lewis' tactics here.
A sanctified imagination.

Or that morning on Perelandra when Ransom, having
descended into hell, emerges into the sweet landscape and
witnesses the handing over to the young king and queen,
Tor and Tinidril, the suzerainty over the planet, up to
this point held in stewardship by Malacandra and Perelandra. Who will move an eyelash in this golden clarity?
Who will cough? Who will so much as clear his throat?
There was silence in heaven for half an hour, we are
told in another story. Surely it is a silence that dissolves
altogether all self-assertion, nay, even all self-consciousness,
that most tedious of all intruders into the precincts of
caritas.

And what about Orual in *Till We Have Faces*? There she describes the coming of the god whom she has loathed for so long in physical terms. "The air was growing brighter and brighter about us; as if something had set it on fire. Each breath I drew let into me new terror, joy, overpowering sweetness. I was pierced through with the arrows of it." [4]

Sanctified imagination. The power we mortals have of conjuring images, of reaching for fancy, if you will, or fantasy, by way of mounting a raid on the inarticulate. It may be that one fine day we will win through to the glorious liberty of discovering that our power of language has suddenly been hugely enlarged so that we may be able to do what we cannot yet do, namely, *say* something about holiness. So far we have had to grope about amongst the nouns *light* and *purity* and *hush* and *dread* and *immensity* and *unapproachability* and *bliss*. Who knows what new powers will be vouchsafed to our speech in heaven? On the other hand, I myself suspect that we may never be able to outstrip the great seraphic immensities, who, as far as we know, make no attempt to explain anything. They cry "Holy!" we are told, and that is all. Perhaps it is enough. In every scene in Lewis in which we are led into the precincts of holiness, language dies away.

I myself think that one of the most exactly accurate pictures of holiness in all of Lewis' fiction comes as we follow Jane Studdock—poor, angry, frustrated, feminist Jane, having herself now been set magnificently free from her vexations—as we follow her, in the very last paragraph of *That Hideous Strength*, down through the warm green garden

---

[4] C. S. Lewis, *Till We Have Faces* (New York: Harcourt Brace Jovanovich, 1984), 307.

at Saint Anne's, to join her poor, vain spouse Mark, himself now chastened, in the pavilion prepared for their nuptials. "And Jane went ... into the liquid light and supernatural warmth of the garden and across the wet lawn (birds were everywhere) and past the see-saw, and the greenhouse and the piggeries, going down all the time, down to the lodge, descending the ladder of humility." [5]

Here we find, not seraphim and incense and deep calling unto deep, but only a seesaw and piggeries and that sort of thing. But what is a seesaw? It is nothing if it does not bespeak innocent and unselfconscious fun. It belongs to childhood. Hum. Childhood and fun: two more images that we need in our sanctified imagination? Is our grasp of holiness incomplete as long as we fail to take these lightweight matters into account? Not to mention our piggeries. What is a pig? One of the great masterpieces of the Most High God— but a masterpiece exhibiting perfections and excellences quite, quite different from the perfections and excellences we see in a lion, an eagle, a porpoise, or an impala. Is there something droll about a pig? Those extravagantly floppy pink ears, those—well, those little *pig* eyes, that great snuffling rubbery pink snout, not to mention the sheer rotundity of the whole enterprise. This creature came from the same workshop, remember, as did your lion and your impala. And we find that it is pigs who are evoked as Jane descends the ladder of humility toward her holy and blissful reunion with her spouse. Is it because sex is piggish? Not if by piggish we mean sordid (although they do love mud). No. Rather, we see under the modality of "pig-ness" (thank you, Plato) an aspect of the holiness crowning all sexuality. Jane and Mark enter into the mystery on a level altogether higher

[5] C. S. Lewis, *That Hideous Strength* (New York: Collier Books, 1965), 382.

than do the pigs, since Jane and Mark belong to the unique species said to have been made in the image of the Most High.

I will borrow from Saint John by way of closing down this topic. The time would fail me to tell—or the world could not contain the books—all that there is to be said about sanctified imagination. But the man whom we celebrate at this conference, born one hundred years ago, has, I suspect, put all of us here very profoundly in debt to him. Having met Jewel the Unicorn, and having seen the pot of boiling potatoes in Mrs. Beaver's house, and the crooked little streams in Edgestow before the Belbury bulldozers got to them, and the Great Snow Dance, and the upstairs room at Saint Anne's where Ransom and Merlin sit as the gods descend—having had all of this salted into our own imaginations, I think we would all agree loudly that our capacity to think of holiness has been greatly assisted by the sanctified imagination of this great storyteller, Mr. C. S. Lewis.

THE LIFE AND LEGACY OF C. S. LEWIS

How do we speak of the life and legacy of C. S. Lewis without betraying all by casting our remarks in an adulatory frame? Certainly there are those in this audience whose response to such a question would be quick and tart: "Adulatory? You don't know Lewis. He was a most difficult man, and he frittered away his latter working life by cobbling up unpardonably frivolous tales of a never-never land altogether *infra dig* for a don." Others of you, starting from an otherwise generally sympathetic point, would, in the interest of dealing a blow to the Lewis cult, cast about for flaws in his work. You would constitute the *advocati diaboli*, whose errand it is to dry up the sheer hagiolatry that threatens to soak the entire Lewis enterprise. I have an impression that my friend Greg Wolfe is somewhat more alive to this danger than I myself am: indeed I am not sure that Greg is sure that I am not one of the hagiolaters. And then there are in this immensely august theater here today, you card-carrying hagiolaters. You organize little dwarvish or elfin societies, stitch little cloaks for yourselves, eat mushrooms, learn to read runes, and quiz each other on trivia about Archenland, the Telmarines, or Uncle Andrew's attic. Lewis' *oeuvre* is Holy

Lecture given in a slightly different form at the C. S. Lewis Foundation Conference, Sheldonian Theatre, the University of Oxford, July 1998.

Writ, and whatever ale he drank is the only ale worthy of the name.

Having thrown up all these demurrals now, by way of little barbicans to defend my flanks against my adversaries, I may address myself to my assignment: "The Life and Legacy of C. S. Lewis".

We want something sweeping, I imagine. Something like one of these steam launches on an aircraft carrier that boost the F-14s into the air so that the next two weeks in Oxford and in the other place will roar along with momentum to spare.

But my success in designing and operating such steam launches, most especially literary launches, has been undistinguished. So let us take the lower road and see what may be said that is to the point.

Lewis' life, for a start. A most drab affair, if you simply tick off the sequence of *events*, as it were. Belfast, with his father intoning like a requiem, "There'll soon be nothing for it but the poor house"—but also the long attic hallways and afternoon sunlight in empty rooms and books stacked in sumptuous plenitude from the top to the bottom of the house. Warnie and Boxen. Arthur Greeves. But then Belsen, with Oldie, the headmaster—who has always sounded to me like Vlad the Impaler. Malvern with its hills: better than Belsen, certainly. The Great Knock, to whom you and I and anyone who has read a syllable of Lewis owe an immeasurable debt (which also means that, if you are Anglican, Orthodox, or Roman Catholic, you will send up a prayer for his agnostic soul, which, I dare say, is no longer agnostic). Oxford, then the trenches in northern France, then Oxford again, with Mrs. Moore and Maureen (the late Lady Dunbar) now somehow to be stirred into the household Lewis and Warnie eventually established.

And Magdalen. Thereby hangs a long and complex tale, and I suspect that most of Lewis' American votaries would much rather visualize him in the Senior Common Room after dinner, with port and coruscating conversation or in the Bird and Baby, with clouds of smoke, great masculine guffaws, Charles Williams dashing off to the bar for more beer, and Tolkien muttering that he never had the smallest clue as to what Williams was chattering about, than on his knees in Mrs. Moore's kitchen, scrubbing the floor or tending great pots of bubbling marmalade. And the tutorials, in one of which, I am told, by J. A. W. Bennett même, I suspect apocryphally, Lewis, having reached the end of his charity with a great lout of a pupil, snatched two swords from the mantel and challenged the hapless lad to a duel. The difficulty with this brave story is that there were no swords in Lewis' rooms.

Which itself brings up a point that must be touched upon no matter what historical figure we are talking about. The myths and the facts. Was Catherine the Great quite as equine in her libidinous adventures as the stories claim? Was Charlemagne two hundred years old? Did Philip II have twenty heads in his collection of saints' relics? Did Saladin send down his own destrier when he saw that Richard's horse had been shot out from under him? We all cling to such titillating bits: they are such fun that we willingly suspend disbelief in the interest of keeping our hero's story pungent.

But Lewis' life. It had no *events* in it, from one point of view. Even his marriage to Joy: well, many a man has married a powerful woman and has found the whole thing to be rhapsodic. And his faculty career: it was drab to the eye of an onlooker interested only in the dust-dry question of academic advancement. His books: Agatha Christie and P. G.

Wodehouse swamped Lewis in the output sweepstakes. Nothing much there. (We are speaking, I do trust you recall, from the point of view that looks for events and people in biographies. If you read the memoirs of Evelyn Waugh or Anthony Powell or Lady Diana Cooper or Sir John Colville, you are swept along on a glittering tide of amusing people. And of course when it comes to the biographies of Churchill, Lord Derby, or Stalin—I read that recently, with my eyes popping out on stems—the great thing is the sheer exaltedness of the whole drama, the Himalayan immensities that seemed to form their metier.)

There is none of this in Lewis. There is lots of drudgery. Besides the tutorials and the marmalade and the unremitting correspondence with people (myself among them) who must have bored him cruelly, and the bus trips to and from Headington, and the R.A.F. lectures during the war, which meant tedious railway trips at most inconvenient hours, then Joy's suffering and death, and then Lewis' own ill health and death: it all seems to supply us with meager fare, if what we want is exciting biography .

And yet. And yet. There is the rub. Here we are, thirty-five years after the man's death, and one hundred years after his birth, having gathered at this ancient university to speak mainly of him. If the life itself scarcely drew a great meteoric stroke across England's historic sky, then we must look to the legacy. And in this we find ourselves squarely in the ancient tradition of English literature. Who will regale us with the life of the author of Beowulf? Or of Gawain? Or of the Pearl poet? Or of Chaucer, forsooth: he was a minor official who lived over Aldgate and had a few contacts with Lionel Clarence and John of Gaunt and so forth, but again, it's meager fare for the biographer. Not to mention our friend Shakespeare. Now there's a life for you. A parish register or two, scattered records of a theater company, a marginal and nettlesome debate as to whether he wasn't in any event Robert de Vere, earl of Oxford, and a folio published after he was dead.

So. What shall we construct from the first half of our title—The Life and Legacy of C. S. Lewis—nothing?

Few of us would allow the matter to rest there. There would be no legacy, for a start, if there had been no life. But beyond that, I think we would all agree that the true drama of the life of C. S. Lewis occurred, as did the life of the Blessed Virgin, or indeed of our Lord himself, in that quiet region beneath the externals. I do not mean to be reaching for laughable analogies here, as though to find Lewis a place next to the Holy Family. And Oxford would certainly appear, especially to tourists, to be a much more exciting place than Nazareth. On the other hand, Oxford, and then Cambridge, were the towns where Lewis did his work, and the flush of romance touching such places tends to diminish if one works there. Evelyn Waugh tells us at the beginning of *Brideshead Revisited*, that in the twenties, Oxford was a city of aquatint. I daresay it was. And we all know that Lewis took pleasure in small things—Addison's Walk and Shotover Hill and so forth. But, like Nazareth, Oxford is a town where there was a life lived in great obscurity—at least until celebrity muddied the waters—but which life turns out to have left a legacy so rich that perhaps millions of people have benefited from the dividends.

Behind the legacy stands this man. None of those books could have been written if Lewis had not been Lewis. This is, of course, to point out the embarrassingly obvious. And Lewis himself argued, in *The Personal Heresy*, against E. M. W. Tillyard, that what we don't need to know when we read a book is everything about the author. I have no doubt at all that Lewis would be embarrassed beyond words at the effort to round up mementi from his life. And this is not an oblique thrust at the Marion C. Wade Collection at Wheaton College in America. It was my own mentor, Clyde Kilby, who put that whole thing together out of his back pocket, so to speak. He got no help from his institution in the early years of his efforts and would come to England and literally knock on doors of people who had known Lewis, without arranging any formal visit ahead of time. One summer I acted as his driver—he was getting old and weary by that time, and since I owed my soul to him, I thought I should try to lend a hand. We went up endless staircases off college quads and steered between high hedgerows down country lanes wide enough to admit only a Mini Minor. On one such trip we went to see A. K. Hamilton Jenkin in Cornwall, whom Lewis mentions in *Surprised by Joy* as having had a hand in his pilgrimage. Mr. Hamilton Jenkin had no recollection of any such thing and seemed embarrassed at the notion that he had ever been a specimen of anything that could be labeled a Christian witness. On another occasion we arrived at Lady Dunbar's front door. She was there, but I cannot remember much of what we talked about except that she excoriated a few people. We had lunch at the Athenaeum with Cecil Harwood, by then very old indeed. Some of his food landed on his necktie, I seem to recall.

But all of this is by way of raising the question of mementi, which always form a part of the scholars' research into an author, whether the author wants his life pillaged or not. I think most of us, whether we care to admit it or not, are at least secretly on Tillyard's side as over against Lewis': we *like* mementi. They are like relics in the Catholic realm.

They bring us closer to the whole enterprise, the man and his work. What good does Cardinal Newman's desk or academic gown do us? Not much, I suppose, but I defy anyone in this theater to go chop up the desk and tear up the gown for dustrags. We are all sacramentalists whether our theology admits it or not: we like physical contact with history. I myself have actually ventured inside the wardrobe and knocked on the back panel to see if I could get through, but with no luck. There were no fur coats hanging in it, for a start, and hence no spruce needles and no Narnia and no Mr. Tumnus. (I know there are two wardrobes, but that is a very moderate score in the relics sweepstakes: there are, I am told, hundreds of relics of the circumcision of our Lord scattered about Europe—and I say that as a Roman Catholic who is not supposed to scoff.)

But I think this topic of relics might form the bridge for us between the two elements of our title: life and legacy. The legacy is the imaginative, intellectual, and spiritual legacy of a life, most of which—at least the part that has affected you and me most directly—was spent sitting at a desk pushing a pen. The letters, the essays, the apologetics, the fiction and fairy tales, the musings on prayer, grief, the Psalms, pain, glory, and sanctity—who here will not send up a prayer of gratitude to the Most High for—for what? For Lewis? Or for his books? The distinction quickly becomes otiose.

But the prose (and the poetry, for that matter) in these books proceeds from matter forged in an intense, intelligent, tough, courageous, articulate, and just mind. My attempt here will be to suggest with a large brush and very few strokes just what we understand to be Lewis' legacy.

Not an easy task. Here was this figure, who will perhaps be recognized by history, despite his detractors, as a colossus, who loomed for not much more than two decades in our century. For one thing, he showed us that literary criticism and scholarship could be both rigorous and gay, shrewd and zesty. For my example, I will take the unlikeliest bit of all of his critical work, namely, his remarks on the late fifteenth-century poet Skelton. If any of you has been lucky enough to have had a course in Tudor literature, you may recall being delighted with Skelton. There is a sense in which he could be said to have been the Ogden Nash of his day— scarcely someone to find in the same volume with Sidney and Spenser. Here are some of Lewis' remarks about Skelton: "[The] subject is a perennial one—the bewilderment, and finally the terror, of a man at his first introduction to what theologians call 'the World'. . . . Things overheard, things misunderstood, a general and steadily growing sense of being out of one's depth, fill the poem with a Kafka-like uneasiness." [Lewis is speaking of Skelton's "The Bowge of Court"]. Or, speaking of Skelton's positively hair-raising bravura in multiplying rhyme, Lewis wrote, "any given rhyme may be repeated as long as the resources of the language hold out. . . . A form whose only constant attribute is rhyme ought to be intolerable: it is indeed the form used by every clown scribbling on the wall in an inn yard. How then does Skelton please? It is, no doubt, true to say that he sometimes does not. . . . [His poems] certainly do not please by the poet's 'facility in rhyme'. . . . On Skelton's terms any man can rhyme as long as he pleases." [1]

Those excerpts come from the famous "Oh hell", that is, the OHEL, *The Oxford History of English Literature*, to which Lewis contributed the sixteenth-century volume. I sometimes open my copy of this text purely in order to

[1] C. S. Lewis, *English Literature in the Sixteenth Century Excluding Drama* (Oxford: The Clarendon Press, 1965), 135–37.

laugh. The margins all the way through my copy are dotted with penciled exclamation points, which are my way of noting something that strikes my funny bone.

In the realm of literary scholarship, we have Lewis' works on Spenser, and his *Allegory of Love*, which is to this day, sixty years later, an unsurpassed work, and, among other items, his *Preface to Paradise Lost*. If you never read a syllable of Milton (which heaven forfend), drop everything and buy, across the road at Blackwell's, this slim volume. It is worth reading all by itself. On pages 17 and 22, Lewis gives the best case ever made for ritual and ceremony, and for liturgical language. I wish I could read both pages for you, but you will have to get the book. In the passage there occurs one of the few places where Lewis waxes patently earnest— speaking to you people who think that spontaneity is the key to worship. Here it is: "Those who dislike ritual in general—ritual in any or every department of life—may be asked most earnestly to reconsider the question. [Ritual] is a pattern imposed on the mere flux of our feelings by reason and will, which renders pleasures less fugitive and griefs more endurable, and which hands over to the power of wise custom the task (to which the individual and his moods are so inadequate) of being festive or sober, gay or reverent, when we choose to be, and not at the bidding of chance." [2]

This would be the natural place for me to make the transition to Lewis' legacy to us in his fiction and fairy stories. But I want to save that to the end (and do not be dispirited: I am well over halfway through my speech, never fear).

But I want to lift an extract from his epilogue to *The Discarded Image*, which, if your Lewis bibliography is rusty,

[2] C. S. Lewis, *Preface to Paradise Lost* (Oxford: Oxford University Press, 1970), 22.

is the book in which he plots out for us in thrilling terms the medieval world picture with its angels, archangels, and seraphim; its tutelary intelligences governing the planets; its gnomes, sylphs, nymphs, and salamanders inhabiting earth, air, water, and fire, the four elements; and the four corresponding humors: blood, phlegm, yellow bile and black bile; and the four personality types in their turn corresponding to the elements and the humors, namely, the sanguine, the phlegmatic, the choleric, and the melancholic. But here is the first paragraph in his epilogue: "I have made no serious effort to hide the fact that the old Model delights me as I believe it delighted our ancestors. Few constructions of the imagination seem to me to have combined splendor, sobriety, and coherence in the same degree. It is possible that some readers have long been itching to remind me that it had a serious defect: it was not true. I agree. It was not true." [3] I may add, however, that Lewis goes on to qualify this "not true" with such astuteness that one is obliged to abandon altogether any chronological snobbery that would maintain that our own picture of things, determined by quantum physics, is any *more* true. Physics may suggest possible contour lines for us for the universe (they themselves claim nothing more), and Lewis has no quarrel with that. But he wishes us to keep firmly in view the rather thin relation between a contour map and a real countryside with its green hills, its hedgerows and meadows full of lambs, the wildflowers, the songs of the winter wren, the veery, the hermitthrush, and the white-throat sparrow, and the brooks splashing over their rocks. (These last instances are my own, drawn from my own hiking in the White Mountains of New

[3] C. S. Lewis, *The Discarded Image* (Cambridge, Eng.: Cambridge University Press, 1970), 216.

Hampshire: Lewis' walking treks would have supplied him with an equally appealing list.) The point about *The Discarded Image* is that it suggested something—and once more we find ourselves having come to the very threshold of Lewis' fiction and fairy tales, which, I may say, incorporate every single one of the ideas we find explicated in Lewis' discursive books and essays.

There were lots of such volumes, and most of them are small. Lewis believed in the worthiness of the small book. We all know most of the titles: *Screwtape, The Problem of Pain, The Four Loves, Letters to Malcolm, The Great Divorce, The Abolition of Man, A Grief Observed,* and, of course, all the collections of essays, for which we all owe an immense debt to Mr. Walter Hooper.

These texts form, it seems to me, a major share in Lewis' legacy. And perhaps I ought to resort to numbering here, so that those of you who take assiduous notes on speeches will be able to show your friends that the keynote speech did have some actual points in it, and was not a mere windy and capricious encomium. Actually, I have reached point number 2 with these small books. Point number 1 comprised my remarks on his literary criticism and scholarship, marked as it was by both acuity and zest.

The small books, then. How many of them have formed perhaps *the* touchstone for our own hitherto somewhat muddled and poorly formed ideas on such and such a topic? (In this connection, I love Lewis' lapidary remark that someone's mind "was not as hard at work as he supposed".) We all blush there. But *Screwtape*: Has anyone here profited from that small book on the matter of temptation? *The Great Divorce*: Has anyone's idea on how egocentrism unfits us altogether for joy been clarified here? *The Problem of Pain*: my own Waterloo is the suffering of animals and the innocent. Do any of you share my gratitude to Lewis for his exquisitely self-effacing efforts to say something to the point on this most perilous topic? Stand up and wave a hanky if you had had things plotted out with such stark clarity before you read Lewis. *A Grief Observed*: I don't know why people cite this as a record of loss of faith: on that accounting, the Psalms must be accounted a similar document. And *Reflections on the Psalms*: Who in this theater had ever thought of the use to which we might possibly put the imprecatory Psalms, by fancying ourselves to be the evil which has forced another soul to the frantic point of wishing that our children's heads might be dashed against the wall? *Letters to Malcolm*: that reminder to pray for Ikhnaton, that protohistoric and monotheistic pharaoh, is one of the most moving paragraphs in all of Lewis' work. *The Abolition of Man*: Has any other book, even a book of a thousand pages, plunged the scalpel with such surgical accuracy right to the tumor that has unmanned our unhappy century?

And one more note on the small books, although the note applies to every line Lewis ever wrote, in any genre. How many of you can cite a boring passage in Lewis? Your difficulty in chasing down such passages is to be attributed, it seems to me, at least partly to two qualities marking Lewis' prose: first, its remorseless clarity, muscularity, and agility; and second, the images. The images. The old slippers in *The Four Loves*, or hell disappearing between the floorboards of heaven in *Divorce*, or The Green Book in *Abolition*. We are carried along, as befits our nature as men not angels, on solid chunks of reality. I repeat what I said a few minutes ago, we are all sacramentalists, willy nilly. (If you disagree, I will quarrel with you afterward, and I will win.)

Also to be numbered in this second category, along with the small books, we may with a certain liberty perhaps

include Lewis' apologetics. Not that these are small necessarily, although *Mere Christianity* is no tome. *Miracles* is a bit
of heavy sledding, but even here, an enormous amount of
what Lewis put forward by way of defending the ancient
Faith is to be found in essays, usually shorter than ten pages
long. And how shall we assess, or summarize Lewis' achievement here? There are perhaps, again, millions of people—
certainly hundreds of thousands—who would attribute their
crossing the line of Christian belief to these works. Lewis'
apologetics have long since won their place on the shelf of
major works of the century. The separate question, namely,
whether his particular mode of doing apologetics, and
whether his philosophical presuppositions are still viable,
is a sticky one. Many orthodox Christian philosophers
suspect that this part of Lewis' *oeuvre* is passé. It all has
to do with what has happened to language at the hands,
first, of the logical positivists, and then of the deconstruc-
tionists. Lewis anticipated this: once when he and Rose
Macaulay were to represent the Christian side in some
debate, he muttered to her before they entered the studio,
"I know what we'll get: we'll get logical positivists, and
you can't talk to them." He dreaded, above all else, I
think, the unmaking of language. *That Hideous Strength*
is his great document here. I myself am not equipped to
venture a prediction as to whether *Mere Christianity* and its
ilk will stay afloat in the long run. I suspect that it will,
since it speaks to our humanness, whereas other philosophical fashions attempt to re-create, or rather to unmake,
reality, and our humanness along with it. Why do we still
read John Bunyan or "Sumer is icumen in, Lhude sing
cuccu"? Because they belong to our humanness. But I
disqualify myself early in this particular question about
Lewis' apologetics.

I now come to my number 3: Lewis' fiction, including, of course, Narnia. And I might, again with a certain liberty, weasel his poetry in here. The early poetry is of interest, certainly, as charting the itinerary of a mind developing. I suppose there are half a dozen dissertations already written on this early stuff, but you will have to read them if you want more commentary on it than this short shrift I am giving it here. But the volume entitled simply *Poems* is brilliant. I make no apology for saying that. I teach English to earn my board and keep, but I must confess that I do not know how to relate Lewis' poetry to other twentieth-century poetry. Perhaps the laconic remark some fashion editor made concerning the highly particular way the late Dowager Queen Mary dressed, would fit here. He simply said that she dressed quite apart from current styles. Lewis and Tolkien, in both their narrative and poetic work, simply ignored current styles. I frankly opine that the dowager queen was not at all a bad example to follow.

If I were to start on the poetry, we would be here for the rest of the day. But if you have not read "On Being Human", then you have missed one of Lewis' most important and most beautiful statements. His sonnet sequence toward the end of the volume pierces with tender but needle-sharp poignance, a matter that lies at the deepest level of the heart of man. And I challenge anyone here this morning to volunteer to read "The Late Passenger" aloud to us without finding your voice breaking. (That is a rhetorical challenge, please: we must not have a rush to the podium just now.)

But the fiction. At the end of my speech, which we are now drawing near, I will attempt some summary generalizations, which will not be easy. Remember, it is the legacy of C. S. Lewis that we are trying to come at here in the keynote address. I feel like the man, whoever he may have been, charged with the task of counting the gold pieces in the great rooms that Atahualpa filled for his ransom (only to be forthwith killed by the Spaniards anyway).

My own guess is that the most vivid memories we all carry away with us from the fiction are the characters. Who of us has not been regaled, frightened, consoled, disgusted, awed, moved, and filled with hope and joy through having met these characters? They run the gamut from Wither to Jewel the Unicorn.

Wither: a wraith, a damned soul, who has specifically chosen hell by busying himself with the unmaking of meaning. How do I stand here? Weston, the scholar who has shriveled himself to a filthy and obscene monkey through his fatuous claim, "I am the Universe! I am your God!" The beautiful beast who sings with music to break your heart, as Ransom emerges from his desolate hell to his sabbath. Mrs. Beaver with her sewing machine, boiled potatoes, and sandwiches, the very archetype of the sheer goodness to which Lewis repeatedly returns. In this connection, we may recall Sarah Smith of Golders Green, the charwoman now glorified and moving along with immense solemnity and grace in *The Great Divorce*. Psyche, the soul hag-ridden with *sehnsucht*, having yearned all her life for the mountains—or rather, the god of the mountains. The Fox, with his fluorescent Greek wisdom, good as far as it goes, but so pitifully inadequate when it comes to the bloody mysteries among which the old priest with his beak and feathers and bladders and amulets, is wholly at home. Mark Studdock, alas: venal, craven, pusillanimous, ready to sell his soul and marriage for a mess worse than pottage. Jane, cerebral, liberated, but oh so sclerotic in her pursuit of a quasi-masculine femininity, and so profoundly transfigured by her encounter with Saint Anne's (who was, you will recall, the mother of the Mother of God) that she is able to be the God-bearer to poor Mark.

Lucy, always the first to be aware of Aslan. She constitutes Lewis' most delicate statement on femininity, I think. His most concentrated statement occurs in the passage at the end of *Perelandra* where Ransom is vouchsafed a vision of the two Oyéresu, Perelandra and Malacandra. Most of the rubbish that has been written on gender need never have burdened the market in the last thirty years, if people had read these few pages. But of course we also have Ivy Maggs and Mother Dimble and Camilla Dennison, revealed in all their feminine dignity and majesty for us when the gods come down upon Saint Anne's.

Edmund and Eustace Clarence Scrubb, tiresome and sniveling little boys who would be sent for counseling now, but who are souls with their first foot on the road to hell. Their salvation gladdens us all. And poor Uncle Andrew and Rabadash and the Black Dwarves, who have so seared their sensibilities that they can see only ennui and ashes where the good creatures see glory. This theme is played out to its inexpugnable end in Orual's story. In *Till We Have Faces*, Queen Urual makes such a plausible case against the gods: How many of us have similar gripes, and which of us will be able, like Orual, to sustain the argument against the Beatific Vision when the purgation specifically fitted for us finally takes us out of ourselves?

And how shall we speak of Puddleglum and Reepicheep? You and I have some inkling now as to what valor is by having met these two creatures. And Jewel. What is a unicorn? Why does its very mention haunt us with a bliss that eludes us? Why does it bid us farther up and farther in?

You have all been wondering if I am actually going to omit the greatest character of all. You would have grounds for shrill complaint if I were to do so. Aslan.

Professor Tolkien may have displayed greater inventiveness in his creation of certain characters—Treebeard, Gollum, Sam Gamgee, and, above all, Tom Bombadil. There is a sheer creative genius visible here.

But this does not diminish Lewis' achievement with Aslan by one scintilla. The thing is different. In those figures from Tolkien, we encounter pure and dazzling originality. In Aslan, the great lion, we see what could almost be called a stock character—the lion as king, which heaven knows, Lewis did not cook up.

But. But. In this figure it seems to me that Lewis has scored perhaps the most important point he ever scored. For he did the thing that is nearly impossible, namely, restored to the imagination of whole generations, entire categories that had vanished from the moral and metaphysical map. Ask yourself how you would even begin to suggest to a generation brought up on MTV, rock music, lewd cinema, pornography, and the omnipotent conspiracy of the whole of academia, political power, and the media, to expunge what T. S. Eliot called "the permanent things" from human imagination, and to replace them with relativism, egocentrism, cynicism, ostentatious squalor, and a sensuality that makes Gomorrah itself look like Mr. McGregor's garden— ask yourself how you would flag down that generation with such notions as majesty, valor, purity, nobility, courtesy, magnanimity, magnificence, glory, and holiness.

We stagger at the very suggestion. I walk down a certain street in Boston where the skinheads gather in their black clothes and black lipstick (on both the females and the males—I can't call them girls and boys, alas), with their

THE LIFE AND LEGACY OF C. S. LEWIS

safety pins through their eyebrows, cheeks, and lips, and I ask myself: How shall we speak of glory? Is there any common footing upon which an approach to sanctity might be mounted here?

In the figure of Aslan, we are regaled with all that has been expunged from our unhappy century. You need only to see the quivering nostrils and pricked-forward ears of the animals at the creation of Narnia, or sail with the Dawn Treader toward the utter East, or go with Digory to the garden where he will pick the apple, or with Susan and Lucy on the night of Aslan's Passion, to see that it can be done.

It is a *weight* of glory that marks Aslan's presence and Aslan's country.

I must end. What is C. S. Lewis' legacy? Who will attempt the summary? Muscular, perspicuous, vastly generous literary criticism; exhaustive but vibrant scholarship; letters of infinite charity; essays unflaggingly engaging and never self-serving; a hardheaded, even tough, handling of moral questions; lucid, nay pellucid, teaching; a prose style that startles us awake again and again in line after line with the sheer delight of the English language; modesty, ebullience, humor, and deep seriousness all in one paragraph; stony severity with all humbug, preening, and tergiversation.

But, arching far, far above all of this, the vision of hell and heaven. The squalor, ennui, vacuousness, wrath, putrescence, and egocentrism of the one; and the bliss, joy, freedom, beatitude, merriment, courtesy, and sheer glory of the other. If I were forced at knifepoint to offer a single word that might suggest Lewis' legacy, I would offer this one word: Glory.

THE WAGES OF READING

A school friend of mine, whom I have not seen for forty-five years, recently sent me a sheaf of articles from *The Atlantic Monthly*, to which he appears to subscribe. Actually, they were book reviews, but of article-length. I found myself galvanized by all of them. They were almost all reviews of recent literary biographies—Evelyn Waugh, Upton Sinclair, Mary McCarthy, H. L. Mencken, Kingsley Amis—that sort of thing.

I began with the Waugh review, since Waugh is a favorite of mine, and I happen to be on his side on every possible topic: manners, the aristocracy, the collapse of civilization, Roman Catholic orthodoxy, bores. I cordially disagreed with the reviewer of the book in question, who clearly was unsympathetic to Waugh's ferocious religious and social outlook. But never mind that.

The reviews that began really to engage my attention were those that concerned themselves with Samuel Pepys (pronounced *Peeps*, if your seventeenth-century English studies have gone a bit rusty), the *enfant terrible* of diarists; Lord Byron, the sensationally romantic figure whose life was at least as fantastic as his poetry; and Oscar Wilde, the acidulous epigrammatist of the late nineteenth century who ended

Originally published in a slightly different form in *Touchstone* (October 2003): 23–25. Reprinted with permission.

up in jail for having sued for libel the marquess of Queens-
berry, who accused Wilde of sodomy (or, as we would more
delicately say nowadays, of having an affair) with the
marquess' son, Lord Alfred Douglas. Wilde, as readers will
all remember, lost the case (the marquess' charges were true,
alas), and went to jail (*gaol* in English) for two years, and
died miserably four years after his release, in 1900.

I was quite swept away as I read these three articles. I
mean, here is Pepys, simply writing down every little thing
of every day of his life in the London of Charles II. His
shoes, his socks, his maid, his food (mustard and tripe was
a favorite dish of his), his "going abroad" (walking) in the
streets of a London, which, by the way, in his day stretched
only from the Tower to Park Lane, and from Oxford Street
to the Thames. (Obviously, things had begun to spill over
into the fields a bit.)

Nothing is of no interest to him. Critics have scratched
their beards over the question as to just wherein we are to
say the genius of all this lies. But genius it seems to be. Of
course, we are also regaled with the most clinical, or shall
we say leering, scrutiny, not only of all of his (daily?) fornication, but of every scrofulous pustule, wen, follicle, boil,
carbuncle, and septic outcropping on every square inch of
his and his ladies' bodies. For a mid-Victorian like me, the
whole thing is beyond being unspeakable. And there are no
smallest details of the scatological aspects of our mortality
upon which he does not descant with the greatest zest.

But on the other hand, Pepys has given us probably the
best descriptions of the Plague of 1664–1665 (not to be
confused with Defoe's *Journal of the Plague Year*, on the same
disaster, but published in 1722) that have ever been written, and also of the Great Fire of London in 1666. On this
latter topic we do, in fact, glimpse details that reveal Pepys'

great and sympathetic heart. After telling about the poor people struggling down the steps of the Embankment with what belongings they could salvage, into boats on the river, he then tells us about the "poor pigeons" who, nonplussed by the conflagration, do not have the sense to leave their perches, and some of whom consequently find their wings burned up and fall to the ground to die.

Well. So much for Pepys, for the moment. He is a "figure" in English literature and has a firm place in the "canon". What about Byron? He, of course, is a colossus, in all senses of the word. He was beautiful, titled, dashing, insatiably adventurous (not to say reckless), restless, brave (although he never actually fought in a battle, much as he tried), and lecherous. He married, but seems to have spent the rest of his days ravishing both boys and women. His interminable poems—*Childe Harold's Pilgrimage, Manfred, Don Juan* (pronounced, by the way, *Joo-un*, by academics), *Mazeppa, The Giaour*—where shall we stop?—extol the super-romantic ideal of the bold, brave, dashing, wildly colorful young man who ravins down (short *a* there, like Claudio's rats in *Measure for Measure*) all conceivable experiences like so much ale. It is all quite breathtaking and intoxicating and is likely to make one look at one's own demure, not to say drab, existence and think, "Life is passing me by."

And then we have Oscar Wilde. Actually, when it comes down to it, he is not much of a literary figure, if we are speaking of major English authors. He didn't write *much* that was good. Oh, to be sure, *The Importance of Being Earnest* (which Wilde was *not*) will last forever, and rightly too. And *The Ballad of Reading Gaol* is deeply moving. But *The Picture of Dorian Gray* cannot be held to be among the great English novels. And most of the rest of Wilde's *oeuvre* has sunk from view.

We all think of Wilde, of course, as being diabolically witty. Here again, rightly so. He could toss off, at the smallest provocation—or without provocation, for that matter—some of the funniest and most withering *obiter dicta* ever uttered by man. In his heyday he was lionized by the rich and fashionable, especially hostesses. And at Oxford he cut a bizarre figure, quite ostentatiously and calculatedly, by the clothes he chose to wear. He is, no doubt, the original of Gilbert and Sullivan's Bunthorne, in *Patience*—your archetypal aesthete—epicene, effete, affected, and suave.

As is the case with both Pepys and Byron, we find ourselves electrified by reading, not only *what* these gentlemen wrote, but also *about* them. Shelves of books have been written about all three of them. How can one resist the wit, the effortless urbanity, the lust for life, the drollery, and the sheer *élan vital* radiating from this trio? *Such* fun!

But. And here is where I found myself, two or three days after the fact, raising a question. It is the sort of question that would interest neither *The Atlantic Monthly* nor its readers. It arises from some *other* reading I have been doing. As a Roman Catholic, I read the breviary and the Office of Readings daily. Here I find myself awash in the Psalms. These poets (I grew up to believe that David wrote most of them, and still do, I suppose) were wholly engaged in matters that seem to have escaped Pepys, Byron, Wilde, their biographers, the critics, and the terribly civilized readers of *The Atlantic*.

They struggled, and cried out, even bellowed, to heaven, over their sins, and over God's wrath, and over matters like grief and death and sickness. And they scrutinized, with myopic punctilio, the smallest matters of virtue: Have I been straightforward with my neighbor? Have I spoken ill of him? Am I guilty of a vituperative spirit? Are my hands clean? Is my spirit pure? When shall I come into the presence of God? Oh, how I love God's house. One thing have I desired of Thee. . . .

And all of this turns out to be of one fabric with what we come upon in the Sermon on the Mount: very drab concerns, from your Pepysian, Byronic, Wildean point of view. Being pure in heart; being poor in spirit; being merciful; hungering for righteousness. Not to mention the various lists put forward by Saint Paul in 1 Corinthians 13 and Galatians 5: love (*not* Byron's notion), joy, peace, long-suffering, gentleness, goodness, faith, meekness, self-control. And so forth and so forth. Pretty dull stuff, by *Atlantic* standards.

I happen also to be reading the Roman martyrology—or, more specifically, Butler's magisterial *Lives of the Saints*. Here you have anywhere from six to fifteen saints' lives for every one of the 365 days of the year. Oh, to be sure, there is plenty of legend there. But Butler, or at least his later editors, Thurston and Attwater, is scrupulous about differentiating between cold history and "pious legend". On the other hand, I am the sort who does not boggle when I read in the Venerable Bede, or in Jacobus de Voragine's *Legenda Aurea*, about the dust on which had been poured water in which some saint's bones had been washed bringing healing to some leper. I mean, hankies went out from Saint Paul with healing virtue, forsooth.

Who is to say that the Holy Ghost stopped everything at the end of Acts 28? I love old Sir Thomas Browne who, though "I am of that Reformed new-cast Religion", nevertheless said, "I am, I confess, naturally inclined to that which misguided Zeal terms *Superstition*. . . . at my Devotion I love to use the civility of my knee, my hat, and hand. . . . I should violate my own arm rather than a Church;

nor willingly deface the name of Saint or Martyr. At the sight of a Cross or Crucifix I can dispense with my hat." [1] I find that same frame of mind at work when I read all of these saints' lives.

I am also reading at present, Eleanor Shipley Duckett's *The Wandering Saints of the Early Middle Ages*. These men (Patrick, Columba, Columban, Fursey, Boniface, Willibrord, et al.) could scarcely turn around without some miracle popping up. Once a granite outcropping rearranged itself into a seat so that two pilgrim saints would be a bit more comfortable. This will not wash in the pages of *The Atlantic*. And the votaries of Pepys, Byron, and Wilde are far more interested in the pustules in the groin of their women (or boys) than in gentleness, goodness, meekness, temperance, faith.

Interested. I think that is the key word. What interests me? I wonder whether, insofar as I pursue the foxfires that flit through my brain in the wake of Byron and company, I am not to that extent "distracted from distraction by distraction" (Eliot, *Four Quartets*, see 141 below). When I read Saint Francis de Sales' *Introduction to the Devout Life*, or Pascal's *Pensées* (I keep a copy by my desk and read a few while I wait for my antiquated computer to crank on to AOL and get itself online and get my e-mail), or the *Imitatio Christi* (this is by my phone: it takes forever to get messages off), I find that the older I get, the more riveting this stuff is.

My grave yawns somewhere here ahead of me. Today? Tomorrow? Another aeonian thirty years (I'd be 98)? When the Angel of Death with his scythe looms blackly at my door, what will I wish I had had my mind on?

[1] Sir Thomas Browne, *Religio Medici and Other Writings* (New York: E. P. Dutton, 1951), 3.

Readers will justifiably be thinking to themselves by this time, "Heigh-ho! What sort of manqué saint is this man? I mean—surely we can enjoy theater and ballet and poetry and Broadway and travel and good wine and feasting and badinage? Are we all to drop to our knees like Carthusians or Cistercians, on freezing stone floors? Come."

Touché. I have a confession. I made my livelihood for forty years teaching English literature. Byron and all. What about that? Was I leading my students down a primrose path?

I don't *think* so. I did, actually, have a most excellent teacher of Victorian literature at Wheaton College, fifty years ago, who left teaching to write Sunday school materials because she could not in conscience go on teaching Ruskin, Pater, Swinburne, and Wilde. Well, that'll show up on her account at the Divine Tribunal as possibly a plus. I don't know. I did not do that. I loved my teaching. Even Chaucer's bawdy.

Perhaps it is a matter of what *finally* engages us and what constitutes "the still point of the turning world" for us (Eliot, see 141 below). Byron does not help me here. Is he all right for study? I could argue the case either way. But I do know one thing: the Romantic Ideal will send you to hell eventually. Luxuriating in fornication and sodomy will, too. The modern world (partly fed by *The Atlantic Monthly*) pursues materials in this connection with the most sober assiduity. Do we (Christians) demur somewhere in here? How countercultural are we?

Here is where a finely tuned question arises. What, we might ask, constitutes the watershed between an interest in, not to say a fascination with, the lurid and the titillating ("Oh—fancy this! Byron was a *pederast* into the bargain! This calls for an article!" And so forth and so forth) and a greater interest in the annals of sanctity? A most piquant question. It is not only the glossy magazines and tabloids that flourish on this. The most desiccated of scholars, and certainly the most dedicated of biographers and critics, not to say the pundits and armchair Freudians, *not* to mention thee and me—all of us have to admit that wickedness, recklessness, disorder, and the bold flouting of convention and "society's taboos" give us a great *frisson*.

Before it is too late, should we, and if so, how are we to, develop a "taste" for the annals of sanctity? And will there come, at last, an actual preference for these over the topics filling the columns, again, not only of the cheap magazines in the airport racks, but also of the highbrow journals? (It is not all, of course, scandal; but totally godless respectability—Virginia Woolf, say—holds the field, surely, over the narratives of souls struggling toward God.)

There is not much modern literature that bespeaks what I am talking about. In our own time, I can think principally of Eliot's *Four Quartets* and Evelyn Waugh's *Brideshead Revisited*. Both, it may be remarked, have suffered a certain amount of obloquy at the hands of the critics and graduate English departments, since they are such objectionably *Christian* tracts, so to speak. Eliot got a lot of the "poor old Tom" sort of thing, and people seem to balk at Charles Ryder's conversion as the thing that eventually spoils *Brideshead*.

Well, then, we may all remark (testily): Do you want us to jettison our libraries and take up hagiography alone? No. But the question of what *interests* me, finally, lurks.

A question to throw us all into a brown study.

BRIDESHEAD REVISITED REVISITED

The late Russell Kirk spoke often of "the moral imagination". By it he referred to that whole backdrop, or set of underpinnings, that corroborates for us mortals the fixities of the moral law. We are not angels: hence we do not encounter reality directly. We are protected ("from heaven and damnation", says Eliot) by the merciful arch, or filter, we might say, of the temporal and spatial, which bring with them the forms and colors that address our imaginations.

When we use this phrase, *moral imagination*, we do not mean that the moral world exists only in the realm of fancy. Rather we refer to the vision of good and evil we find in works of fiction. It is a vision that not only suffuses these works, but also presides over the terms of these fictions, nay, that determines the very stuff and texture of them.

Take, for example, the fourteenth-century *Vision of William concerning Piers the Plowman:* here we have, in an allegory to be sure, not merely the picture of a personality, or of a whole world, but, beyond these, the vision of what constitutes goodness and badness. Or take *Gawain:* the trouble in that poem is that Gawain has sinned (not that he is "out of touch with his feelings" or that he has been "victimized"). There is a *moral* litmus test brought to

Originally published in a slightly different form in *Touchstone* (Summer 1996): 27–32. Reprinted with permission.

bear on his behavior. In *The Faerie Queene*, all the thick woods and grottoes and hags and perils are to be understood in moral, and not merely psychological, or linguistic, terms. In *Measure for Measure*, the thing that has them all apoplectic in Vienna is the matter of sin and its punishment. We playgoers may enjoy the leisure and luxury of beholding fascinating personalities at work—Isabella and Angelo and Lucio and Claudio—but the nub of the drama is a moral matter.

It is not without significance that we often reach for Renaissance and pre-Renaissance fiction when we speak of the moral imagination. By the time we get to Fielding, and then Jane Austen, Trollope, Henry James, and Virginia Woolf, we are not sure that "moral" is altogether the apt word. To be sure, all of these authors undergird their stories, in some sense, with a world of moral suppositions. Trollope, for example, shows how all the dramatic currents and countercurrents flow over a bed, so to speak, of moral assumptions. The sanctity of marriage is there, for example, and truthfulness, and generosity, and fidelity to one's duties, and benevolence: it is all there. But the main thing that engages our attention in Barset, or among the Pallisers, is not a rock-bottom question about goodness and evil; Trollope has not set out primarily to extol morality or religious truth.

Walker Percy makes this distinction, speaking of fiction:

Let me define the sort of novelist I have in mind.... He is ... a writer who has an explicit and ultimate concern with the nature of man and the nature of reality.... One might apply to the novelist such adjectives as "philosophical," "metaphysical," "prophetic," "eschatological," and even "religious.".... Such a class might include writers as diverse as Dostoevsky, Tolstoy, Camus, Sartre, Faulkner, Flannery

O'Connor. Sartre, one might object, is an atheist. He is, but his atheism is "religious" in the sense intended here: that the novelist betrays a passionate conviction about man's nature, the world, and man's obligation in the world. By the same token, I would exclude much of the English novel—without prejudice: I am quite willing to believe that Jane Austen and Samuel Richardson are better novelists than Sartre and O'Connor. The 19th century Russian novelists were haunted by God; many of the French existentialists are haunted by his absence. The English novelist is not much interested one way or another. The English novel traditionally takes place in a society as every one sees it and takes it for granted. If there are vicars and churches prominent in the society, there will be vicars and churches in the novel. If not, not. So much for vicars and churches.[1]

It is not to be urged that Evelyn Waugh should be thought the equal of Tolstoy, or even of Jane Austen. Nevertheless, his fiction raises piquant questions, if we are speaking of the moral imagination and twentieth-century English language fiction—particularly *Brideshead Revisited*. But his *Sword of Honour* trilogy also would certainly raise similar questions, most notably in the figure of the protagonist's father, old Gervase Crouchback. We would need to undertake a wide canvass in order to discover another character in recent fiction who exhibits in such stark colors the quality we can only call holiness. We, jades that we moderns are, find ourselves hailed, against all plausibility, with holiness—that is the only word for it—in the figure of Gervase Crouchback. And it is done, *mirabile dictu*, without the faintest whiff of sentimentality.

But in *Brideshead Revisited*, Waugh has done the almost unthinkable. He has given us (jades, if the accusation is not

[1] Walker Percy, *The Message in the Bottle* (New York: Farrar, Straus and Giroux, 1982), 102–3.

too fierce) a full-blown acclamation of Catholic piety, vision, morals, and dogma, but in terms that steal a march past merely modern sensibilities, and in fact virtually swamp those sensibilities.

It might be put this way: we are a skeptical epoch. Waugh's book is full of skepticism: indeed, the narrator is a card-carrying skeptic. Charles Ryder, the protagonist, is a thoroughly modern man. We might congratulate ourselves on being a somewhat cynical epoch—and the book is redolent of cynicism. Again, we are an unbelieving era, and the whole drama in *Brideshead* is seen through the lens of unbelief. Yet again, we are most certainly a highly self-conscious era— and the narrator in *Brideshead* is agonizingly self-conscious, almost paralytically so. (In the BBC television series, Jeremy Irons, in depicting Charles Ryder, displayed incredible dramatic prowess by making the reticent, self-conscious, laconic Charles a figure who seizes and holds our attention, and affection even.)

Oddly, *Brideshead* would seem able to take its place entirely comfortably on the shelf of modern fiction (as opposed to other fiction with religious overtones, like that of Tolkien or Williams or Chesterton, for whom categories like "fantasy" and "metaphysical thriller" have to be invoked). And yet *Brideshead* takes us all the way in to the world of Christian belief, piety, and dogma.

How does Waugh do it? My hunch is that he does it by *bravado*. It is bravado that is Waugh's trump card. Knowing that he is writing in a highly blasé, weary, and urbane world (and fifty weary years have passed since then), he first of all trumps that world, so to speak. He upstages us all by making his novel ten times more blasé, weary, and urbane than we are.

For example, the tale is set in the 1920s, in Oxford, London, and Venice, and at a great country house. Any reader

ignorant enough to congratulate himself on his own clev-
erness is very quickly left in the dust by the sheer agility,
the prowess, the *vivace* tempo of the badinage flying about
his ears. You thought you were urbane? Meet Sebastian:
you will feel yourself an oaf. You thought you were witty?
Meet Anthony Blanche: you will retire in confusion from
the lists. You thought you had fine sensibilities? Next to
Charles you are a churl. You thought you were civilized?
In the family circle at Marchmain House you find that you
are the merest rustic, left mute by your own solecisms.

But Waugh's strategy goes much further than this. After
upstaging our supposititious urbanity, he goes on to disarm
our routine and self-congratulatory unbelief, again by sheer
bravado. That is, we find ourselves in thick Catholic piety
and faith, but deprived, somehow, of our usual ability to
patronize that piety and faith. We have lost our vantage
point, and it is no longer these pious people who are under
our avuncular surveillance, but we who are under theirs.
For example, in one conversation with Lord Brideshead,
Charles announces that he is an agnostic. Bridey is only
mildly diverted by this, the way he would be if Charles had
announced himself a vegetarian or a necrophiliac. "Really?"
says Bridey. "Is there much of that at your college?" [2]

Now that is bravado. But it is not bravado from the characters themselves. Indeed, there is nothing ostentatious, or
swashbuckling, about any of them. The bravado is at work
in the challenge that the narrative mounts against the reader.
We find that we have been angled into the uncomfortable
position of being the ones under scrutiny. We no longer
have the luxury of patting faith on the head. Faith is looking at us, quizzically, ironically, and slightly incredulously.
"An unbeliever?" it seems to say. "Fancy." Somehow

[2] Evelyn Waugh, *Brideshead Revisited* (Boston: Little, Brown, 1973), 92.

"unbeliever" and "bumpkin" seem to have become synonymous here.

But a much greater subtlety is at work in Waugh's narrative than any brief exchange like that might suggest. The subtle strategy comes in the form of a challenge: the reader finds himself drawn into the story, and losing thereby his agnostic footing. (This, of course, is to assume, for the argument, that your archetypal "modern" reader *is* agnostic.) We enter a brilliant world in the story, but it is a peculiar world, namely, the world of the Catholic aristocracy in England. By locating his story here, Waugh throws down a gauntlet.

Catholicism in England always has been in the minority: for some centuries it was a beleaguered minority. So to be Catholic in England was to be entirely free from the burden under which the Church of England always seems to stagger, namely, the burden of being agreeable. Anglican bishops seem anxious to assure everyone that what they are retailing is, after all, nothing but good, modern, sensible English fare. Don't for a moment suppose that I am purveying zeal, or miracles, or revival. To be Anglican is to be *au courant.*

This is an unfair caricature, of course, but one which, for good or ill, finds itself echoed in English fiction (and also in television: the late Malcolm Muggeridge was wickedly merciless in tweaking the noses of just this sort of churchman).

By locating his story among the English Catholic aristocracy, Waugh has, with one leap, made it immune from having to be acceptable. Catholicism through the centuries has not ordinarily been found pawing the arm of contemporaneity, as it were, and pleading, "But you can be Catholic without crowding your Englishness, or your respectability." To be Catholic is to be different—but not different, Waugh would have urged, in the way cults, sects, or conventicles are. It is easy to dismiss the religion in those quarters by pointing out that it is tacky, or marginal, or haywire, or *arriviste*, whereas to be Catholic is to belong to the most ancient and august organism in the world. It is older than the oldest dynasties and universities. To be Catholic is to be free from ever having to temporize. (If this sounds triumphalist, we may remind ourselves that Waugh might not have demurred at the charge.) To be Catholic is to be identified as someone who espouses a whole fabric of ideas—Virgin Birth, miracles, transubstantiation, and so forth—but who cannot be dismissed with exactly the same insouciance with which one might dismiss you if you belonged to a sect.

This matter never comes up in the story in so many words, but the way in which the Flyte family hold their faith is a vastly different business from the way in which, say, a devout Evangelical, middle-class family might hold theirs. The Flytes are immemorially at home in their serene and lofty faith and entirely untroubled by the disjuncture between that faith and the rest of England. They have, as it were, nothing to prove.

Thus Waugh outflanks his readers. He does not have to try to weasel religion into the narrative: it is of the very texture—a highly civilized texture—of the narrative. But there is more. Waugh manages a sort of narrative alchemy, so to speak, whereby the troubles of the Flyte family take on the aspect of *sin*.

This is unheard-of in modern fiction. Which of Henry James' or D. H. Lawrence's or E. M. Forster's characters must make his agonizing choices in life under the scrutiny of the Church's teaching on sin (unless it be by shucking off that teaching)? Stephen Dedalus must leave the world of Jesuit sermons. But in *Brideshead*, we find that everyone, sooner

or later, must come to terms with God, not in an attenuated or leached-out version that might be acceptable to William Ellery Channing's Boston, or our own New Age sibyls.
No. What is asked of the characters is that they squeeze
through the needle's eye of sacramental confession and abso-
lution, and *thus* find dignity and freedom and authenticity.
It offends our fastidiousness.

This tactic, or alchemy, if you will, whereby Waugh obliges
us to take seriously the demand laid on his characters that
they face their choices in the light of Catholic teaching, is
paralleled by another tactic, namely, that even though the
Faith is, in some sense, the heroine of the story, nevertheless, every single exemplar of that Faith is a very poor icon.

We may survey the characters to see if this is so. First, of
course, there is Sebastian. What a dazzling, coruscating figure he is. Young, beautiful, witty, acerb, cavalier, infinitely
cultivated: Which of us is not left plodding in the dust as
his barouche-landau whirls by? He seems to know, and be
long since at home in, everything that marks the precincts
where life is lived with grace and civility: cigars, wine, clothes,
art, repartee, persiflage, eccentricity—Sebastian is the very
avatar of all of this. He would seem to stand at a polar
extreme from the dowdy world of religious belief. But when
Charles ventures to raise the matter of Sebastian's faith, ever
so gingerly, we have this:

"Oh dear, it's very difficult being a Catholic."

"Does it make much difference to you?"

"Of course. All the time."

"Well, I can't say I've noticed it. Are you struggling
against temptation? You don't seem much more virtuous
than me."

"I'm very, very much wickeder," said Sebastian indignantly.

". . . I suppose they try to make you believe an awful lot of nonsense?"

"Is it nonsense? I wish it were. It sometimes sounds terribly sensible to me" (86).

This is the note struck in *Brideshead Revisited*. Whereas religion ordinarily has to creep apologetically, or lurch awkwardly, onto the stage, here it dances out in front of our eyes, daring us to cavil or carp. We haven't often encountered religion in these bravura terms. We are not sure how we might gainsay it.

And there is Sebastian's older brother, Lord Brideshead (Bridey). The satanically witty Anthony Blanche, in his thumbnail sketch of the whole family, says Brideshead is "something archaic, out of a cave that's been sealed for centuries" (54). And indeed, we find ourselves writhing at times over Brideshead's lack of apparent tact.

There is something vastly civilized about Bridey. He has no vanity at all, and he is transparent and utterly without malice. But he can be heavy-footed. We find this when Bridey explains why his fiancée, Beryl Muspratt, must not visit the Flyte household, where Julia is now present with her husband and Charles, her lover: "You must understand that Beryl is a woman of strict Catholic principle fortified by the prejudices of the middle class. I couldn't possibly bring her here. It is a matter of indifference whether you choose to live in sin with Rex or Charles or both—I have always avoided enquiry into the details of your ménage— but in no case would Beryl consent to be your guest" (285).

So far, Catholicism is not being very compellingly, or attractively, represented by the Catholics among whom our agnostic narrator Charles finds himself. Sebastian's Catholicism seems to exist in a category with Mother Goose;

and Brideshead sounds like an inquisitor. But there is their wonderful little sister Cordelia. She promises to pray for Charles and tells him she can't spare a whole Rosary for him, only one decade. She implies that it would be a good idea if Charles chipped in five shillings so she can buy yet another African goddaughter. "I've got six black Cordelias already. Isn't it lovely?" (94). We seem to be being invited to write Catholicism off with our worst prejudices confirmed about how mercenary and idolatrous it is.

But Cordelia turns out to be a girl, and presently a young woman, of vast integrity, generosity of spirit, joy, and self-effacement. Much later in the story, speaking to Charles of the disordered lives of her older brother and sister, Sebastian and Julia, she quotes Chesterton's Father Brown: " 'I caught him . . . with an unseen hook and an invisible line which is long enough to let him wander to the ends of the world and still to bring him back with a twitch upon the thread' " (220). With charity and faith like this at work in Cordelia, we readers scarcely feel inclined to snipe at her five-shilling goddaughters in Africa.

In this same conversation with Charles, she speaks of Lady Marchmain, their mother. Lady Marchmain has died by this late point in the story. Cordelia says to Charles, "You didn't like her. I sometimes think when people wanted to hate God they hated Mummy. . . . You see, she was saintly, but she wasn't a saint. No one could really hate a saint, could they? They can't really hate God either. When they want to hate Him and His saints they have to find something like themselves and pretend it's God and hate that. I suppose you think that's all bosh" (221).

The reader, it seems, has been angled into Charles' position: Do I wish to sit in judgment on such sentiments as these, when the thing that so patently glimmers through it all is goodness?

But what are we to make of Lady Marchmain? Early in the story, Charles, the narrator, says this: "Religion predominated in the house; not only in its practices—the daily mass and rosary, morning and evening in the chapel—but in all its intercourse. 'We must make a Catholic of Charles,' Lady Marchmain said" (126).

This is all innocent enough, but we discover in the story that Lady Marchmain is something of a dragon. It may be because of her sheer power over her children, exercised ever so softly and elegantly, that they all have such problems. And so once again, we find a reason why Catholicism need not win us over. Look at what a termagant Catholic piety has made of Lady Marchmain.

But then we come to this, Julia's sympathy for her mother uttered through the bitter tears of remorse: "Mummy carrying my sin with her to church, bowed under it and the black lace veil, in the chapel; slipping out with it in London before the fires were lit; taking it with her through the empty streets, where the milkman's ponies stood with their forefeet on the pavement; Mummy dying with my sin eating at her, more cruelly than her own deadly illness" (288).

Which brings us to Julia, long since deeply embroiled in a life of sexual havoc. At the end of the story, she renounces Charles, for whom she has divorced her husband: "I can't marry you, Charles. . . . I saw to-day that there was one thing unforgivable . . . the bad thing I was on the point of doing, that I'm not quite bad enough to do; to set up a rival good to God's" (340).

Just a day or two earlier, when the family insists that their father, the renegade Lord Marchmain, be given the last rites on his deathbed, and Charles fiercely objects that extreme unction is "a lot of witchcraft and hypocrisy," Julia asks, "Is it? Anyway, it's been going on for nearly two thousand years" (325).

The scene at Lord Marchmain's deathbed is one of the most delicate in all of fiction. Waugh's tact as a narrator is put to the fiery test here. How do you present a drawn-out, highly charged deathbed scene without sloshing into the worst sort of bathos and treacle? Victorian novels and Hollywood movies have made us all quite justifiably skittish about deathbed scenes.

But Waugh seems to bring this one off. It is doubly threatened with sentimentalism, since not only do we have the dying man surrounded by his family, we also have our agnostic Charles, having reached the crisis in his own recalcitrant itinerary though at the same time scandalized by the dogged faith of the family. Nevertheless, Charles utters a feeble prayer and in response a sign is given.

"Then I knew that the sign I had asked for was not a little thing, not a passing nod of recognition, and a phrase came back to me from my childhood of the veil of the temple being rent from top to bottom" (338–39).

How do you do a conversion scene? The perils are legion. But Waugh's tact is in control: we never see Charles converting. In the epilogue, when we are back in the bleak present with Charles, nineteen years later, we find him, in 1943, with his army unit having been ordered to bivouac, unbeknownst to him, on the immense Brideshead estate. He steps into the little chapel in the house, and there he finds "a small red flame—a beaten-copper lamp of deplorable design, relit before the beaten-copper doors of a tabernacle; the flame which the old knights saw from their tombs . . . that flame burns again for other soldiers, far from home. . . . It could not have been lit but for the builders and the tragedians, and there I found it this morning, burning anew among the old stones" (351).

That is language that sails very near the wind. One false word, and we would capsize into sentimentalism. But I think Waugh brings it off. Reticence is what saves it all. We are not given the conversion scene: that would have been unmanageable (we may recall similar reticence on Shakespeare's part, in refraining from giving us the marriage scene of Romeo and Juliet, and in having Falstaff's death scene only reported by the maladroit Mistress Quickly). But we do see Captain Charles Ryder, in the chapel, offer an "ancient" prayer, "newly learned". Somebody has been teaching him the prayers of the Church. Obviously he has been received into that ancient Church.

Brideshead Revisited is the story of a religious conversion, whatever else it may be. Conversion is one of the topics that is most intractable, and most inhospitable to any attempt to come at it narratively. There is one sense in which the Catholic Faith itself may be said to be the heroine of the story. Certainly Charles is the protagonist. But the victor is the Faith that, in spite of—or, paradoxically, and far more profoundly because of—its shabby look when clothed with the flesh of Catholics themselves, triumphs, both in Charles, and also in each of the characters before they make their exits.

Waugh would have urged that this is the way it is. God shows up in the most inauspicious precincts: Israel—not one of the more impressive tribes of antiquity; Bethlehem—not one of the watering spots of the world; Calvary—scarcely an appropriate purlieu for the King of Heaven; the Church—not exactly a select group; and a flat, white, tasteless wafer—not a hopeful entry in the baked-goods sweepstakes. But the thing about all of these items is that God is to be found there.

Waugh has caught this in his novel and consequently offers the modern reader a work of moral imagination rare in modern fiction. The squalor, the bad taste, the *sturm und drang*, the ineptness, show up, not just in remote contrast to some austere vision of the Faith. They are the very modality in which that Faith is, as often as not, mediated to us.

AVE, MUGGERIDGE

Offering a speech about Muggeridge is a somewhat rum enterprise—a bit like offering to paint a picture of Caravaggio or Cimabue: they did the thing better themselves. Who will step forward and speak about this man whose hilarious mastery of the English language leaves most other wordsmiths in the ditch at the side of the road? I say "most other wordsmiths", since Muggeridge himself delighted in few things more than the prose of accomplished practitioners of the art. He once told me that he and Kitty were reading Edward Gibbon aloud, for recreation. There is the mark of a vastly civilized man—or couple, I should say: Kitty was his equal, if not in writing, at least in sheer agility, civility, and urbanity of mind.

I have entitled my remarks "Ave". I do not mean to be frivolous, much less blasphemous, in seeming to place Muggeridge in the category with our Lady, to whose name this salutation, *Ave*, immediately attaches itself in our minds. I mean only "Hail".

What would I like to hail in this man? Well, for one thing, his odd pilgrimage toward Christian faith and, finally, the ancient Church, which so galvanized the American Evangelical world, and hence, Wheaton College, the Oxford,

Lecture given in a slightly different form at the Malcolm Muggeridge Centenary, Wheaton College, May 23, 2003.

shall we say, of that world (although I may have bumbled into a solecism here, since Muggeridge was a Cambridge man—whose time at that university, I may add, was, on his own testimony, "scandalously desultory", to co-opt the phrase he used concerning Tolstoy's efforts at school; he always maintained that he was useless as a student). But any talk about Muggeridge would be missing a very great deal if it did not hail his zest for the English language.

For example, one does not get very many pages into his autobiography before one finds that the town hall in Croydon (I think I have this right) was "a building of quite exceptional architectural confusion". There you have it. Muggeridge did not depend on polysyllables, or on arcane words for his effects. These (effects) spring up at us from the rich and quizzical matrix of his natural sensibility. Here is another example, found literally at random by flipping the pages of my copy of his memoirs. "Working for Scott [at the *Manchester Guardian*] was like waltzing with some sedate old dowager at a mayoral reception in Manchester; for Beaverbrook [another press lord], it was like taking the floor in a night-club in the early hours of the morning, when everyone is more or less drunk." [1] But one did not have to have read Muggeridge's writing to come upon this zest. Once at our breakfast table, my daughter, then about eleven years old, I think, announced out of the blue, "I think I am growing up to be like Papa." Without one second's hesitation, Muggeridge put in, "This is grievous news." Or again, one morning when my son, then about eight, came into the kitchen in a state of some pique over something or other, Muggeridge remarked to

[1] Malcolm Muggeridge, *Chronicles of Wasted Time*, vol. 2: *The Infernal Grove* (New York: William Morris & Co., 1974), 53.

me that the boy was "a bit peppery this morning". That sort of thing.

Having itemized a few instances of Muggeridge's zest for the English language, I must remark that I owe a very great debt to a man whose name I can no longer recall. He was the editor of a sort of Christian underground journal in Cambridge, Massachusetts, during the seventies, when most underground journals had for their apostolate the business of undermining the seawall that stood between traditional Western civilization as Jews, Greeks, and Christians had known it, and barbarism. They succeeded, by the way: that seawall collapsed, and we now live in the ruins of that civilization. If you think I am being too gloomy here, go out and look at the clothes, and listen to the argot, and discover the moral categories and the manners, of the MTV generation, and you will come away dismayed and agreeing with me. "Grunge" is a word not to be found in the vocabulary of Plato, Maimonides, Avicenna, or Alcuin. But back to this man whose name I forget. He asked me to review the two-volume autobiography of one Malcolm Muggeridge for his paper. I agreed happily, since I knew Muggeridge from afar as the editor of *Punch*, to which I subscribed during the late 1950s when I was myself trying to creep out of the encircled camp of Philadelphia Fundamentalism and to see what was going on in the big world.

They sent me the two volumes for review. I began reading. Within the first three pages I found myself ravished by the man's prose. I am one of those people who put marks in the margins of books I am reading. In my script, an exclamation point means that I have found some line or lines to be funny. My copy of the autobiography is sprinkled with these exclamation points. I was going to regale you with a great barrage of amusing and trenchant quotations from my copy, but just now, as I was typing this page, I went to my shelf and pulled out the two volumes. Fancy my chagrin when I found that the only copy I have of volume I is a copy that belonged to my mother, who did not mark up her margins the way I do. So I cannot find all the *bon mots* I wanted to salt my speech with. What can have possessed me to let my own copy of the volume go, I cannot imagine: but there it is. *Sic transit gloria mundi.*

But back to Point One. Muggeridge's religious pilgrimage, which bemused the world, and astonished and thrilled American Christians, most especially those of an Evangelical stripe. I will plagiarize some paragraphs I wrote on this topic many years ago, and since these paragraphs appeared as the introduction in a book that sank without a ripple (actually, all of my books have adopted that melancholy habit), I think I can indulge in this plagiarizing without anyone's rising to his feet and protesting, "But we've all read this already, in that book." There is no danger of that. The following, then, is what I wrote, so long ago.[2]

It is always a piquant curiosity when a public figure converts to something. The Beatles seek out a guru; Cassius Clay becomes a Muslim; Sammy Davis, Jr., converts to Judaism; an astronaut takes up Transcendental Meditation; T. S. Eliot declares himself an Anglo-Catholic; and so forth. People never know quite what to do. If the figure is magnetic enough, there may be a small momentary popular surge toward whatever the thing is. Or there may be an amused and hearty "Right on, man! You do your thing, and we'll do ours." Or perhaps some knowing head-wagging: "Well,

---

[2] Malcolm Muggeridge, *A Twentieth Century Testimony*, introd. by Thomas Howard (New York: Thomas Nelson, 1978).

I could have told you this", or "Mmm ... Poor duffer's gone soft in the head, you know."

That last remark, I think, was the general, cultivated reaction to the spiritual odyssey of one of the most electrifying figures of our own time. He would not have been picked as a likely candidate for religious conversion, being not only an enormously civilized and urbane man of letters, but an *enfant terrible* of letters, a hard-headed journalist, a bodkin-tongued critic of the passing scene, and a general man-about-modern-affairs. One ordinarily thinks of men in this category as being cynics.

The man, of course, is Malcolm Muggeridge. A sometime journalist for British newspapers and the editor of *Punch*, he eventually emerged as a figure on British and American television—a personality who, everyone soon discovered, would regale and startle any audience with his wit, and who would insist, with implacable iteration, that the modern world is busy abuilding, not the City of God, nor even the classless Eden of optimist liberalism, but, quite simply, Babel. There was nothing that gave him greater pleasure than baiting woolly-minded Church of England bishops in his TV interviews. He would often mimic himself for my delectation as he told me about these interviews. "BISHOP!" he would begin, and then proceed to lure the hapless hierarch into a logical cleft-stick.

He might have been merely another crazy and unclassifiable exhibit for the eyes of mankind, in the lineage of Ezekiel, John the Baptist, Saint Simeon the Stylite, or Saint Francis of Assisi (who, you will remember, threw all of his clothes off in public at one point). But Muggeridge, like these gentlemen, was a figure who, in his ferocious and single-minded attack on the spirit of his age, and in his dedication to the task and message given him, appeared as a warning and comfort to honest minds, and as a dunce or a bore to fools.

The thing that stuck in everyone's craw was, of course, that the man eventually explicitly identified himself as a *Christian*. Alack. Here is all of this urbanity and wit, and all this trove of knowledge amassed during several decades at the center of twentieth-century affairs—all this promise that we would now have a real elder prophet for our time who would help us with our agenda of dismantling history and superstition, and of putting together a truly enlightened, liberal, and multicultural society. And what do we get? Doom. Jeremiads. Brickbats. *Jesus*.

For that is what the man was on about. Jesus. Of all the tiresome and dismaying backwaters for a modern eminence to dodge into, this, surely, was the most tiresome. Pulpy and rabbity minds have always fled from the hurly-burly and ambiguity of existence to the consolations of superstition. They have always chosen to placate the gods or hope for pie in the sky, rather than to address themselves courageously and humbly to the hard, light-of-day realities of life. But that is for pulpy and rabbity minds. Here we had *Muggeridge* doing this. What ailed the man?

If we wanted to find out what ailed the man, we could have done worse than to find out something about him by reading his own account of things in the two volumes entitled (with archetypical Muggeridgean self-deprecation) *Chronicles of Wasted Time*. Here he told us of his Fabian Socialist upbringing, with the whole gray troupe of leftist votaries of the earthly (read, Marxist) paradise plodding through his parents' living room, with Beatrice and Sidney Webb, whose niece Muggeridge had married, in the van. He also told us of his years at Cambridge, where, if we credit his wry portrait of himself as a feckless ne'er-do-well, we will conclude that his academic career was a total washout.

After Cambridge, he went to India as a teacher, as we all know. His reflections on the British Raj are a bellwether of the sort of piercing and unsettling remarks on the world scene he would be making for the rest of his life. One finds him poking pins into the balloon-like pretentions of pith-helmeted, be-braided, be-plumed colonels and other pukka types, not, as one might confidently expect, by way of clearing the ground for a fierce tract on the virtues of local self-government and the villainy of imperialism, but rather by way of letting the air out of *all* pretentiousness, imperial or local. In his descriptions of other British colonies, the wigged, plumed, and cockaded local chiefs who supplanted the moustachioed governors-general and viceroys do not appear on stage as necessarily wiser and nobler men than their imperialist Anglo-Saxon predecessors. Muggeridge was bemused by the whole phenomenon of man's lust for power and glory. His reaction to the puffing and strutting of politicians, tycoons, and plenipotentiaries, is not so much disgust as incredulity. What *can* they have thought they were about? Did they really believe it all? he seems to ask. This motif ran through his writings for decades before he was flagged down by the teaching of Christ and found divine corroboration for his own distrust of man's vanity. Actually, it should be remarked here that from very early on, Muggeridge, secular man though he felt himself to be, had the lurking notion that what one found in the teaching of Christ might just possibly be on the mark. This, incidentally, turned out to be something of a stumbling block to his American Evangelical fans when he came to the U.S. in the 1970s. They all wanted to know when he had got "saved", or when he had become a Christian. I daresay some of them even asked him when he had accepted the Lord Jesus Christ as his personal Savior. They were discomfited to find that Muggeridge did not at all understand their question. The point was, as he told me later himself, that he had always been en route, so to speak, and that his eventual putting of his Christian cards on the table was really only the upshot of a whole life of moving toward that point.

We all know the tale of Muggeridge's experience as a journalist. He was a foreign correspondent in Russia during the high and palmy days of Stalinist terror in the 1930s. He and his wife, like good English liberal intellectuals, had gone to the Soviet Union as pilgrims with Utopian stars in their eyes. Here now was the City of God come to earth, with the added advantage of its having jettisoned God. The City of Man. The classless society. The dictatorship of the proletariat. The only difficulty in the enterprise was that it looked suspiciously like hell.

No one would see it, of course. Cadres of rumpled humanitarian zealots from England and America made their pilgrimages and were shown the props and pasteboard sets of the Stalinist stage. They chose not to hear the shrieks coming from backstage, nor to see the Cheka hurrying half the population off to torture and the salt mines, nor to log the statistics of starvation following Stalin's gigantic collective agricultural plans. Once again, Muggeridge was bemused, more, if possible, by the murderously unctuous gullibility and humbug of these Western observers than by the plain atrocities and banalities of the Soviet system. What he saw extinguished forever from his eyes the stars glimmering over any conceivable secular Utopia. What you get in these Utopias, he came to see, is horror, tumescence, and megalosaurian tyranny.

And once again, we find in his writings, not the mere bitter fervor of the disenchanted partisan, but rather the more subtle and difficult awareness that *all* statecraft is shot through with this fearsome cupidity, vanity, and voraciousness, and that all of us exhibit it unless some great love or suffering has begun to purge it away. Long before he became enamored of such figures as Jesus, Augustine, Francis, Tolstoy, or Mother Teresa, Muggeridge seems to have avoided the mistake common to passionate moral conviction, that it is *those guys* (Stalin, or Hitler, or Pol Pot—or Saddam Hussein)—that it is *they* who are the evildoers, and that *we* were immaculately conceived. There is a wry awareness running all through his work of the unhappy irony that what prevents most of us from being Attilas or Ivans the Terrible is not goodness so much as lack of the chance to lord it over our colleagues. But again, this did not make him a cynic. He winced, as it were, over the awareness that it is all true of himself first of all. Indeed, he makes the point that he has never come across any atrocity, any plunder, any outrage, or any perversion anywhere in history or society that he did not recognize as all too familiar: he had encountered it at close quarters in his own bosom, so to speak.

The salt that saves Muggeridge's mordant awareness of man's fallibility from being merely mordant is, of course, his humor. He cannot stop chuckling. His sheer zest for life, people, and words tumbles out all over. There was, then, an elegant dramatic fitness in his having been elected editor of *Punch*. The note struck in that journal was a sharp, urbane, agile mockery, the butt of it all ordinarily being the Establishment pachyderm. Nothing was sacred. Even Her Britannic Majesty did not escape. (This was, as far as I know, the only point on which I might have squabbled with Muggeridge.)

But Muggeridge looked back on his *Punch* editorship with a wry demurral. He found himself struck by a sort of gruesome irony in it all—a sort of macabre poetic justice in the enterprise of trying to dredge up laughter from the bog of the modern West, especially from England in its decline. He came to feel that the news, somewhere in there, becomes pure fantasy, creating bogus events out of nothing, and then magnifying them into diurnal apocalypses in order to keep the populace tuning in and buying the sponsors' products, if nothing else. And the humor becomes more and more abrasive and metallic until nothing at all is left behind but sophistication, ennui, and eventually, inanity. (Parenthesis here: he would have found a wicked satisfaction in the invention of the word "spin" and in the ponderous solemnity of such spin doctors as Dan Rather, Peter Jennings, and Tom Brokaw).

What galvanized Muggeridge's curiosity was the spectacle of communication deified (it is to be kept in mind here that he earned his board and keep as a *journalist*: the irony did not escape him). Mass communication. Instant everything (again, the coverage of the Iraq war surely corroborates everything the old man saw coming down the pike). Communication as The Juggernaut. The Demiurge. Implacable, omniscient, omnipresent, omnipotent.

Anyone—pagan, Christian, or Jew—who has read anything Muggeridge wrote in the last decade or so of his life, or who ever saw him as a guest on some television program (we may thank our friend William F. Buckley for giving Muggeridge so generous a hearing)—anyone, I say, who knows of Muggeridge's later work, knows well enough that he was obsessed with one topic, finally, the way the prophets, apostles, and saints were obsessed with one topic. Goodness. Purity of heart. Truth. Sanity. Sanctity. God. (If you counted those nouns, you will have totted up six items there, whereas I approached the list by urging that Muggeridge had *one* topic in mind. My rejoinder here would be that, somehow, those six categories all come down to one thing in the end.) He was *vox clamantis in deserto*. In the precincts of Vanity Fair, Muggeridge was like the poet or sage or seer who stands on the hill outside of the city, calling out to the shopkeepers and holidaymakers, "That way lies madness and destruction!"

Sometimes people like this turn into bores—monomaniacal, garrulous, wild-eyed. But anyone who ever met Muggeridge and his wife Kitty will have had any fears on this point dispelled. You spent most of your time, if you had the slightest love for words and wit, in paroxysms of laughter. The repartee, the badinage, the persiflage, the sheer merriment darting and flashing through the air the whole time were like water from the fountain of Helicon. And readers of his work find that what they have come upon there is true of the man himself: razor-sharp wit, passionate moral conviction, unsentimental common sense, an appetite for sheer goodness, a noble capacity for disgust in the face of what is disgusting, and boundless mirth. But with this, nothing tawdry, nothing snide, nothing harsh or raucous or pettifogging or vulgar. All is clarity, agility, and charity.

When did the man become a Christian? Who knows? For one thing, we would all have welcomed a third volume to his memoirs. Oh, to be sure, he did come out with a small effort in this connection. But I think he was tired out by the time he addressed himself to this task, and we got only farthings from the huge treasury of his wisdom and wit. But in any event, Muggeridge would have sidestepped this question as to his conversion. When did I become a

Christian? Well now, if you are asking for a date when I "decided for Christ", I'd prefer to say that I'm trying to decide for Christ all the way along now. It has not been so much a matter of one jump through a hoop as of beginning to follow in The Way, as the early Christians used to call it.

But I am putting words into his mouth. I can only guess, on the basis of having read everything that I can get my hands on that he wrote, and of a few gloriously happy visits with him (he once spent five days at our house in Beverly Farms, Massachusetts, and we howled and cackled the whole time). No one needs to speak for Muggeridge. Anything that the rest of us say is a matter of gilding the lily. If he cannot satisfy us, then we will have to moot the melancholy supposition that the English language itself has failed us.

A Portrait of
Dietrich von Hildebrand

The name Dietrich von Hildebrand is not, perhaps, as well known as it should be among intelligent and literate Catholics—or, for that matter, among Christians of any ilk. He is a man whom Pius XII referred to as "a twentieth-century doctor of the Church". Those who remember this Pontiff will recall that he was not a man who spoke lightly or extravagantly.

Who was Dietrich von Hildebrand? We would not be far from the mark if we accorded him the dignity of the present tense of the verb—who *is* Dietrich von Hildebrand?—as we do with many figures in history (J. S. Bach, Augustine, Giotto, Tolstoy, et al.) whose work abides in such a manner as to lift them above the mere flux of time and to place them in a sort of "perenniality", if a clumsy neologism may be permitted. It is inconceivable that the writings of von Hildebrand will ever be dated, no matter what tortuous metamorphoses the coming centuries may bring.

This is because von Hildebrand's intellect and imagination—and heart, really—dwelt above the dust and skirmish of Vanity Fair. He seldom wrote or spoke on mere topicality—the vogues, causes, and notions that dash themselves like surf

Originally published in a slightly different form in *Crisis* (February 2000): 21–26. Reprinted with permission.

on the jetties of contemporaneity. Although, it must be said in this connection that he was far from being unaware of such turbulence: when he saw foolishness, heresy, or infidelity brewing, as happened in the wake of Vatican II when popinjays of all sorts used the council as a warrant to substitute a Punch and Judy show for the ancient mysteries, he was not above wading into the broil, as in his *Trojan Horse in the City of God* (newly reprinted by Sophia Institute Press).

But the characteristic venue of his mind was amongst what T. S. Eliot called "the permanent things". His remarks on gender, liturgy, morality, and the human person must be accounted among the great monoliths marking the path through the history of the Church as she moves on her pilgrimage nearer and nearer to the Last Things.

But again, who is he? The most exiguous sketch of his life would include the following. He was born in Florence in 1889 (on the same day as Christopher Dawson) and died in New Rochelle, New York, on January 26, 1977. His father, an eminent German sculptor, lived and worked in Florence and was knighted in 1904 by the king of Bavaria. Hence, von Hildebrand had as his own familiar neighborhood that world of Dante, the Academia, the Pitti Palace, the Duomo, and the whole efflorescence of beauty and civility that sprang up so astonishingly in the Italian Renaissance and that was so revered by Bernard Berenson, Harold Acton, and other astute minds (many of whom, alas, never surpassed the merely aesthetic).

It may suggest something of the rarefied atmosphere of this household when we consider that visitors to the family included Gladstone, Henry James, Rilke, Rudolf Otto, Wilhelm Furtwängler, Hugo von Hofmannsthal, Ricard Strauss, Liszt, and Giraudoux. Even though von Hildebrand was an unbeliever in his youth, his young imagination and spirit drank deeply at the wells of beauty, truth, and virtue. At university, he studied philosophy under Adolf Reinach and Max Scheler, the latter of whom largely formed the mind of John Paul II. Von Hildebrand took his Ph.D. under Husserl. In 1914, he was received into the Roman Catholic Church.

When Hitler's national socialism began to emerge in the 1920s, von Hildebrand recognized it as the epochal evil it turned out to be (despite Hitler having fooled almost a whole nation by the early '30s) and became a vocal and implacable foe of Nazism. Because of this, he was forced to flee to Vienna from his faculty position at the University of Munich. There he established the journal *Der Christliche Ständestaat* (Christian Corporative State) and was consequently condemned to death personally by Hitler, who loathed him.

The harrowing escapades that attended his flight from Vienna (e.g., leaving the city on the day of the *Anschluss* at 9:00 A.M. and having the Gestapo arrive looking for him in less than 24 hours) are the stuff of spy fiction—or fact, rather. He eventually fetched up in New York in 1940, without a *sou* in his pocket. He was appointed to the faculty at Fordham University and taught philosophy there for nineteen years, retiring in 1960. He spent the remaining seventeen years between his retirement and death writing. It may interest readers to know that, emerging briefly from a coma, he requested that the *Te Deum* be sung at his deathbed.

What sort of a figure did von Hildebrand "cut" during his life in New York? Who formed his "clientele"? The answers to both questions seem bleak on the surface. He was always poor (a state of affairs widely known among academics), and he rarely commanded the headlines, even in the American Catholic press. He attracted the profound admiration of orthodox Catholic scholars (William Marra and Bernard Gilligan among them) and had the ear of both Paul VI and John Paul II. In a private talk with Paul VI in 1965, he warned the Pope of forthcoming grave perils to the Church, and similarly in 1970, he sounded the alarm in the Holy Father's ear as to what the Church might encounter in the wake of Vatican II. Two contemporary Catholic scholars who might be accounted "Hildebrandians" are Joseph Seifert, head of the International Academy of Philosophy in Liechtenstein, and John Crosby, a member of the philosophy department at Franciscan University in Steubenville, Ohio. Both owe their profound knowledge of von Hildebrand's thought mainly to personal conversation with him during his retirement.

His *oeuvre* (body of work), as they say, is massive. His untranslated work on aesthetics (which he wrote in German) consists of two five-hundred-page volumes, and his *Das Wesen der Liebe* (*The Nature of Love*) is five hundred pages. In an audience granted to von Hildebrand's widow in January 1980, John Paul II forthrightly acknowledged his own intellectual debt to von Hildebrand, especially in the matter of marriage. In a gesture of personal gratitude, this Pope baptized, confirmed, and gave Holy Communion to one of Dr. Alice von Hildebrand's Hunter College students, a former atheist, in April 1985. In addition to the previously mentioned works, von Hildebrand wrote 5,000 pages of autobiography, which was edited to around 300 pages by Alice and published under the title *The Soul of a Lion*.[1]

How shall we approach his immense work? Fewer than a dozen of his books have been translated into English (many

---

[1] Alice von Hildebrand, *The Soul of a Lion: Dietrich von Hildebrand* (San Francisco: Ignatius Press, 2000).

are available from Sophia Institute Press, in Manchester, New Hampshire). A systematic progress through these dozen would turn into a tome. It may be fruitful, then, to touch on only a few of the notions that formed the underpinnings of his work.

Undoubtedly, two words supply us with an excellent gateway into the world of Dietrich von Hildebrand's thought: value and reverence.

The word *value* has been nearly wrecked for us in recent decades, dragooned by moral relativists who did not wish any absolute hierarchy of the good to be imposed on our schoolchildren and who, hence, cobbled up a grotesque industry called "values clarification". The notion was that each small Tom, Dick, and Harry must "get comfortable" with his own notions as to what constitutes acceptable or unsuitable behavior. Ironically, a few intractable absolutes studded the scheme, such as "sexist" remarks and other politically incorrect utterances. Pronouns became a battleground. It never became clear, under this scheme, just what sort of rejoinder we might mount, say, to Mao Zedong, whose values placed the state above the individual, with genocide as one of its corollaries. Having jettisoned absolutes, what strictures could we put forward to stem such activities? Pol Pot was another one who defied the amiable quagmire we cultivated with such assiduity.

The work of von Hildebrand stands at a polar extreme from all of this fatuity. By *value*, he did not mean the windy generalities invoked by presidents and mayors in Fourth of July speeches but rather (shall we capitalize it?) That Which is excellent *in itself* and is to be *admired* (a very weighty word for von Hildebrand). Interestingly enough, the word *value* is so massively basic for him that it is far from easy to wring succinct definitions of the word from his work, so to speak. He virtually always refers to value by way of affirming something *else*, rather as the rest of us presuppose the word of God. In *Liturgy and Personality*, he says:

> The meaning of all creation is the imitation and glorification of God.... That which is created ... exists only in order to imitate and glorify God, in fulfilling the divine idea in its regard and simultaneously bringing to fruition the fullness of values to which it is ordained. For all values— goodness, beauty, the mystery of life, the noble light of truth, and even the dignity of being itself ... all these are rays which radiate from God's being.[2]

Or again:

> Values are not only like a dew falling from heaven, but also like incense rising to God; each value, in itself, addresses to God a specific word of glorification. A being, in praising God, praises Him through its value, through that inner preciousness which marks it as having been drawn out of the indifferent. Nature praises God.... This is true of every work of art, every perfect community, every truth, every moral attitude. Man ... must first of all respond adequately to each value as a reflection of God; he must respond with joy, enthusiasm, veneration, love ... and lovingly adore God, Who is the fullness of all value (12).

Value, far from being a subjective vibration trembling from my individuality, is "out there"—a quality of the immense backdrop against which our lives are played out. Or we could put it thus: ultimately, all value derives, like a cataract flowing, not from a mere That Which: it is He Who. God is not, of course, an abstraction, and hence, we cannot quite

[2] Dietrich von Hildebrand, *Liturgy and Personality* (Manchester, N.H.: Sophia Institute Press, 1986), 11.

assign to him an ontological category called value. But he is, on the other hand, the wellspring of all that is excellent in itself and, hence, of value. The Matterhorn is not a value in so many words, but it towers there, shimmering in its might, and bids admiration forth from souls who exult in might, majesty, purity (the snow), form, grandeur, gravity, serenity, and so forth. The Mozart *Requiem* is not a value, but its music draws us into the precincts of sheer beauty: sublimity, perfection of form, decorum (the notes "fit" the text), awe, terror (*"Quantus tremor est futurus . . . tuba mirum spargens sonum"*), rescue (*"Recordare, Jesu pie"*), and repose (*"Hostias et preces, tibi, Domine, laudis offerimus"*). These are matters that call for admiration from souls well-formed.

Another major theme in von Hildebrand's work, which he writes about in *Transformation in Christ*, is "the succession of stages that leads from Baptism . . . to our actual transformation in Christ . . . the shaping of that life which lights up the face of the 'new man in Christ' . . . the state of fluidity, openness, and receptivity to formative action from above." [3] What is our task on this earth, we mortals? It is, as Milton would have it, to "tune our instrument" to the Music of the Spheres. That is to say, to permit ourselves to be shaped, formed, chiseled, smelted, kneaded, plied (choose your metaphor) into that image that discloses the very heart of the Most Holy Trinity to us, namely, Jesus Christ. Man was created to be in all grace, nobility, dignity, magnificence, and solemnity—in the *imago Dei* (image of God), that is. Von Hildebrand says in *Transformation in Christ*, "Christ, the Messiah, is not merely the Redeemer who breaks

---

[3] Dietrich von Hildebrand, *Transformation in Christ: On the Christian Attitude* (San Francisco: Ignatius Press, 2001), xix–xx.

apart the bond and cleanses us from sin. He is also the
Dispenser of a new divine life which shall wholly transform us into new men.... Our surrender to Christ implies
a readiness to let Him fully transform us" (4–5). When evil,
alas, does its obscene work on this image, we end up with
a horror: wretched, pusillanimous, venal, craven, and
debauched, but, ironically, vain, strutting, and pompous at
the same time.

Such a soul has squandered its capacity to admire that
which is admirable. (The Greeks called this property *aidos*,
and for them, it had to be learned. It represents the stark
opposite of "doin' what comes naturally", or "letting it all
hang out".) All has been perverted. We need only recall
the jaded souls at the arena in Rome: "Darlings, peel me
another grape: I'm so bored with these crucifixions that I
don't know what I'm going to do. Not to mention the
gladiators they've got these days. So tedious." What place
is left, when we reach this point of surfeit, for wonder—
wonder at an edelweiss, a Jack Russell terrier, Vermeer's
Young Woman Reading a Letter, or the sight of a boy from
the innermost city offering his seat on the trolley to a
woman? Cynicism, irony, sophistication, and ennui all cauter-
ize the moral nerve-endings necessary to perceive and admire
value in such phenomena. But it takes training to cultivate
the agile, delicate, and self-forgetful frame of mind that puts
forth such nerve-endings.

Von Hildebrand was himself a case in point. His taste
had been formed, almost inevitably it would seem, by that
Florentine background, so that even his natural being (aside
from his regenerate spirit, which sprang into life presently) was attuned to beauty and sickened by squalor, oafish-
ness, and gaudiness. His wife speaks frequently, both in
private conversation and from the lectern, of this *gravitas*,

this discrimination (but not snobbery), this flawless simplicity even, that registered like litmus the responses of his
innermost being to beauty or ugliness. He himself speaks
of "this progress toward simplicity, which is a part of the
spiritual significance of advancing in age" (*Transformation
in Christ*, 15).

Ultimately, of course, all of this is drawn up into the
realm of grace, which, according to Catholic teaching, builds
on nature. It is not a mere matter of being highbrow. The
twittering persiflage of mere aesthetes—at Lady Ottoline
Morell's Garsington, in Bloomsbury, Greenwich Village or
the Museum of Modern Art—is as far from the admiration that regales pure souls as hell is from heaven. But we
don't come by it naturally. It takes pedagogy (the Greeks
again): years of discipline and training to tune us to the
Music of the Spheres—to that perfection of harmony, equi-
poise, power, grace, fitness, and splendor we call beauty
but that may also be accorded to truth and goodness. A
good moral choice (of, say, generosity, self-effacement, courage, or service) is beautiful under its own modality, as is
the song of the winter wren under its modality. Both are
also true, since they accord with perfect correspondence
with reality.

It is not for nothing that this one of von Hildebrand's
major works is entitled *Transformation in Christ*. The perfection of stature in store for all souls who will undergo
the necessary schooling is measured by that highest measure, namely, the perfection exhibited in the figure of
the Incarnate Word. At the very end of the book, there
is a summary, as it were, of all the foregoing chapters
with their remorseless and microscopic scrutiny of the tactics to which we turn in our efforts to protect ourselves
from God:

It is extremely important for us to profit by the moments when God draws us nearer to Him, when He allows us to be possessed by true values ... all such possession by high natural values must be *ordained to our true surrender of self to Christ*. If this is not the case, we do not hear the call of God; nay, we even abuse His gifts.... It is in such moments ... that our vision is given a valid perspective. It is then that we see the true countenance of things, which we must engrave in our mind. (497)

All perfections—aesthetic, moral, or verbal—point to this figure. This theme, of course, is very much the animating spirit in Dante's work. The beauty of which the eyes of the lover are vouchsafed a true glimpse in the figure of Beatrice, is the beauty of the Godhead. All point to the Beatific Vision. I doubt whether von Hildebrand was familiar with the Protestant hymn "Eternal Light, Eternal Light", but he would have applauded this stanza:

> Oh, how shall I, whose native sphere
> Is dark, whose mind is dim
> Before th'Ineffable appear
> And on my naked spirit bear
> The uncreated beam?

How shall a worm like me (this is Scripture's assessment, not self-hatred) entertain even the most forlorn hope of ever achieving that transformation that will enable me not only to see but to exult in and be ravished by the Beatific Vision?

Transformation in Christ is our handbook (always excepting Sacred Scripture, of course). Handbook? In effect, yes. The unsuspecting reader will not remain unsuspecting for long. Von Hildebrand bangs the gong on page 1. Taking Saint Paul's daunting challenge in Ephesians 4:22–23 ("Put off your old nature which ... is corrupted ... and be renewed in the spirit of your minds"), he strides briskly to his task. It is no use for us to halt, salaam, and circumnavigate: the man to whom the book is addressed (as is the New Testament) must be "ready to change". Grace does not put poultices, patches, and simples on original sin. It's death (baptism) and then the long haul toward sanctity, that state of being wherein alone I will be able to bear the radiance of glory flashing from the Sapphire Throne. Chapter after chapter subjects us to the unendurable scrutiny of the truth. "Contrition", "true simplicity", "striving for perfection", and sequence after sequence on freedom, patience, meekness, mercy, sorrow, sobriety, and self-surrender harrow us with a holy harrowing. Von Hildebrand's method commonly entails the demolition of every conceivable dodge, strategy, and obfuscation by which we are pleased to maintain our self-satisfaction and then the opening up of the virtue, or of the aspect of *caritas*, that corresponds to these squalid ruses.

Thus value. Used by von Hildebrand, the word sheds the flimsy rags that have cloaked it in our own bland era and takes on, as it were, seraphic wings. We are hailed every moment of our lives with the titanic majesty of reality. Have we eyes to see it, and a heart to admire—nay, to adore it? Or will we end up like the damned souls who, when they taste beauty, taste only ashes, pumice, and sulphur?

The second word that I have mentioned as standing close to the center of von Hildebrand's vision is *reverence*. Here again, as with the word *value*, the force of the word has been leached away by its use in modern argot. In this case, it is sentimentalism that is the villain. "Ah! Reverence! So uplifting. Let us reverence all things—trees, saw-whet owls, rich loam, sphagnum moss. How ennobling!" If we embarked

on that line of sentiment in the presence of von Hildebrand, we would be met with a tart "No!"

Our reverent friend is, of course, not altogether adrift. Von
Hildebrand himself would say (and so far so good for our
friend), "an adequate response is due to each value according to its rank ... *because it is a value.*" [4] And as he also says
in the same work, "The cosmic value of the objective fact
that everything possessing a value should receive an adequate response of will, of joy, enthusiasm, and love according to the kind of value it represents, finds its highest, ultimate
causa exemplaris in the eternal loving response between the
First and Second Divine Persons" (64). But we weren't speaking of theology on this nature-outing of ours.

Well, you should have been, von Hildebrand would wish
to add. And here is the kernel of his small volume, *Liturgy
and Personality*:

> The person formed by the Liturgy has absorbed in his flesh
> and blood the notion that he owes a suitable response to
> every value. He will rejoice in every exalted spectacle of
> nature, the beauty of the starlight sky, the majesty of the
> sea and mountains, the charm of life, the world of plants
> and animals, the nobility of a profound truth, the mysteri-
> ous glow of a man's purity.... The man formed by the
> Liturgy will affirm all this as a reflection of the eternal glory
> of God (71).

And again, "His entire value-responding attitude, his heart
and spirit will be turned completely toward the world of
values and God in the first place" (ibid.).

Those perfections of the creation are most emphatically the
handiwork of the Most High and, hence, are to be greeted

[4] Dietrich von Hildebrand, *Liturgy and Personality*, 64.

by us as by worshippers of that deity. Nothing that we mortals can make can compare to the perfection we descry in all of that. Something serious has gone wrong with the man who, when he thinks of those things, thinks only of scoring the valleys and hillsides with the satanic treads on the tires of his all-terrain vehicle and of spitting din and carbon monoxide into the silent purity that ought to reign in such purlieus.

However, there is a difference between reverence and loyal custodianship. We mortals, in our descent from Adam and Eve, are to be "lords" of the creation. Not tyrants, bosses, or dictators but good lords or stewards, in a sense in which that notion would have been understood by the true hierarch who knows that his rank obliges him to guarantee and defend the well-being of every creature and acre under his suzerainty. In the strictest sense, we are not to "reverence" the creation, with the implication here that we in some way do obeisance to it or take up an inferior attitude toward ourselves vis-à-vis, say, dolphins, Douglas firs, or the Thames River. No fir tree, no matter how soaring, is to be placed above the lowliest child in the hierarchy. We must keep in mind here von Hildebrand's remarks in *Liturgy and Personality* on the man whose "self-surrender to Christ, and through Christ to God, is complete" (49). For this man, "Reverence is the essential basis for such a perception of values, and for a true relationship with the whole realm of values ... with the Absolute, the supernatural, and the divine. Reverence is the mother of all virtues, of all religion ... [it] is thus the foundation of all perception and sense of values" (49–50).

Much as we deplore and mourn the tearing up of acreage by great, filthy diesel monsters, if that acreage is necessary to the well-being of the populace who live there, then up it comes. (I speak as one who wishes the internal combustion engine had never been invented.) On the other hand, if mammals (dolphins) are being swept up in great Russian, Norwegian, or Japanese seines and allowed to drown or if rhesus monkeys are being tortured in psychological experiments about loneliness and its corresponding neuroses, we should rise up in fury in behalf of these cousins of ours. (I am not a Darwinist in even the remotest sense; I mean "cousins" only in so far as we share a whole category of creaturehood with the beasts.)

It is a blurring of the English language to bring the word *reverence* into play when speaking of our relationship with nature. One reverences that which is above one. Speaking of the man whose response to value accords with the hierarchy of things, von Hildebrand says in *Liturgy and Personality*, "His entire attitude toward the world of values must take this hierarchy into account. The admiration and veneration which he offers a value must correspond to its objective height, and so, too, the joy which he feels about something, the place he reserves in his soul for a good" (81–82).

We may *admire* anything at all that is admirable (an ichneumon fly, the *Madonna of the Rocks*, or Chartres), but we stand in reverence before that in whose being there subsists something that outstrips our own peculiar rank or station—or "estate", as the Middle Ages called it. Hence, of course, angels are to be reverenced and, in a limited sense, any man whose rank (the queen, the bishop, the general) places him above us. There would be a thin line between honor and reverence here: certainly, it is permitted to speak of reverencing our parents, even though we know that they share our mortality and our sinfulness. But they are "above" us in the hierarchy.

Von Hildebrand expended immense energy in trying to awaken us to both the duty and fitness of reverence. It is our duty because, in a manner of speaking, that is how it is. The duty derives from the same source as does the appropriateness of the man stepping forward and the woman backward in the fox-trot. It's the choreography of the thing, we say, and in a sense, there is no further court of appeal. If a truculent child in a rage demands why he should honor his father and mother, our final answer is a bold "Because that is the way it is." Von Hildebrand speaks in *Liturgy and Personality* of "the inner structure of every communion-situation", by which he means the "That's how it is" we have been invoking. The ability to perceive and honor this structure (the choreography, we might say) in a given situation he calls *discretio* in *Liturgy and Personality*. "The spirit of *discretio* implies . . . a sense for the strata or depth at which one moves, and should move, not mixing up the levels, and not passing unaware from one level to the other" (115, 121). Perhaps the manner in which waitresses nowadays address their customers as "you guys" (even if it is a party of dowagers) would be just such a mixing up of the levels.

There is a piquant aspect to this. Reverencing that which is to be reverenced reaches further toward the central mysteries than mere surface splendor (the queen's scepter) or impressiveness (the general's stars) would call for. What about the untouchable in the gutter in Calcutta? What about the thalidomide child? The well-tutored eye will descry glory—glory stained or twisted by tragedy, but nonetheless glory. For here is the image of God.

On the other hand, what happens to us when our moral nerve-endings are bludgeoned with the assault of obscenity, brutishness, or surfeit—an assault mounted with all the power that the media command, a power to be envied most wistfully by your Genghis Khans or your Tamburlaines? The capacity to accord reverence to that which ought to be reverenced is extinguished. The mystery of sexuality would be the dramatic case in point in our own time. Von Hildebrand says in *In Defense of Purity*: "Either the mysterious union of two human beings takes place in the sight of God (*in conspectu Dei*) or man flings himself away, surrenders his secret, delivers himself over to the flesh, desecrates and violates the secret of another." [5] The true man and woman know the sexual phenomenon lies on the cusp between the temporal and the eternal and is, hence, to be accorded immense reverence. The debauch, alas (and here we find most of Generation X, with its black lipstick and leather), sees only the prurient, the lurid, and the sultry. How on earth is the nature of reality, with its corollary of reverence, to be introduced at all into such a wasted epoch as our own? Well, without being frivolous, we can say, "Read Dietrich von Hildebrand."

Von Hildebrand writes on many other topics. Gender: His book *Man and Woman* leads us into such noble precincts that virtually all of the last twenty-five years suddenly look consumptive. It is thus with *Marriage: The Mystery of Faithful Love* (Sophia) and *Purity*. Here we are on the high ground where the air has the tang of heaven in it. Von Hildebrand would have been heartsick over the efforts (mendacious, really) of brisk, religious types both Protestant and Catholic, during the last twenty-five years to rewrite Scripture and redraw the moral map of the universe in the interest of making the Christian view of gender palatable to a world crazed with questions of power and political equality. C. S. Lewis once used the phrase "sordid trumpery" in

[5] Dietrich von Hildebrand, *In Defense of Purity: An Analysis of the Catholic Ideals of Purity and Virginity* (Baltimore: Helicon Press, 1962), 15.

reference to his own smarmy attitude during adolescence. The stacks and stacks of books and articles written in the interest of accommodating Christian notions of sexuality and marriage to a modern agenda would have looked to von Hildebrand as just such trumpery.

Gender. Art. Aesthetics. Liturgy. Sex. Sacrament. Civility. Sanctity. These are the topics among which one finds oneself on opening the work of von Hildebrand. In virtually all of these areas, we are flooded with late-arriving propaganda. Von Hildebrand points to another, and more ancient, way.

LIGHT ON CHARLES WILLIAMS

Charles Williams was doubtless the oddest figure in the Inklings. His work never won the immense readership enjoyed by Tolkien and Lewis, but since the 1930s he has always had a small, enthusiastic, and at times impressive (e.g., Auden and Eliot) audience. Most of his books are long since out of print, and it seems to be a difficult matter for publishers (Eerdmans in the U.S.) to keep even his seven novels alive. Ironically, despite this semi-obscurity, Williams was to some extent the agitating figure in the Inklings. The publican at The Bird and Baby in Saint Giles' remarked that when the Inklings were in session in one of the rooms there, it was Williams who rushed back and forth to and from the bar, keeping everyone supplied with beer (and scotch, I seem to recall), while great clouds of smoke and roars of masculine laughter rolled out from the room. But he was not only the waiter, so to speak: he was often the one to moot some piquant topic for discussion, and he could be depended upon to bring to any such topic a point of view at least quirky, if not positively crotchety. Tolkien complained that he never had the foggiest notion what Williams was on about. Williams looked a little bit like a monkey, and Eliot recalls his jumpy method

Originally published in a slightly different form in *Touchstone* (Dec. 2004). Reprinted with permission.

of lecturing, continually shifting about, perching on the table, hopping off, and jingling coins in his pocket (this would have been during Williams' public lectures, but the same ganglion of nerves animated his approach to the Inklings meetings).

For readers unfamiliar with Williams, it may be apposite to mention that he was born in 1886 and died, quite suddenly and unexpectedly, during minor surgery at the Radcliffe Infirmary in 1945. Lewis grieved deeply over Williams' death, and wrote a beautiful ten-line threnody to the effect that this death changed the whole world for Lewis, and that he would love to talk a whole night about it with a friend: "But with whom ... oh unless it were you?" [1] Williams married a woman named Florence, whom he renamed Michal. Why he should have picked the name of Saul's daughter has always eluded me. He named his only son Michael. They lived in unremitting penury, and during the Blitz, Williams moved with the Oxford University Press, where he was an editor, from London to Oxford. His wife and son remained in London, an arrangement belonging in the same bin with many other unaccountable points about Williams. (His relationships with women, who fell all over themselves under his spell, were *most* peculiar, but, after many years of study, I am absolutely convinced that he went to his grave never having defrauded his wife.)

Williams would have pleased old George I, who remarked to Alexander Pope one time, "Scribble, scribble, scribble, eh, Mr. Pope?" (I may have both king and poet wrong here, but the point remains.) Williams never stopped scribbling—on bits of paper, the backs of envelopes, in

---

[1] C. S. Lewis, *Poems* (London: Geoffrey Bles, 1964), 105.

margins and endpapers, and on every other surface he could find. He wrote historical biographies, drama, poetry, fiction, and essays theological and literary. His most serious piece of semi-scholarship was *The Figure of Beatrice*, written in the 1930s, and still admired by Dante students. His poetry, besides seemingly hundreds of unpublished sonnets and lyrics, many of them either to Michal or to some other (supposititious?) woman, will be remembered, if at all, for his Arthurian cycle, published in two slim volumes under the titles *Taliessin through Logres*, and *The Region of the Summer Stars*. These short lyrics are as difficult to read at first as is Eliot's *Four Quartets*. They are like the Rosetta Stone: one needs a crib. Williams left a sheaf of interpretive notes about them, and Lewis finished off the commentary, publishing the whole lot under the title *Arthurian Torso*, which is also now out of print.

It is in Williams' seven novels that we find in most accessible form his highly idiosyncratic set of ideas. It may as well be said at the outset that these volumes will never take their place on the shelf of major English literature. So, unacceptable as the following method may be if we are speaking of literary criticism, we must adopt an "ideas" approach to them. (My dissertation advisor at New York University kept objecting that my work on Williams' fiction was "too ideational", so I had to cobble up some simulacrum of a literary approach: but it was a *pis aller*, I must confess.) In this connection, I find solace in the difficulty Eliot found in commenting on Williams' fiction in his introduction to *All Hallows' Eve:* "Much of his work may appear to realise its form only imperfectly; but it is also true in a measure to say that Williams invented his own forms—or to say that no form, if he had obeyed all its conventional laws, could have been satisfactory for what he wanted to say. What it is, essentially, that he had to say, comes near to defying definition." [2]

There is a short list of notions, or images, which lead us into the world of Williams' imagination. Any such list would have to include at least the following: "the theology of romantic love", the Beatrician Vision, The City, The Empire, and the Index of the Body. We may attempt to come at the list piecemeal, but readers of Williams' work will know that, at the end of the day, what we have is a seamless fabric.

By the *theology of romantic love*, Williams means simply that, in the experience of an intense love (ordinarily to be found between a man and a woman), we mortals have served up to us in quotidian form the immense mystery that lies at the trinitarian heart of the universe, namely, that self-giving is a mode of joy. Any true lover knows that to give himself (and a thousand gifts) to and for his lady, far from seeming drudgery, is bliss. One cannot do nearly enough to satisfy the joyous demands of one's own love. Giving and receiving become indistinguishable. And, says Williams, this paradox lies at the heart of things. In the Blessed Trinity, we descry just such a state of affairs, where the Son eternally gives himself in love to the Father, the Holy Ghost being, in some sense, the "agent" of this love. So "romantic love" may be said to be the hint, universal among us men, as to the final nature of things. And insofar as I begin to learn this lesson, to that extent I am learning the steps of the Dance, which is, shall we say, the choreography of heaven and of the whole universe, actually. My life for yours. Hell loathes this and snaps, "Out of my way, fool." The angels and saints have learned to love this, and to know it as ecstasy.

[2] T. S. Eliot, introduction to *All Hallows' Eve* by Charles Williams (Vancouver: Regent College Publishing, 2003), xiii.

Any smallest gesture in this direction may constitute an early lesson in the Dance. "Here—let me give you a hand with that bag of groceries." Or "Oh—someone has thrown down an empty cigarette pack here in the park; I'll just pick it up and put it in this trash can over here." Or to one's wife in the middle of the night: "What? A glass of water? Here—let me get it." All of this is quintessential Williams. He *sees* the Divine Love mediated down, down, down, through the whole fabric of things, even to the picking up of a bit of trash. My life for yours: it may mean three seconds of my time to redeem some thoughtless bit of self-indulgence on the part of someone else, or it may mean, or did mean, Golgotha, where My Life for Yours was supremely dramatized and entails our eternal joy.

And, in Williams' vision, any such gesture may be "counted unto one for righteousness", as in the case of Abraham who pulled up his tent pegs in Ur. The characters in any Williams tale who refuse such chances set themselves on the road to hell. Those who embrace such chances begin to ready themselves to receive the Great and Salvific Sacrifice.

Three words that occur over and over in Williams' work, especially in his essays, are *substitution*, *exchange*, and *co-inherence*. By giving you a hand, or by standing in for you in any ordeal, I begin to learn about *substitution*—my life for yours. *Exchange*: let me do that for you: Christ died for us. *Co-inherence*: no one can stand alone. I cannot do without help and, by both offering and accepting help in ten thousand ways, I embrace this principle of co-inherence, which is yet another way of describing the choreography of the Dance. Hell abominates it all: it is the joy of heaven. And Williams' characters are all in school, as are all of us.

The Beatrician Vision: As Dante saw in the little Florentine girl some hint of the Divine Perfection, so one may see, if

one has eyes for it, in every case in point of beauty, something that points toward that Perfection—toward the Beatific
Vision, ultimately. To stop short and adore Beatrice for herself alone is precisely to stop short. Therein lies idolatry.
One sees Beatrice (or an edelweiss, or the Matterhorn, or
the West Highlands, or the Cotswolds, or hears a Mozart
flute sonata, or the overture to the second act of *Die Zauber-
flöte*, or smells the fresh peaches espaliered on the warm
brick wall of the kitchen garden, or looks at one's beloved,
or at a Golden Retriever, or an arctic tern) and one says,
"*Benedicite, omnia opera Domini!*"

Williams' phrase for this, which he thought he had come
across somewhere, but could never recover the source, was
"This also is Thou ... neither is this Thou." The syntax
should be clear. Beatrice (or the peaches) derives from, and
hints at, Thou: but she is not quite Thou. All creation whis-
pers "Not yet. Not here. Keep going." Idolatry stops in its
tracks, and thus loses both Beatrice and the Beatific Vision.

The City is one of Williams' oddest images, and one on
the hither side of which Lewis drew the line, since he loved
the countryside and, with Tolkien, hated the roar and stink
and clangor of the Oxford that had been ruined by the
Morris Motor Company. For Williams, however, one cannot take one step in the city without encountering the
Dance. Oh, to be sure, it is forced upon us by law, but the
Dance is still there. For example, red and green traffic lights.
They impose on us the principle by which alone things can
work at all: you first. I must wait (red light) while you proceed (green light). Does one not see this in the inter-
changes of a Nureyev and a Margot Fonteyn, where the
man "presents" the ballerina to the audience, as it were,
saying in effect, "Look! Here is beauty! I step back with all
of my own grace and power and render the humble service

of steadying her while she executes this breathtakingly delicate movement." Or in any (traditional) dance floor: you cannot waltz or fox-trot without this graceful receding and proceeding on the part of both partners. In paradise, the red and green lights have long since disappeared, since we have all learned both to wait for the other one (with joy) and to accept (with grace) the other's waiting. For Williams this was all too obvious on any city street.

Or take money, upon which any city functions. What is a coin? It has the sovereign's head on it, for a start, a detail not left unnoticed by Williams. And it says, in effect, "My labor for yours. I depend on what you have worked for, and vice versa. We will both starve if we refuse such exchanges." In another century one might have proffered a lamb, or a basket of apples, in payment for some commodity that one needed. Coins are nothing but icons of that principle. My work for yours. My life for yours. The self-giving exchanges (of love, eventually) are not some peculiarity of the precincts of felicity. They are omnipresent, and any life or work at all, let alone any joy anywhere, depends altogether on one's either refusing or welcoming the principle. Heaven and hell are under every bush—or at every corner in The City. If we had asked Williams whether he meant the London financial district or the *Civitas Dei* by "The City" he would have demurred. Have it whichever way you want. It all comes to the same thing in the end. Insofar as the banks and the stock exchange give over wholly to avarice, then the image is wrecked, and hell looms.

The Empire in Williams is the Byzantine Empire. And a highly idiosyncratic notion it is of that thousand-year labyrinth of patricide, fratricide, matricide, duplicity, and subtlety. Williams simply chose to press into service the notion of widespread authority (he has the empire reaching to

Britain) deriving from the sacred emperor, and served by "logothetes" (Williams loved that sort of *arcana*) speeding in all directions to do the emperor's will. It is thus with reality, says Williams. Do not the angels speed to do the will of the Sacred Emperor? And must I not learn that same zeal and speed in carrying out his will? In one bizarre attempt to elicit the fullest possible potency from the image, Williams superimposed a sketch of a nude woman's body over the map of the empire, with Logres (Britain) being the head, France the breasts, Rome the navel, and Jerusalem the pudenda. One has to admit that Williams taxes our assent to the limit at times.

In this connection, however, we have his *Index of the Body*. This is really nothing more than the medieval and Renaissance notion of the body as being a holograph (scarcely their word) of Truth, as it were. That is, the head sits atop the body because reason ought to rule; then we have the affections in the chest; and the appetites in the guts. This is the right ordering of things hierarchically, and any tinkering with that hierarchy will land us in Babylon, Sodom, or hell. In fact, Williams used Gomorrah to indicate the false city at the very end of the line: if Sodom is the attempt at union with the mirror image of myself, which is fruitless, then Gomorrah is the final solitude where I have rejected *any* union at all, and have insisted that I be alone. Any other self at all would raise for me the intolerable business of "relating" to that self, and that way lies heaven, which I loathe. The main character in Williams' best novel, *Descent into Hell*, one Lawrence Wentworth, a respectable historian, ends by insisting on Gomorrah, against a thousand chances that have been offered to him to choose otherwise.

It will have been obvious from the above paragraph that Williams' images run in and out of each other. We begin a paragraph speaking of the Index of the Body, and end with The City (or, in this case, the Anti-city).

In each of his seven novels, Williams summons some *thing* that crops up in ordinary 1930s English common life and tears the scrim between immediacy and ultimacy, or time and eternity, or the ordinary and the unconditioned. This tactic, it will be clear upon a moment's reflection, entails the reverse of what Lewis and Tolkien do in their tales of faerie. In those, we are summoned *away* from ordinariness, to either a time that is unlocatable on our calendars (Middle Earth) or a place that cannot be located in our geography or cosmography (Narnia). Thus, a certain distance and leverage are gained. Williams has ultimacy muscling *in* on people's lives, and suddenly all is in question. It is a literary device brought into play in the interest of plucking us by the sleeve and awakening us to the stark fact that just such ultimacy lies all about us at every moment and attends every choice we make, every attitude we adopt, and every habit we cultivate. One example may suffice for all here: Lawrence Wentworth, being a historian, especially of battles in England, knows exactly the detail of the military uniforms needed for a local summer theatrical being rehearsed in his neighborhood. But, because he is a misanthrope generally, and is particularly nettled by one or two recent developments in his own life, he petulantly refuses to help the drama group who approach him for advice. One syllable ("Yes") would push the door to joy ajar for him (I offer what I have—knowledge of military history—for your sakes), but he chooses petulance and hence advances another step toward the Gomorrah he wants.

In a visit which I made in 1963 to Lewis at his house in Headington, he remarked to me something to the effect that "God is not going to force anyone into heaven." Williams would have agreed.

PERPLEXITY IN THE EDGEWARE ROAD

A Note on T. S. Eliot

In the poetry of T. S. Eliot, most particularly in his *Four Quartets*, we find a modern instance of the phenomenon bespoken by all art since the beginning.

The place of art in any civilization or tribe is always the same. It is to articulate—that is, to give shape to what is otherwise formless or shapeless. The thing that would be otherwise formless, in the case of art, is human experience.

The people of antiquity, and of the Middle Ages, and thence of the modern and postmodern epoch, all exhibit a proclivity that is unique to our species among all the species of life that inhabit this planet, namely, the desire to *utter* experience and not simply to *undergo* experience. (I am here setting on one side, I hope not rashly, the whole question of gorillas and dolphins. Whatever may be said of their "language", it does not seem to develop; nor have we any tablets or inscriptions or manuscripts they have made in the effort to preserve whatever it is they "say".) We (men) share all kinds of experience with the other species of animal life: we get hungry and so do our dogs; we run out of energy and become fatigued, and so do our dogs; we suffer disappointment, and so do our dogs (witness the dog's tail ceasing to wag, and then drooping, as it becomes clear that he is to stay in the house when the rest of us set out for our walk). Dogs seem to have a capacity for embarrassment, and even for shame (upon being discovered, for example, curled up on some forbidden sofa). But the point here is that dogs never *do* anything about these experiences, and we do. We not only suffer experience: we must say something about it afterward. All art—all sculpture, drama, dance, painting, poetry, and narrative—bespeaks this proclivity in us to articulate our experience. (Music presents a conundrum here: In what sense does it articulate something? Yet we feel that indeed it does—time and form, if nothing else. I am thinking of Bach more than of Wagner here.)

In the case of drama, of course, it is easy enough to see what I am talking about. We all know, before we get to the theater, much too much about the experience of jealousy, but nonetheless, we have paid good money, and we wish to see this unhappy component of our experience played out for us yet again by following the fortunes of Othello. Not, of course, that the play *Othello* exists solely as the dramatic projecting of the single experience, jealousy. It is a complex entity, this play, but we can at least say this, that every nuance in that drama is altogether recognizable to us, the audience, as being too true of our own experience of life. Nothing is false. We do not have to be wife-smotherers to recognize our own vulnerability to the very thing that overthrew Othello.

Similarly with painting. Why should Monet bother about all those water lilies, or Renoir about that man in the rowboat in the park with the young lady, or Frans Hals about all those apple-cheeked burghers, or Hieronymus Bosch about all those damned souls, when these things already exist in the real world? Aren't the artists gilding the lily, so to speak?

No, we say, they are plucking us by the sleeve. They are laying a hand on our arm and saying, "Look! Look well!"

Or dance. Ballet, ballroom, folk dance: it is all a very peculiar phenomenon, when you think about it. Why should we get up on our toes and caper like this? Surely it is at best a trifle *infra dig*?

But no again, we say. The rejoinder to this sort of stricture arises from the profoundest depths of man's spirit. We must dance. We will dance. Nay, one has only to look at the shape of Slavonic dance, Siamese dance, flamenco, Morris, the Highland Fling, Watusi dance, Navajo dance, to see that here we witness the exquisite articulation by many tribes, of the whole range and scope of man's experience: joy, grief, pride, yearning, rage, desolation, anticipation, delight, love. It is a giving of shape, under the condition of the human body itself, and its movements to our experience of mortal existence,

And so it would go with all of the arts—even, I think, with architecture. Surely the shape of our buildings, whether we are referring to the temple at Karnak, the palace at Versailles, the cathedral at Chartres, or the World Trade Center, not to mention our dwellings, speaks volumes about our own self-image, and about what constitutes appropriate space and material for our life and our work?

The artist, we might say, is the *one* who is able both to see the possibilities of form in our experience, and to achieve an analogy to that form in some specific and lasting modality—in oil and canvas, in words, in movements, or in marble.

T. S. Eliot's material was words. All of mankind had, long before Eliot appeared on the scene, experienced disenchantment and ennui, but somehow his having given a particular verbal shape to that experience in such utterances as "I should have been a pair of ragged claws / Scuttling across the floors of silent seas" or the business about "... muttering retreats / Of restless nights in one-night cheap hotels / And sawdust restaurants with oyster shells: / Streets that follow like a tedious argument", not to mention spitting out the butt-ends of our days—somehow those ways of saying it not only express what more than a few of us have felt, but also bring into being some capacity to experience experience.[1]

Eliot very quickly became the darling of the generation that was achieving self-consciousness just after World War I. Innocence lost, ideals decimated, world weariness, and the refusal ever again to be taken in by the politicians: it was a bleak moment, touched ironically with the eat-drink-and-be-merry of the 1920s.

Eliot's tactics seem to have entailed the finding of a voice that would speak words of ennui, impotence, restlessness, and demurral, but which would at the same time ring with enough authority to flag us all down. This is not an easy set of tactics. How do you speak in a somnolent, attenuated, febrile murmur without lulling your readers into the very lassitude your work as an artist fears most of all? Music that puts us to sleep loses its *raison d'etre* at the point when we succumb. Drama that draws us into the precincts of boredom by boring us fails.

Somehow Eliot kept us reading and rereading his chronicles of dereliction. "Prufrock", *The Waste Land*, and the Sweeney poems, for all of their torpor and squalor, galvanized us. Eliot found himself lionized by a world from whose eyes the stars had been rudely put out. They loved him.

But then the joker. Eliot converted. In 1927, he announced that he had converted to orthodox Christian belief of the most austere and rigorous sort.

How nettlesome. How tiresome for his votaries. It is as though the high priest in the polytheistic court of the pharoah had turned from the altar to the throng one fine morning

---

[1] T. S. Eliot. "The Love Song of Alfred Prufrock" in *The Complete Poems and Plays, 1909–1950* (New York: Harcourt, Brace & World, 1952), 3, 5, et passim; all quotations are from this edition.

and had said, "I believe in one God ..." The consterna-
tion, dismay, and fury that would have greeted this perfidy
on his part would have known no bounds. Eliot found himself to be the object of a not dissimilar outrage. He had
betrayed his trust as the oracle of the modern West.

But from his own point of view, his conversion did not
at all change his office as poet, nor did it make lighter the
burden he as poet carried, namely, the burden of speaking
truth. It is difficult enough work to carry on with your
craft as poet if what you produce wins accolades for you,
but your task becomes onerous indeed if what you are saying invites catcalls and brickbats.

What did Eliot do? For one thing, he produced no major
poetic work for almost a decade. Some essays appeared and,
presently, his plays. But then, in 1943 there appeared *Four
Quartets*.

In this work, it seems to me, Eliot took the truths that
are platitudinous (we all die; time carries all away; ecstasy
beckons in fugitive moments) and denied us the luxury, so
dear to self-congratulatory existentialists, of pitching camp
on those melancholy truths. The great theme of "pointing" that appears early in the work, forces us to acknowledge that these platitudes are themselves pointers. Pointers
to Something Else.

Twenty-five years before he wrote *Four Quartets*, he had
had his Prufrock recoil from such implacable platitudes. "Oh
do not ask, 'What is it?'" Prufrock knows that if we allow
the question at all, we put ourselves in the awful danger, to
be skirted at all costs, of blundering upon an Answer that
will destroy our pitiable attempts to garrison ourselves against
the Truth. So long as we dodge and dodge, we might make
shift to escape the dread confrontation.

In *Four Quartets*, the modern cover is blown, so to speak.

For example, in "Burnt Norton" we hear this:

> What might have been and what has been
> Point to one end, which is always present.
>
> ("Burnt Norton", 1:9–10)

Anyone's experience of the mystery of time bothers him with just this point, namely, that the claim the present moment has on me somehow arrives at the hither end of both what has actually been and also of what might have been. In other words, I find myself under an imperative that ignores the distinction that I myself might like to put forward: that, if things had been different, I would have done better, and so forth and so forth—all the miserable protestations I would like to offer the jury.

And in that same passage, Eliot speaks of "disturbing the dust on a bowl of rose-leaves". What bowl of rose-leaves? We do not need footnotes to help us conjure the picture of that bowl—that sad potpourri on the library table of some lonely soul whose life now consists in the sad and dry effort to relive past loves, with the nosegays and corsages now all dusty and desiccated. The voice in "Burnt Norton" asks, "But to what purpose / Disturbing the dust on a bowl of rose-leaves" (16–17). We find out before we have finished the poem that *memory* has a purpose far more serious than merely to swamp us with nostalgia. It is meant to regale us with the remorseless fact of time's passing, and so to make present to us all that has happened. And at this point a Christian recognizes the true shape of things, namely, that memory, rightly used, brings us to confession. Or put it this way: fruitful confession, which is necessary to salvation, obliges me to take the past and not merely to bewail it, but to place it here, in full view of myself and the Judge and the jury, and to say, "*Miserere mei, Domine.*" Furthermore, a Christian will recognize in this shape of things the Eucharist itself, since the Christian liturgy is an *anamnesis*, that is, a remembering that is also a making present. We do not indulge in lachrymose nostalgia at the Lord's Table. Things are much more serious than that. The veil between time and eternity is drawn aside, and we are "here", in a past eternity when the counsels of God conceived our salvation, and at Golgotha, and in the Upper Room, and in heaven with the seraphim.

This would seem to have carried us very far from the bowl of rose leaves. But Eliot would urge that all memory, if it is not to land us in a bottomless fen of sentimentalism, must be briskly marshaled and made to serve the present, which is, as Saint Paul insists, the accepted time, the day of salvation.

In the next section of "Burnt Norton", we find ourselves hailed with the circulation of the blood, and then with our lymphatic system, and then with the orbits of the stars, and then a boar hunt. What sort of rummage sale of ideas have we here?

But the poetry quietly obliges us to admit that in each of these phenomena we have a *pattern* of movement—even the chase that draws the boarhounds and the boar into a kind of dance. But, like the unhappy boar, one cannot always descry the pattern of the dance; so the poetry lifts us above the trees of the forest where we may

> ... hear upon the sodden floor
> Below, the boar-hound and the boar
> Pursue their pattern as before
> But reconciled among the stars.

> (Ibid., 2:12–14)

Reconciled among the stars. A hint of what any reflective person hopes for: that there is—there must be—somewhere, some center from which the chaotic choreography takes its impulses. One wishes for such a center. And Eliot's poetry pursues us, going on to say:

At the still point of the turning world. Neither flesh
   nor fleshless;
Neither from nor towards; at the still point, there the
   dance is
But neither arrest nor movement. And do not call it fixity,
Where past and future are gathered. Neither movement from
   nor towards,
Neither ascent nor decline. Except for the point, the
   still point,
There would be no dance, and there is only the dance.
                                        (Ibid., 2:16–21)

Who needs footnotes here? The sheer lucidity of it arrests us. Ah. The still point of the turning world. Not fixity, with its suggestion of something mechanical bolted down, but not mere movement either, with its suggestion of mutability. Rather, that stillness which, in its very stillness, is more vibrant and energetic than all the thrashings and strugglings that mark our experience of time. The words of the poetry supply us with a way of imagining eternity—even the Godhead—that, left to our own poor resources, we probably would not have come up with.

Or again, what tactics may we observe here, when the poetry speaks of something we have all seen, say, on the faces of the people in the subway?

> Only a flicker
> Over the strained time-ridden faces
> Distracted from distraction by distraction
> Filled with fancies and empty of meaning
> Tumid apathy with no concentration.
>   (Ibid., 3:10–14)

Alack. Such dereliction. How revolting. The very air itself poisoned with the eructation—the vomiting forth, if you will—of used-up breath from the lungs of these forlorn souls. And the poetry proceeds on its inexorable way:

> Not here
> Not here the darkness, in this twittering world.
> Descend lower, descend only
> Into the world of perpetual solitude.

> (Ibid., 3:24–26)

One does not have to have read Saint John of the Cross to recognize here the state of soul to which the poetry bids us, namely, the darkness and solitude to which we all must press, through and beyond the dereliction that surrounds us in our mortal life—that darkness and solitude which alone, like the tomb of Christ, precedes any notion of resurrection.

Or take this. The next section of *Four Quartets*, "East Coker", opens with these words: "In my beginning is my end." Again, no footnotes about Mary, Queen of Scots (who is reported to have said this, or the reverse, actually, as she approached the scaffold) are necessary. Anyone who will stop and think will know that indeed his "end" (his death) is both implied, and already at work, in his beginning (his birth). But, profounder than that, he will know that his end—the fruition of his whole personhood, the *telos*, the destiny for which he was made—is implicit in his beginning, his conception, the way the oak is implicit in the acorn. And this realization prods him to keep asking, "Well, then, what is it all *about*?" which is precisely what Eliot's poetry prods us to ask, for there will be no salvation for the man who fails to ask such a question (poor Prufrock was terrified of such questions).

In "East Coker" we also find this:

Do not let me hear
Of the wisdom of old men, but rather of their folly,
Their fear of fear and frenzy, their fear of possession,
Of belonging to another, or to others, or to God.

("East Coker", 2:43–46)

Oh dear. There it is. Mere age, in the sense of birthdays
totted up, is very far from being any guarantee of wisdom.
Indeed, it may well be a tragicomic aggregation of folly—a
lifetime's efforts to avoid facing things, and a sort of apo-
theosis of fatuity. Alas. As we get older we do indeed fear
belonging to another—to the staff in the nursing home especially. But what if our eternal destiny *is* to belong to
Another—The Other? That is the most frightening destiny
of all, for the man whose whole effort in life has been toward
what is so bravely called "self-determination" or "self-
actualization". Alas for that man on the day when he finds
that he must either belong wholly to Another or be damned.

Toward the end of "East Coker", we find this:

And so each venture
Is a new beginning, a raid on the inarticulate
With shabby equipment always deteriorating
In the general mess of imprecision of feeling,
Undisciplined squads of emotion

(Ibid., 5:7–11)

Here is the challenge that taxes any artist, and any Christian for that matter: How shall he begin, yet again, with his
shabby mental and emotional and spiritual equipment, to
mount, yet again, a raid on the inarticulate, that is, an attempt
to take the jumble that is our mortal experience and to
shape it and call it into significant form the way the Holy

Ghost did at the creation? Most of us most of the time live in a general mess of imprecision of feeling. Our very syntax betrays this mess. Words. Eliot remarks in "Burnt Norton",

> Words strain,
> Crack and sometimes break, under the burden,
> Under the tension, slip, slide, perish,
> Decay with imprecision, will not stay in place.
> ("Burnt Norton", 5:13–16)

But beyond words there is the Word—The Word in the desert, says Eliot. It is to this that we turn, rather than to horoscopes, haruspications, omens, pentagrams, and palmists,

> "When there is distress of nations and perplexity
> Whether on the shores of Asia, or in the Edgeware Road.
> ("The Dry Salvages", 5:14–15)

When Eliot wrote those words, distress had reached the shores of Asia—Japan had invaded China, and distress was to reach those shores at least twice again in Eliot's century: Korea and Viet Nam. The distress in the Edgeware Road—domestic infidelity and strife, abortion, the collapse of public morals, the wreck of education, private *angst* and aimlessness—has only increased since he wrote.

Four Quartets remains today, more than fifty years after it was written, as a case in point of what the artist, and a fortiori the Christian who is an artist, has for his task. To articulate what is true, *pace* the art-for-art's-sake caucus.

Let Us Purify the Dialect
of the Tribe

When I was very young my mother used to read to me, as she had done for all of my brothers and sisters, from the books of Beatrix Potter. Those fortunate enough to have had these books read to them will remember this enchanting set of very small books with their gray-green, matte-finish bindings, each with a small watercolor in the middle of the front cover, showing the Two Bad Mice, say; or Mr. Jeremy Fisher; or Simkin, the Tailor of Gloucester's cat, leaving deep pawprints in the snow as he trails up a narrow lane on Christmas Eve between the jutting gables of the half-timbered houses of Gloucester.

No one whose young eyes ever looked into the innocent and often sunlit depths of those watercolors can ever, it seems to me, quite forget the yearning aroused by these pictures. The little path up the hillside where Lucy found Mrs. Tiggy-Winkle's tiny house; or the warm rockery where Mrs. Tabitha Twitchit's three naughty kittens lost their frocks; or the sandy floor of the forest where we see Old Mrs. Rabbit with her shawl and basket, setting out to buy currant buns at the baker's: What, we ask ourselves, is it all about? Wherein lies the power of that spell? Why is it that the yearning awakened in us when we look at these pictures surpasses anything that we ever encounter in the real world?

For one thing, of course, we are sadly aware that the real world has long since bulldozed and covered with asphalt most of such vistas, and decked them with neon. As it happens, while I sit writing this speech I can look up, straight into a bucolic landscape painted by the seventeenth-century Dutch painter Hobbema. There is a rutted, sandy road, three peasant cottages, a few passersby, and a gigantic gnarled tree looming up to touch billowing cumulus clouds that seem to arch over things with immense benevolence. Nothing would be gained, however, if I booked myself a flight to Holland hoping to find this place. The effect has long since been compromised by the tens of thousands of other people arriving by charabanc and motorcycle who tell themselves that they would like to see the land painted by Hobbema and van Ruysdael. We would all have to settle for shuffling along through the Rijksmuseum in long lines of people all tricked out in jeans, shorts, halters, Reeboks, and sunglasses.

We find, in painting like this, and in the prose of Beatrix Potter, a case in point of what we look for in good stories: some fragment of the world or of our experience taken and translated into pictures or words that paradoxically give the thing back to us with more force and clarity than the original itself.

When you see a painting you are set free for the moment from the clutter that ordinarily beleaguers you—the time of day, and how many minutes you have until you must push on, and the racket of jets overhead and weed-eaters and so forth: you are set free from these distractions and are able to enter in to what is circumscribed by the borders of the picture, whether it is a landscape, a girl pouring milk from a ceramic jug, or *Aristotle Contemplating the Bust of Homer*. Somehow we seem able to get *in* to the world of the picture, or of the story, in a way which eludes us with respect to our own real world.

This paradox is at work in all of art. The unreal thing—the make-believe—in the poetry, the ballet, the opera, the sculpture, the drama, or the painting, often presents itself to us as reality intensified. We are more struck, for example, with the "reality" of the girl with the milk jug in Vermeer's painting than we ever are with anyone in our own world pouring milk into a glass. In Beatrix Potter's watercolors and prose we find ourselves drawn into a world that both convinces and enchants us.

One of my earliest recollections in this connection is of the friendly and anxious sparrows who came upon Peter Rabbit with his coat buttons entangled in a net in Mr. McGregor's garden and "implored him to exert himself". Now there are other words in English that might have been brought into play here: they besought him; they begged him; they petitioned him; they urged him; they encouraged him. But if we canvassed this list of words we would agree that *implored* was *le mot juste*. As, also, was *exert*.

It is next to impossible to say precisely why a given word or phrase fits, and why alternatives would have diluted, or muddied, the effect. This is true of every line of poetry, and every brushstroke of painting. If Rembrandt, for example, had smoothed out, ever so slightly, the rather nubbly nose on that old man there, we would never have missed the nose as he gives it to us, but we would have missed it in the sense that we would never have known the face of the man as he is *with* the nubbly nose that Rembrandt was pleased to give him.

Once I came across the following in a small book about poetry. The author spoke of Coleridge's *Ancient Mariner* and pointed out the line about the bride pacing into the hall as the agitated wedding guest tries to extricate himself from the clutches of the glittery-eyed and grizzled mariner. Coleridge's lines are "The bride hath paced into the hall / Red as a rose is she." The author of the poetry text suggests that the effect would have been altered if we were to try "The bride hath paced into the hall / Red as a beet is she." The images are not interchangeable, but it is only a matter of one syllable. Perhaps later in the bride's life, when she is toiling over steaming laundry tubs and great kettles of boiling soup, with squalling infants and a loutish husband all over her kitchen, we might evoke the beet. But not now, on her wedding day.

My own memory is full of happy phrases from Beatrix Potter. In Mr. Jeremy Fisher's house, for example, we find that "the water was all slippy-sloppy in the larder and in the back passage." Or, when the two bad mice are pulling feathers from the bolster in the doll house of Lucinda and Jane, Hunca Munca reflects that they would do better to take the bolster for their own use rather than pull it to pieces. "Hunca Munca had a frugal mind", says the narrative. Or, when she and Tom Thumb can't get the plaster fish off the platter on the dolls' dining room table, they throw it into "the red-hot crinkly paper fire". Or, when Mr. Jackson the toad refuses some dainty offered to him by poor Mrs. Tittlemouse into whose tidy house he has pushed his obese way, we find this: "'Tiddly-widdly-widdly! ... Mrs. Tittlemouse! No teeth, no teeth, no teeth.' He opened his mouth most unnecessarily wide. He certainly had not a tooth in his head."

This is very nice stuff for small children. But most of us would admit that it is very nice stuff for any of us. Love for the language will augment the pleasures of reading for us all, but love for the language is the first requirement for anyone who wishes to write. It precedes such elements as insight, and the burden to get a message across, and the urge to write (often invoked by starry-eyed would-be writers). The English language is an entity so rich, so exquisite, so inexhaustible, that no one—not Shakespeare himself— has yet wrung dry its possibilities. Its syntax and vocabulary are a treasury that is still full. This is itself a sad paradox, inasmuch as the last twenty or thirty years have witnessed an impoverishment of the general fund of vocabulary, nay, of discourse itself, so calamitous that the failure of the banks in 1929 seems paltry by comparison; so that we find verbal paupers all around us, tattered, emaciated, and reduced to the stark penury of such verbal resources as "It's like wow" or using "interface" or "office" as verbs.

I am not speaking of fancy writing or speaking, however. Take the following paragraph from Anthony Trollope:

> Mrs. Marsham was by no means satisfied with the way in which she was treated. She would not have cared to go at all to Lady Monk's party had she supposed that she would have to make her entry there alone. With Lady Glencora she would have seemed to receive some of that homage which would certainly have been paid to her companion. The carriage called, moreover, before she was fully ready, and the footman, as he stood at the door to hand her in, had been very sulky. She understood it all. She knew that Lady Glencora had positively declined her companionship; and if she resolved to be revenged, such resolution on her part was only natural.[1]

Those lines are to prose what baked potatoes are to food. One is not dazzled by them; but one admits that it would be difficult to find more satisfactory substance.

[1] Anthony Trollope, *Can You Forgive Her*, vol. 2 (Oxford: Oxford University Press, 1977), 91.

On the other hand, equally good writing may call attention to itself, like caviar. Here is a description of Cyrus'
tomb in Persia from the travel diarist Robert Byron: "It
looks its age: every stone has been separately kissed, and
every joint stroked hollow, as though by the action of the
sea. No ornament or cry for notice disturbs its lonely serenity." Or the scenery in Cyprus: "The affinity of the landscape is with Asia rather than the other Greek islands. The
earth is bleached to whiteness; only a green patch of vines
or a flock of black and tawny goats relieves its arid solitude.... Over the whole scene hangs a peculiar light, a
glaze of steel and lilac, which sharpens the contours and
perspectives, and makes each vagrant goat, each isolated carob
tree, stand out from the white earth as though seen through
a stereoscope." Or an Arab gentleman "who was dressed
like a wasp in a gown of black and yellow stripes".

Many years ago, Malcolm Muggeridge stayed at my house
for several days. One morning at breakfast my daughter, then
about twelve, announced, "I think I am growing up to be like
Papa." Without one second's hesitation, Muggeridge put in,
"This is grievous news." Or again, of Lady Violet Bonham-
Carter: "She had a crop." (Crop? Then you remember
your childhood picture books that pointed out the dangling
fold of skin under a hen's beak, and your picture of Lady
Violet is just what Muggeridge wanted it to be.)

Once in his memoirs Muggeridge remarked that the town
hall in the Croydon section of London was "a building of
quite exceptional architectural confusion".[2] Who of us, upon
hearing this adroit fillip dealt to the impressive expectations
roused by the crescendo of "quite exceptional architectural

[2] Malcolm Muggeridge, *Chronicles of Wasted Time*, vol. 2: *The Green Stick*
(London: William Collins Sons and Co., 1972), 25.

. . ." by the sudden word "confusion", will not agree that at a stroke everything has tumbled into bathos? One is prepared for a quite exceptional architectural grandeur or achievement, but we will remember forever the egregiously unmemorable design of the building because of one word brought to bear upon it by a man who loved English.

My own zeal for the language owes itself to my father and his droll use of English. Once when he was opening his briefcase, which had latches that flew up smartly when you drew two little brass keys aside with your thumbs, we heard him exclaim with mock vexation, "Say! Every time I open this case I flay my knuckles." Flay. Or again, during an evening when we were all sitting next to a fierce blaze in the fireplace of someone's living room, he moved his chair back with the *sotto voce* complaint, "Say! This fire has burned the nap off my suit." The nap. In one syllable he had caught a detail about one of the vagaries of sitting in front of blazing logs. One night he had made a small pile of laundry—a shirt perhaps, and some socks—in the corner of the bedroom, to be put in the hamper the next morning. My mother objected mildly. Says my father: "Do you think some lethal miasma will arise from them during the night?"

I can remember going about as a small boy saying over and over again to myself the line from *Pilgrim's Progress* about the Giant Despair: "He getteth him a grievous crabtree cudgel." The three words regaled me, and still do, I suppose. I loved Kipling's *Just So Stories*, with "the really-truly twirly-whirly eel", and "yonder self-propelling man-of-war with the armor-plated upper deck" (a crocodile), and the refrain, "Then up jumped Dingo, Yellow Dog Dingo, always hungry, grinning like a coal scuttle." And best of all, "the great, grey, green, greasy Limpopo River, all set about with fever trees." Who can expunge lines like that from his mind? I imagine that, if I live to be 95 and have forgotten almost everything, I will still be able to repeat my Kipling. The prose matters.

I keep a sheet of paper inside the front cover of my OED—I have the two-volume micrograph edition, with which you have to use a magnifying glass that sits on a little revolving stand near my desk. When I come across a word that I don't know, or whose pronunciation I want to check, I write it down on this sheet of paper so I can look it up at my leisure. I seem to have written down, among other words, the following: capercailzie, paravanes, vaticination, oneiromancy, esemplastic, gravamen, vicegerent (not to be confused with vice-regent), emunctory, syzygy, farrago, sessile, tantivy, spagyrite, pnigos, quincunx.

T. S. Eliot, in his *Four Quartets*, spoke of the poet's task (and we may broaden that category "poet"—or rather, invest it again with its full Aristotelian meaning—to embrace all serious handlers of words) as "the intolerable wrestle with words and meanings" ("East Coker", 2:20–21). The voice speaking in "Burnt Norton" seems fairly to groan with this:

> Words strain,
> Crack, and sometimes break, under the burden,
> Under the tension, slip, slide, perish,
> Decay with imprecision, will not stay in place,
> Will not stay still.
>
> ("East Coker", 5:13–17)

What sort of agony, in the old sense of *agon*—a wrestling—do we glimpse in those words, wrung from the writer struggling with English words? Whatever else it is, certainly we may say that we hear the groanings of a writer who was painfully aware of the weight and worth of his materials—words. And, in one of the most intense scenes in the entire *Four Quartets*, in "Little Gidding", where Dante appears to Eliot as Eliot walks amongst the rubble of London on the morning after the blitz, and they are speaking of their office as poets, Dante says to Eliot, "our concern was speech, and speech impelled us / To purify the dialect of the tribe." (2:126).[3]

For any Catholic, who has at the center of his vision the mystery of the Incarnation of the Word that was in the beginning with God, and without whom nothing was made that was made, this whole topic takes on great piquance.

---

[3] For all these quotes, I utilized T. S. Eliot, *The Complete Poems & Plays: 1909–1950* (New York: Harcourt, Brace and World, 1971), 125, 121, 141, respectively.

THE CATHOLIC ANGLER

An Interview with Thomas Howard
by the Editors of Touchstone

TOUCHSTONE: *One of the things C. S. Lewis is now notable for is his intellectual dissent from, in a way his assault on, feminism. I mean not only the ordination of women as in his essay "Priestesses in the Church?", but the feminist ideology in general.*

HOWARD: That's one of those questions that has to be chased all the way through the corpus of Lewis' works, because, obviously, feminism as such was not then a major or articulate force. He wrote the essay "Priestesses in the Church?" because the question had surfaced in a mild Anglican sort of way, but there was nothing very imminent about it.

Lewis presents a view of reality at a polar extreme from the frame of mind that ends up demanding ordination of women as presbyters. Obviously, he believes in hierarchy, but it's not a hierarchy of power, which seems to be the feminist understanding. The whole discussion of priestesses in the last thirty years has run along sociological and political lines, with theology dragged in, when necessary, from the sidelines and various attempts made to rewrite the Bible

Professor Howard was interviewed by senior editors Patrick Henry Reardon and David Mills while at Trinity Episcopal School of Ministry to teach a weeklong course on the novels of C. S. Lewis. A more lengthy version was originally published in a slightly different form in *Touchstone* (September/October 1999). Reprinted with permission.

to show that Saint Paul said you should ordain women as presbyters.

In Lewis, you get a vision of things—of everything—in which the whole question of masculine and feminine is a subdivision of tremendous, prior considerations that he understands to characterize the universe. Lewis felt that those categories are of the very stuff of the universe, prior to male and female. Male is the way masculinity exhibits itself under biological species or terms, and female is the way femininity manifests itself under biological species.

For him, hierarchy is obviously the way the Dance is choreographed, or the way the map of the universe is drawn. He points out in one place that in a hierarchy one has the duty of obedience to those above one in the hierarchy and the duty of magnanimity and stewardship and *noblesse oblige* to those below one. I seriously doubt that Lewis would use the words "above" and "below" with respect to masculine and feminine, because they don't apply. They are terms used by people who can only think of a dance in terms of power—which makes for a pretty poor dance.

The *locus classicus* for his view of gender is, I think, the scene toward the end of *Perelandra* when Ransom sees the two eldila: Perelandra, who is feminine, and Malacandra, who is masculine. The feminine eldil, Perelandra, participates in equal majesty, dignity, authority, and so on, with the masculine figure, Malacandra, but she has a receptiveness, a nurturing side. All these words have become buzzwords now, but they weren't when Lewis wrote them in the 1940s.

I think he would feel that it's turning things upside down to try to come at the mystery of femininity and masculinity with a power glint in one's eye, or with an egalitarian, calculating set of categories to try to even up the slices of the pie.

You see this mind in That Hideous Strength.

HOWARD: There's a sense in which the entire book *That Hideous Strength* is a document in the case. Jane Studdock is clearly deeply confused at the beginning of the book in her effort to avoid being thought of as "little wifey"—and who wants to be thought of as little wifey? Fairy Hardcastle calls her that.

But she doesn't want to be identified with what she would think of as stereotypes, but which are actually archetypes, having to do with womanhood and being wife or mother, etc. She is an intellectual, she is writing her dissertation on John Donne's "triumphant vindication of the body", and yet poor Jane is a Gnostic without knowing it. She hasn't got a *clue* about the vindication of the body. She doesn't know that her body will turn out to be virtually Mark's salvation, not just because he remembers her with lust or concupiscence in the toils of Belbury, but because it is her womanhood that stands with clarity and truth and good sense and resilience and toughness over against the bottomless deception and disintegration that is Belbury.

It is Jane *embodied*, not just the idea of Jane, not just Jane's intellect—far from it—but Jane as his *spouse* that saves Mark. And, of course, the very last paragraph of the book is, in one sense, the beginning. We have now come up to the real beginning of the marriage. Mark is about to be saved. He has escaped hell, and Jane is to be his salvation.

You've spoken before about women being naturally religious, having some natural intuition or instinct for the spiritual, and about men being the activists who go dashing around trying to make up for a lack of spiritual instinct.

HOWARD: I cannot prove it, but I deeply suspect that this is indeed the case. I think Lewis felt this, too. His picture of Lucy, for example, would sustain the following line of thought, namely, that there is a profound ontological sense in which the woman is *there*, wherever we mean by "there". She is at home. Woman is *the place*, so to speak. She carries it in her. She creates it around her. There's something that women know in their bones and marrow and lymph system and womb about being human. They are profoundly at home in being human.

Men, on the other hand, are vexed and perplexed about life. It may be a form of the wish for power. Obviously, women are susceptible to certain kinds of vanity, but men are not only equally so, but also may be susceptible in more serious ways. Take Mark Studdock: he will mortgage his soul to get into the inner ring. And you see that sort of thing with men all the time.

It's my hunch that this is the reason that trying, as some of the feminists did early in the game, to dredge up names of women conquerors or women composers or women painters, through the ten thousand years of myth and history that we have, ends up being farcical. It's a lost game. The list is short. There are not that many good women composers. There are not that many good women philosophers or mathematicians. There are not many good women painters.

I'm intrigued by the question of women novelists. A case could be made that among the English novelists, they're the best—George Eliot, Jane Austen, and so on. None of the men ever quite equal them. One could go off on a disquisition about that. It may spring from their profound understanding of the immediate and familiar, and of domestic situations.

But anyway, back to the main point. This will sound fanciful and almost Jungian, which I would hate to be thought to be, but nevertheless, I suspect that the reason it has been the men who have been charging around—slaying woolly mammoths, conquering kingdoms, furrowing their brows over mathematical formulae and physics and astrophysics, writing symphonies, you name it—is that men are aware of being in some sense on the periphery, and they want to find out: What is it? what is it? *what is it?* The woman is already there, says my theory. So women aren't hag-ridden with this need to know or to find out.

This doesn't mean a woman can't be a physicist or a statesman. In our own time, three of the toughest and most successful heads of state—Margaret Thatcher, Indira Gandhi, and Golda Meir—certainly have shown no lack of ability, but my guess is that your archetypal woman—woman *qua* woman—doesn't aspire to that. Even Margaret Thatcher is not a feminist as such. She didn't become prime minister to show that women could do it, to score a point for the women. She liked politics. She liked running a government. And she could do it. She was jolly good at it. She was better than most of the men.

But anyway, there's my theory. It gets right down to the sexual imagery, you know. The man is seeking the place. He's the aggressor; he's one who is probing, if you will, trying to find the place. The woman is already there.

Relative to language, at Saint Anne's in That Hideous Strength, *both the men and the women work in the kitchen, but the Fisher King will not let them work there simultaneously because they do not share the same vocabulary.*

HOWARD: Yes. That's interesting. And this is one of the things that scandalizes Jane. She thinks of herself as being a liberal with all the right liberal attitudes, and she gets into Saint Anne's and finds this simultaneous egalitarianism *and* hierarchy, and she *cannot* put it together. It scandalizes her and bothers her. She finds that Ivy Maggs, who is lower class, is considered to be an equal member of the community, and so on and so on.

I think the men and women do not work in the kitchen at the same time because they do not have the same vocabulary, and obviously their vocabulary springs from their inner substance and their way of coming at work and life. Lewis has a marvelous aside somewhere where he speaks of a great "purgatorial kitchen . . . with milk boiling over, toast burning, and crockery smashing". The women will have to learn to calm down about it, and the men will have to learn to lend a hand.

There's no notion in Lewis that something is proved by men giving the baby the bottle or washing the dishes. Among a lot of couples nowadays, of course, the woman is almost afraid to carry the baby, and the man has to push the stroller and change the diapers. I don't think Lewis would have been comfortable or happy with that notion, but it's natural to him to picture Saint Anne's as being such a place where there is this strange simultaneous egalitarianism and hierarchy.

But when hierarchy is called upon, then it exercises itself. When the Fisher King needs to be boss, he's boss.

If I recall the differences in the way men and women speak, Lewis says that a man says, "Put this on the third shelf on the north wall", whereas a woman says, "Put this over there." The second is direct and the first is quite specific by giving a grid, an outline.

HOWARD: And for reasons incomprehensible to the men, it works for the women! "Put it over there" doesn't worry another woman. The man wants to say, "Well, which shelf? Which end of the shelf?" Yes, I had forgotten about that. That's a good component, if you want to try to put together a whole picture of Lewis' ideas.

He had his tongue a little bit in his cheek sometimes about all this, but I think one should. Lewis had a notion that there is probably a lot of drollery in heaven, too, and it's rather amusing, that sort of thing. And yet it touches on an ontology. It's profound.

You said that when the Fisher King needs to be boss, he's boss. But he's never a fisher queen. What is it in headship that requires masculinity? Why is the Fisher King a Fisher King?

HOWARD: Well, there's the question. Again, you have to keep recalling the fact that you can have a queen, a Catherine the Great, a Maria Theresa, a Victoria, an Elizabeth, who can jolly well run the show. But I think this connection of headship and masculinity derives from God's revelation of himself as *he*. God is not male, of course, but certainly he is masculine in the Judeo-Christian vision. And in most pantheons the head honcho is masculine. There are not nearly as many matriarchal pantheons as the feminists would have us believe, with the creator as the absolute sovereign being a female or a feminine figure.

One of the reasons would be that in good medieval and renaissance fashion we encounter the doctrine of correspondences. We reflect in our circumstances the nature of the Deity, and the head in the universe is king, not queen. I don't know any place where Lewis tries to itemize properties that add up to a better crowned head.

On the other hand, back to *Perelandra*. The description of Malacandra as opposed to Perelandra is certainly, if one buys Lewis' ontology and vision at all, magnificent. It is not only convincing, it is also a magnificent unfurling of antiphonal dignity, antiphonal majesty. The whole story of *Perelandra* is Tinidril being trained to be queen and mother. Tor, who is going through lessons we never see, is being trained to be king and father. We don't see his part. It's interesting that Lewis picked the female, the feminine figure, to pursue, to follow with great punctilio.

Why does one need to have a king? I think Lewis would finally demur a little bit on that question. He would not retreat on it, but he would appeal to mystery. He would tick off the various items and say a woman can do this and that, and that women are just as bright as men, and just as important as men ... and yet, and yet, and yet: there is something about the masculine mystery that is asked to bear the yoke of authority, for whatever reason.

In "Priestesses in the Church?", Lewis says that a child who prays to "God the Mother" will have a radically different religious life, spiritual life, from one who prays to God the Father, but he doesn't argue the point. He just drops it. One intuits the truth of his insight, but how do you convey it? It is not a self-evident proposition anymore, even to Christians. It may have been obvious when Lewis wrote, but not now. Is there some way of making an argument for that, or do you have to do it imaginatively?

HOWARD: I suspect that your last clause there may be the key. It may have to be done narratively or imaginatively in a sense analogous to the following: namely, it would be laborious, at best, to try to write a disquisition on a state of affairs where absolute power is characterized by absolute love and mercy and grace. When we think of absolute power, we immediately think of Hitler and Mao and Stalin. It would be a laborious task to plot out how absolute power could show itself as absolutely merciful as well. But all you need is one page about Aslan, and you've got it. You've got the whole picture: absolute power with absolute mercy and grace and love and tenderness.

The paradox, the terrible good, would be a hard proposition to cope with in a propositional disquisition, but you see it in a paragraph or two about Aslan. By the same token, it would be laborious if not impossible to show why masculinity is asked to bear the yoke of authority, and why a feminine deity leads to confusion and chaos. To describe a child who prays to goddesses, I think you'd just have to get down to specifics and talk about Isis and Diana, or Ungit in Glome. There's a lot of truth in the religion of Glome, by the way. They certainly know about shed blood and propitiation and liturgy and so on.

There's a non-answer! I don't know. I wouldn't be able to argue it. Lewis never does argue it in so many words.

To switch subjects sharply, who are your heroes and why?

HOWARD: Well, Enoch, who walked with God and God took him—that's all we know about him. I like Simeon and Anna because there they were, waiting for the salvation of Israel with no trumpets and drums. Saint Joseph is a major figure in my martyrology. Then, moving along, and skipping lots of the Fathers and saints down through the centuries, I am always intrigued by Saint Vladimir. And Saint Michael the Archangel.

Among the literary figures who have had the most impact on the shape of my imagination would be T. S. Eliot, most notably in *The Four Quartets*. Obviously, Lewis and Tolkien and Charles Williams, no question about that. Flannery O'Connor because of the toughness and sinewiness and ebullience of her Catholic orthodoxy.

Then of Catholic and Orthodox writers, I'd list Romano Guardini, Dietrich von Hildebrand, Karl Adam, Alexander Schmemann, and Georges Florovsky, although I have only read one small book of his. Is that a long enough list of heroes?

Dante?

HOWARD: Oh, heavens, yes. Dante. He's got the whole thing. And Samuel Johnson, of course, and Newman.

Why Saint Joseph?

HOWARD: Because he's almost a patron of the obscure and of the anonymous—of all those whose walk in life is simply to put one foot in front of the other, with no limelight, no flashbulbs, no headlines. Obscurity and anonymity: that is something that I have wrestled a lot with myself. Obviously, I have written a few books and a few articles, but they are in a very tiny, almost invisible, corner of the cotton patch.

I think a man is harried or has his metaphorical elbow plucked now and again with the desire to move and shake, to be listened to, to be read, to be heard. And that has passed me by. That has eluded me, and I need to take Joseph seriously as a patron who is outside the carbon arc lamps on the stage. And yet, and yet: he's right up there with half a dozen saints.

Who are your models as a writer?

HOWARD: T. S. Eliot's prose is wonderful. And C. S. Lewis, of course. Two English writers, Anthony Powell and Eve-lyn Waugh, have had a major, major effect on my prose in the books I have written in the last eight or ten years. Everybody—including my wife—says my style is more irenic, less pugilistic now than it used to be. That is to be attrib-uted, I think, to my reading of Anthony Powell and Evelyn Waugh.

What is it in their prose style that you've picked up? They are all my [Mills'] models, as well, with Orwell and a few writers like that.

HOWARD: There is a—how shall I put it?—there is a del-icate tact and a circumlocution in the interest of directness—which sounds like a paradox, which it is—that somehow began to appeal to me and get under my skin.

I'll give you one example from my own writing. In the little book called *Lead, Kindly Light*, which was about my odyssey from Anglicanism to Rome, I give a page or two of description of Fundamentalism, mentioning some of the stereotypes that Hollywood likes to indulge. Then I had a sentence starting another paragraph saying, "I myself am not disposed to scoff in this connection."

Whoppo! So much for the people who were thinking, "Yippee, he hates the Fundamentalists, and he's really going after them." And I say, "I myself am not disposed to scoff in this connection." That would be an example of a sen-tence that I think I would have to attribute to those writers.

What is it in this prose style? I don't like to say self-effacement. One doesn't want to accuse oneself of self-effacement.

He said self-effacingly.

HOWARD: Yes! [Laughs.] Well, you tell me.

We're interviewing you.

HOWARD: Touché. I think it has to do with a lowering of the decibel level and a dependence on courtesy and tact in prose, and a certain circuitousness that angles around the topic. Here's another example: Christopher Hollis, who was nobody in particular himself, but was a friend of all those people in England we've been talking about. He's referring to what he believes and what he doesn't believe. He says, Purgatory, that's fine. As to hell, I'm a little more skittish, but "Whoever it is that has the arrangements for the Last Judgment, it will not be me, so it makes very little difference what I think about it." That's the sort of thing that appeals to me.

That's very helpful. Lewis, and even more so Chesterton, argued by analogy in a way that makes a point that, if you just laid out the argument in logical form for people, it would escape them. When you say, "This that you don't believe is exactly the same thing as this other thing that you already believe", that is when the light goes on.

HOWARD: Absolutely. Probably anybody who has moved into Anglicanism or Orthodoxy or Catholicism from free-church Evangelicalism would agree that by far the real zinger for them was the argument that shows by analogy that they had already bought into the principle of incense, kneeling, vestments, things like that. If they say they don't like read prayers or anything "canned", they had better quit singing hymns. "Amazing grace, how sweet the sound"—John Newton wrote that 250 years ago. It's canned; it's shopworn; it's warmed over; you're not expressing yourself ad hoc, off the cuff; it's not spontaneous. Forget it.

So you're exactly right. Even with questions about the Mother of God, you can angle them into Catholic belief step by step by step with things that they already know. They've never thought of it, but there is no other creature in the universe who has been so privileged—no seraph bore any offspring to God, no seraph suckled the Son of God, the second Person of the Trinity. And so on. You're off and running. If you proceed by noncontroversial steps you can lead them right into the Catholic lobster trap.

Back when you were talking about characteristics of the particular writers you followed, of angling things instead of hitting them directly, I [Reardon] was thinking that what you were describing is very, very Anglican. When you used the word "angled" it brought back Gregory the Great's "not Angles but angels". All of us who write for Touchstone *share a store of writers from whom all of us borrow. With a few exceptions like S. M. Hutchens, who doesn't like Flannery O'Connor and most of Dostoyevsky.*

[MILLS]:   *And Jim Hitchcock doesn't like Chesterton.*

HOWARD: And I don't like Belloc.

One other thing I'd like you to comment on. Lewis is not afraid to be obvious. Look at Mere Christianity, *for example. He'll say, "There are four arguments for this. First, . . . Second, . . . Third, . . . Fourth, . . . Therefore, we've seen there are four arguments for this. And there are two arguments against it. First, . . ." It's all very clear.*

HOWARD: Of course, he had a *ferociously* rigorous training from the Great Knock, Kirkpatrick. Lucky Lewis, he had the training. I can't do it. Peter Kreeft writes that way. He got up at one conference and said, "I have twenty-one points." My heart sank into my boots. But he got through them in forty-five minutes. He has that kind of training and discipline. I don't.

You are heuristic in finding divisions that are already there. In your book on Charles Williams, the divisions were already there: he wrote this number of novels, this is how many chapters we will have in the book. These are the subjects he covered, this is what I'm going to cover. But I think that's part of your genius. You can find the divisions in which the subject naturally falls; you don't have to impose your own categories on it. It's one of your values as a writer.

HOWARD: Yes, I suppose I do try to stick to the obvious.

That's not what I meant.

HOWARD: Well, let's say that I try to pluck people's sleeves and make them see what's right there in front of them. I dedicated *Chance or the Dance*, which was then called *An Antique Drum*, to my professor Clyde Kilby, "who took my arm and said, 'Look.' " He made us look at what was there.

    If one were to analyze the effort at persuasion in my sequence of books—I never have, until now—I think I'd urge that I try to keep it on the level of "This is right there, chaps." It isn't as though I'm trying to introduce Protestants to monstrosities or grotesqueries from somewhere off in the universe. I'm telling them, it's here, you already count on highly similar notions.

Do you have sort of a mere Christianity reading list, I mean "mere Christianity" in Lewis' sense, the sort of thing Touchstone is about? If someone said that he has a year and wants to read ten or fifteen books to get the general outline of mere Christianity, what would you recommend to him? Besides Mere Christianity.

HOWARD: Well, of course, my list would be loaded in the Roman Catholic direction. But on mere Christianity, obviously Chesterton's *The Everlasting Man* and *Orthodoxy* I would certainly recommend. Romano Guardini's book, *The Lord*, which is his magnum opus, has very, very little that is explicitly or polemically Roman, so I would tell people to drop everything and read that.

Dietrich von Hildebrand's magnum opus, *Transformation in Christ*, I would loudly recommend that. Alexander Schmemann's *For the Life of the World* opens up the sacramental vision of the world.

You earlier mentioned Karl Adam.

HOWARD: Yes. Karl Adam wrote a book called *The Spirit of Catholicism*. I think it is probably the best single book one could give to a thinking person who is looking at the Church, and specifically the Roman Church.

Then, I think, with a certain amount of indirection, of Walker Percy and Flannery O'Connor's essays: Percy's *The Message in the Bottle* and Flannery O'Connor's *Mystery and Manners*. And her letters, in *The Habit of Being*. There are lots of others that I'm not as familiar with now as I used to be: people like Eric Mascall and Austin Farrer. And there's that whole French Catholic intellectual movement that is bone-crushingly difficult but very good: Péguy, Claudel, Maritain, and Bernanos.

Of course, I've left out T. S. Eliot, if only his *Selected Essays*. And *The Idea of a Christian Society* and *Christianity and Culture*.

What about imaginative works? Almost everything you mentioned is discursive. What about someone who wanted to form a Christian mind or imagination through imaginative literature? What books would you recommend he read?

HOWARD: Well, strange as it may seem, I would start at a place that would appear to be way out in the hinterland, having nothing to do with Christianity, but I maintain that it participates in the same pattern. I would tell them to get the whole set of Beatrix Potter's books and read them. *Mrs. Tiggly-Winkle, Squirrel Nutkin, Jeremy Fisher*. You have to read those. I was brought up on them. And Lewis loved them. He said *Squirrel Nutkin* opened up to him the *idea* of autumn in the sense of *sehnsucht*.

Anyway, Beatrix Potter. And the Christopher Robin books. These are good things. But after that, it's embarrassingly predictable what I would say: Tolkien, Lewis, and Charles Williams. What else am I going to say?

There are all these other efforts to come up with new three-volume sagas. God bless them. I have friends who tried to make the effort. But it's no good. Mozart has done it, you can't write Mozart symphonies. Haydn has done it, you can't write Haydn symphonies.

Tolkien has done it. And even if little John Jones loves elves and fairyland and all that kind of thing, he doesn't have the philology at his disposal. Tolkien came at it with a titanic grasp of and love for and immersion in English and mythology, and the Greek and Roman classics, and "northernness". It can't be done again.

By imagination, I didn't just mean fantasy, though. For example, I was thinking of the Norwegian writer, Sigrid Undset.

HOWARD: Well, yes, of course her *Kristin Lavransdatter* is a wonderful book. And then I would say Evelyn Waugh, most particularly *Brideshead Revisited*, which I think is the most successful piece of fiction from the Christian point of view in the twentieth century. It is a magnificent story of a conversion. And he never misses a step. There are a thousand places where he could have slipped into the mire of sentimentalism, and he didn't. It's flawless.

I would say Waugh's military trilogy, *The Sword of Honour*, if only for the two or three pages in the second volume that give the funeral of Guy Crouchback's old father. It is a portrait of a Christian gentleman the likes of which has never been drawn before.

And then, of course, Flannery O'Connor and Walker Percy. I happen to like both of them. I know it's easier to get your toe into O'Connor through her essays and her letters, and that people are often stumped by her stories. But if one can get the skeleton key to Flannery O'Connor and what she's on about, it's tremendous, particularly *The Violent Bear It Away*.

Of Walker Percy's novels, I think *The Moviegoer* and *Love in the Ruins* are my favorites. I actually do bog down eventually in Walker Percy. I've never been able to get through *The Last Gentleman*. I don't think I've ever been able to quite get through *The Second Coming*. But certainly *The Moviegoer* and *Love in the Ruins* are major works.

What about Anthony Powell?

HOWARD: Only from the standpoint of honing one's prose style. And, if you will, maybe honing one's sensibilities. There's an urbanity, and a reserve, and a rather droll, dry self-deprecation in him that's very, very salutary. It saves one from being sanctimonious or too solemn about oneself. I think there's an awful lot of trumpery in Christian journalism and speechifying by people who are just too impressed with themselves and too pontifical. In reading Tony Powell you are taken into a world where understatement or the oblique statement or the allusion is the zinger.

I was thinking that Powell's A Dance to the Music of Time *gives such an extraordinary portrait, in Widmerpool, of the archetypal modern man who is simply pure will, and of the eventual chaos and destruction that this enslavement to the will leads to. It's a horrifying image of modern man.*

HOWARD: Oh yes. I mean there isn't much religion in Tony Powell, but he certainly gives an acute, and exquisite, portrait of modernity, and almost postmodernity. If you want a portrait of modernity, *A Dance to the Music of Time* would be it.

One more question along this same line: What would you give for a C. S. Lewis reading list? If someone had a year to read five or ten books of Lewis' and wanted to know which ones to start with, what would you tell him, to get an overview of his prose and fiction?

HOWARD: There would be an obvious case for telling someone to start with *Mere Christianity*. I wouldn't quarrel with that, but I, myself, might say, start with the *Narnia Chronicles*. Reading the *Narnia Chronicles* has the advantage of almost inevitably drawing a reader in, head over heels, to a world— *the* world, the world of truth, of reality—that is Lewis' whole world. So I would say the *Narnia Chronicles*, *The Abolition of Man*, *The Great Divorce*, "The Weight of Glory" and

"Transpositions"—which last two appear in a book of essays called *The Weight of Glory*—*The Space Trilogy, Till We Have Faces.*

Then, of his apologetic books, *Miracles* I think in one sense is a special-interest book. I think *Mere Christianity* does that job well for general readers. Of his scholarly books, the books on Edmund Spenser and his *English Literature in the Sixteenth Century* from the Oxford History of English Literature—the "OHEL"—are wonderful. They're glorious reading. Other works like *Studies in Words* and *Experiment in Criticism* are good, but they're not center stage.

I think I would include *Preface to Paradise Lost*, interestingly enough, even if the reader has never read and will never read Milton. Lewis touches on some very, very fundamental things there.

The Problem of Pain?

HOWARD: Yes, I would certainly include that.

Last night in your lecture you told everyone to drop everything and read The Discarded Image.

HOWARD: Ah! Yes! You see, the list gets longer. That's a glorious book. And he pursued an absolutely faultless course. He never drops into the error of nostalgia for the Middle Ages or of complaining that "Oh, we've gone down the tubes since then." He describes the mind of the Middle Ages, and at the very end of the book he says, "It will be obvious to the reader where my sympathies lie", but he doesn't argue it.

Yes, I think one could even make *The Discarded Image* number one because it will lead you in a sober, classroom way or a Lewis tutorial way into the world that you are going to encounter one fine morning at the Last Trump.

THINGS SACRED

The Power of Wise Custom

Two words cast a pall over the imagination of those who have grown up since 1960—during this forty years, that is, when *spontaneity*, *naturalness*, *creativity*, *sincerity*, and what we might call the *visceral*, have been so earnestly extolled. The two words are *ritual* and *ceremony*.

Spirits wither straightaway. "Dull!" we hear from one corner. "Repressive!" from another. "An imposition! A straitjacket!" we hear from various quarters. "What we want is freedom to be ourselves—our natural, real, unconstrained selves. Ritual and ceremony are guaranteed to stifle all vitality and genuineness. They are a recipe for ennui."

Well, yes, we might say, your frantic objections are not altogether without warrant. But we need, clearly, to revisit the topic. If we leave things with those objections granted, we settle for an impoverishment of human life so tragic that famine itself is not too strong a word to bring into play.

Strong words, indeed, from all sides. What nerve have we touched, that we get this leaping response? What spot have we lanced that people recoil so? It is a matter, we begin to think, of challenging certain modern assumptions so deep that those who hold them feel threatened, and those of us (those

Originally published in a slightly different form in *Touchstone* (December 2000): 10–12. Reprinted with permission.

few of us, it often seems) who reject them root and branch
feel a certain desperation.

Our century flounders along in the wake of the Promethean
and Faustian Romanticism that stole over the entire West
from Germany in the eighteenth century (helped along a
good bit by Rousseau). Prometheus was the Titan who (God
love him) stole fire from Zeus because he saw us mortals
shivering in the cold. Faust was the scholar who, finally
bored with the usual academic fields, decided on magic and
made a pact with Mephistopheles, or Satan (Mephisto was
only a lackey), to the effect that he could have his wishes if
he signed over his soul to Satan for eventual disposal.

Prometheus and Faust became the heroes of everyone who
wished to call his own shots, so to speak, to shape his own
destiny free of meddlesome gods or moral codes. A spin-off
from this center is the distrust of ritual and ceremony that is
almost universal now, for a man who objects to ritual and ceremony is a man who would prefer to "do his own thing" rather
than be clamped into a preordered scheme.

This preference began to show itself extravagantly in the
sixties and seventies. In clothes, for example. Costume and
uniform have always borne great significance. They bespeak
the occasion. A nurse on duty appears in starched, immac-
ulate white (the idea being hygiene). A policeman on duty
appears in blue, with a special hat (the London bobbies had
the best ones), the idea being: here we have a man with
authority.

A housewife wore a "house dress" during her working
hours—decent, but not "dressy". Your dressy dresses (velvet, silk, and brocade) meant church, or the opera, or a
dinner party. Men wore a suit, including waistcoat, stiff collar, necktie, and fedora, to work (look at any news photo

up through the 1950s for proof). And of course tribal costume, regimental costume, royal attire, and priestly vestments would be the most colorful cases in point of ceremonial
dress—dress, that is, prescribed by the identity of the wearer
and the demands of the occasion (crowning a new king, or
opening parliament, or going up to meet the gods).

This has all disappeared, as we know, or most of it. It
lingers, of course, in a few contexts. But such contexts are
dwindling. My son, for example, goes to work on Wall
Street—certainly the last bastion of your man-in-a-three-
piece-suit. Firm after firm is now permitting informal dress
for the workday. I have not seen a nurse in white for, I
suppose, thirty years.

And my peers and fellow travelers on airplanes (you used
to "dress up" to travel): tank tops, shorts, or anything your
whim may have suggested to you is the order of the day.
We must all travel amiably with hairy legs, elephantine legs,
hairy shoulders, and nipples straining at the T-shirt. The
rubric is "Well, hey! I dress the way I want to. It's me,
everybody. Sorry if you're so uptight as to notice, much
less be offended."

We seem to have strayed from our topic. But clothes,
along with language, posture, attitude, décor, and "special
events", all furnish us with indices of how a given civilization or era stands vis-à-vis existence itself; and public ritual and ceremony, of which these are all a part, were, for
ten thousand years of myth and history, looked upon
as—known, let me say, to *be*—the very guarantors of both
significance and of our humanity itself.

What does this mean? We may take as an extreme example
the coronation of a monarch. Not one single gewgaw of
the whole business is "necessary". Crowns, scepters, orbs,

ermine, state trumpets, processions, velvet, diamonds, bow-
ings, heralds in tabards—not one molecule of all that par-
aphernalia is actually necessary. But somehow we want it
all. And in so wanting, we have taken our place along with
every tribe, culture, civilization, and society ever known.
Whether the crown is of feathers or of gold is not the point.
The monarch is, must be, set apart.

Or, somewhat closer to home, a wedding: none of the
"rules" accomplishes a thing, pragmatically. (The bride's train
just drags along the floor and gets *dirty*, for heaven's sake.)
The slow, measured walk down the aisle, the special clothes,
the book from which the minister reads, the canned vows:
it is all increasingly called into question now.

Couples write their own vows, the idea being, "But we
want this to be *our* wedding. We want it to express who we
are. We want our friends to share our joy, and they can't do
that if we have to say words someone else wrote a long
time ago. If things are going to be real, they have to spring
spontaneously from our love, and not from a printed page."

Hmm. Are you sure you are on firm ground there? We
might ponder a few embarrassingly obvious items.

First, spontaneous or not, we would all agree that there
are *some* spontaneous displays that we *don't* want just now
(we are still talking of weddings here). An infant vomiting,
for example. Very spontaneous, and natural, and perfectly
sincere, but somewhat disconcerting to the rest of us. Or
some well-meaning relative who rushes out to rumple the
bride's hair lovingly as she comes in. Or some bright soul
who jumps up in the middle of the proceedings to share a
reading that has meant a lot to her.

No. Oddly, some "rule" is presiding here. Some decorum, some appropriateness, some acknowledgment of a
weight of significance suffusing the occasion. We can't *quite*

do what we want. At some point the rest of us have to lapse into silence and focus our entire attention on the ceremony that is occurring.

Second, it turns out that we do, after all, most earnestly wish the occasion to be a ceremonial one. A couple doesn't get married, be they never so blithe and earthy, on the fly in the middle of a game of hide-and-seek. Everything else has to stop. And what occurs now must have *some* forethought investing it.

If we do not like Thomas Cranmer's angelic English, that, of course, is a very great pity. God himself will not prevent our cobbling up our vows. But, one way or another, they have got to be cobbled up. It may indeed be the case that some wedding has occurred somewhere, in which the man and woman (they would scarcely wish to be called by such heavily ornamented words as *bride* and *groom*) sauntered up to some random spot, accompanied by the ragtag and bobtail of their friends, and "chatted" their vows. Perhaps so. But such an event will not serve, we suspect, as any sort of paradigm for weddings. All of anthropology, sociology, and religion cry out against it.

Third, our spontaneity caucus is missing something. It is missing the paradox that lies at the root of all ceremony and ritual, namely, that by reaching for the seemingly artificial phenomenon of ceremony, lo and behold, we are all carried beyond the shallow puddles of the spontaneous, into the deeps of genuine significance.

Through the imposed, we meet the natural. Through the prescribed, we meet the sincere. This is always and everywhere true. No tribe, culture, civilization, or society has ever operated on any other assumption.

Birth rites, puberty rites, marriage rites, death rites: no one gives the back of his hand to these things. Huns, Florentines,

Saxons, Watusi, and Athenians all agree here. If you are approaching something significant, or *if you want to discern the significance of an event*, you must submit to ceremony. (It might be apposite here to make a small distinction: the word *ritual* refers to the words of the ceremony, and the word *ceremony* refers to the movements entailed.)

We do not, for example, hunt up the nearest dumpster when a death has occurred. That would be practical; the body, after all, is of no more use to its owner. The event calls loudly for elaboration, not so that we may all escape the awful meaning of it all, but, contrarily, so that we may all enter more fully into the awful meaning. Hence, slow processions, solemn music, hush, and courtesy.

Birth: the frippery of blue versus pink, and of showers, and nurseries all bedecked, and cigars and champagne—these all appear in the service of immense significance (the mystery of a new personhood is amongst us) and assist us in grasping the mystery. Ceremony gives us something to *do*, when doing nothing would leave us frantic and awash, or else (and this is worse) as oblivious to the mystery before us as the animals.

Now obviously, the topic that is being held in abeyance here is worship. Here is the point of all of our ruminations. How should we worship?

It would seem presumptuous in the extreme for any mortal to take upon himself the authority to dictate to another how to worship. "Good heavens, man, are you serious? You are outgodding God. Don't tell me how to worship."

Who, indeed, will presume to legislate here? Surely God loves the spontaneous noises of his creatures: the buzzing of the wasp, the croaking of the frog, the scream of the eagle. Would this not include my own staggering efforts to find impromptu words with which to praise him? The form, or formlessness, of public worship is purely a matter of taste.

Not altogether. Those who urge this upon us forget two things: first, there is no such thing as spontaneity in any regularly recurring public occasion. Quakers, Brethren, and Pentecostals all would testify to this. Anyone from any of those "informal" purlieus will tell us that everyone present knows exactly what is going to happen, and when, and with what phraseology. There is an unmistakable beginning to the "service" and an unmistakable end; and what happens in between is what happened last Sunday, and the Sunday before that, *ad infinitum*.

Second, we all must recognize the Himalayan watershed between the public and the private. The private (my own prayers and praises and devotional exercises) may take any of a hundred forms, depending on what I like, or want, or need. But, from the beginning, public worship has been ordered. (We may consult ancient Judaism for corroboration here, as well as Islam, Hinduism, the Aztecs, or Egyptians.)

You can't have a stampede, or a jamboree, or an off-the-cuff "happening" for your public solemnities. People have to know, and expect, what's coming next. The prayers set down in the great English Book of Common Prayer of 1662, or in the Roman Missal, are not more "set" than the sequence of stock phrases that pour from the mouths of people who suppose that they are approaching the Sapphire Throne spontaneously.

Anyone who has lived with the burden of producing perennially impromptu prayers knows what an ordeal it is to keep those prayers "fresh". In fact, such a person knows that you cannot. You are reduced to piecing together a sequence of phrases familiar in your tradition.

And (perhaps the most important point yet) ritual and ceremony raise us all to a level unattainable by our own spontaneous efforts. What language shall we use in the precincts of holiness? Think of "Almighty God, our heavenly Father, who of thy tender mercy didst give thine only Son Jesus Christ to suffer death upon the Cross for our redemption; who made there (by his one oblation of himself once offered . . .)" or "we most heartily thank thee, for that thou dost vouchsafe to feed us, who have duly received these holy mysteries, with the spiritual food of the most precious body and blood of thy Son our Saviour Jesus Christ; and dost assure us thereby of thy favour and goodness towards us."

Can we excel that? Who of us will wish to enter these ritual sweepstakes with any notion of doing a better job? The words become rote? No more than (and perhaps rather less than) the shopworn phrases we piece together in our spontaneous attempts.

But God doesn't need all that stilted sixteenth-century English. No. But perhaps we do? Or at least something freighted by common usage in the Church for centuries. We no longer use Latin, but who of us who has ever assisted at the old Mass, or even who has only heard the Byrd *Mass for Three Voices*, will suppose that language can do better than "*Laudamus te, benedicimus te, adoramus te, glorificamus te; Gratias agimus tibi propter magnam gloriam tuam*"?

C. S. Lewis felt rather strongly in this matter (though he considered himself a man who did not naturally like ritual; it embarrassed him). Speaking of ritual, he wrote, in *Preface to Paradise Lost*, "those who dislike ritual in general—ritual in any and every department of life—may be asked most earnestly to reconsider the question. It is a pattern imposed on the mere flux of our feelings by reason and will, which renders pleasures less fugitive and griefs more endurable, which hands over to the power of wise custom the task (to which the individual and his moods are so inadequate) of being festive or sober, gay or reverent, when we choose to be, and not at the bidding of chance."[1]

One last point: the desire for ritual and ceremony has nothing to do with taste, nor with being highbrow, as some people claim. Consult history. Most of the people on this poor earth of ours, from the beginning, have been anything but highbrow. Your ancient Antiochenes, your ninth-century French peasants, your fifteenth-century Russian crones, your nineteenth-century English laborers, and most of the rest of us mortals, have only very rarely come anywhere near an outlook that could by any stretch be called highbrow.

And yet this is the very multitude for whom public, regular worship meant ritual and ceremony. They would have had immense difficulty with the historically recent paradigm of the "meeting" focused on a very long speech.

[1] C. S. Lewis, *A Preface to Paradise Lost* (London: Oxford University Press, 1970), 21.

The Image of the Cross

At the center of Christian vision and imagery stands a great and enigmatic sign, the sign of the Cross. Like the brass serpent held aloft on a pole by Moses in the desert, the Cross has drawn and fixed the gazes of men ever since it was raised. It is there at the center of Christian vision because it is there at the center of the divine drama celebrated in that vision—the drama unfolded on the stage of our history in the sequence of Annunciation, Nativity, Passion, Resurrection, and Ascension. And, like all these mighty mysteries in this sequence, the Cross defies all our efforts to grasp its full significance, and all our attempts to respond adequately. Shall we approach in sackcloth or in festal garments? Shall we sing songs of penitence or of triumph? Shall we bring ashes or garlands?

The difficulty we mortal men have in the presence of the events that make up the Gospel is that, while the events themselves are straightforward enough for any peasant to understand (the angels appeared to *shepherds*), the significance of those events exhausts the efforts of the most sublime intellects to grasp them. The plain Gospel story is told, century after century, to peasants, children, and philosophers and calls forth adoration and faith from all alike. The

Originally published in a slightly different form in *Christianity Today* (April 9, 1976): 6–10. Reprinted with permission.

stable, the Upper Room, the garden, the Cross, the tomb, and so forth: these are points in a tale that is plain enough for all of us. But these are also points on the frontier between the seen and the unseen, the historic and the eternal, the contingent and the unconditioned, and hence open out onto vistas where the divine immensities loom in all their terror and splendor.

For this reason, the Cross, which is a clear enough object, attracts the unceasing efforts of man's intellect and imagination and affection to respond in some manner fitting its significance. It is carried in procession with great pomp in Rome and hangs on a string around the neck of an Irish farmer. It glimmers from a plaque next to a child's crib and shines from the pages of Aquinas, Calvin, and Barth. It is hailed in sorrowful chants (*"O vos omnes . . . videte si est dolor sicut dolor mei"*) and in hymns of contrition ("When I survey the wondrous Cross") and of triumph ("Onward, Christian soldiers"). There are gold crosses, plastic crosses, wooden crosses, jeweled crosses, and stone crosses. There are huge crosses towering in the Alps and the Andes and tiny crosses on dashboards and shelves. There are crosses on spires and crosses on gravestones. There are Celtic crosses, Crusaders' crosses, crosses of Saint Anne, and Coptic crosses. There is the bare cross, the crucifix, and the Christus Rex (Christ crowned and in royal robes on the Cross). And of course there is no counting the frescoes, mosaics, icons, and oil paintings that have for their subject the crucifixion scene.

What can we say of the Cross—this mystery celebrated, extolled, lauded, adored, and followed for two thousand years? Nothing new, certainly.

For Protestant imagination, the focus has always been not so much on the *image* of the Cross as on the *work* on the Cross: the work of atonement wrought by Christ there for

us, from which proceed our redemption and the forgiveness of our sins; and the work of the Cross in the heart of
the Christian who embraces it, dealing death to the Adam
in us with all of his sin, and opening the way to new life.
Hence, in this imagination, the Cross is thought about, and
spoken about, and preached and written about, but not much
depicted. The idea here is that if you externalize and visualize your representations of the Cross, you will get to looking at the thing you have made and miss the significance
behind it. It is a caution that has been alive in the Church
from the beginning, and one that will need to be kept alive
until we pass from faith to sight in the final triumph.

But whether Christians' meditations on the Cross have
been accompanied by any sort of visual representation or
not, all Christians have known that this Cross is right at the
center for them. The story that they call Good News antici-
pates and moves straight toward the Cross from the outset;
nay, there is shed blood and the promise of bruising some
thousands of years before that story itself unfolds. And there
is no victorious denouement to the Gospel story (what Professor Tolkien calls the "eucatastrophe"—the *good* out-
come) in Resurrection and Ascension without the Cross
first. There is no question of eternal life for us without our
going down into crucifixion and burial with Christ, like
seeds of wheat planted in the ground before the crop and
harvest. There is no putting away of sin by any method
other than crucifixion. There is no doing away with the
debt piled against us unless it is nailed to the Cross.

Christians see themselves, then, as a people under the
sign of the Cross. It is the sign of their salvation; it is their
ensign, their banner, their cover, their plea, and their glory.
It is an interesting datum in the history of the Church that
there has never been defined for Christian orthodoxy one

universally satisfactory doctrine as to what happened at the Cross. All creeds and councils agree that at the Cross Christ effected our salvation, and that our debt was, somehow, paid there (paid to whom? God? the Devil?), and that we have forgiveness of sins and eternal life on the basis of that event. But the fullness of the transaction remains a mystery. The words *offering, sacrifice, substitution, atonement, example,* and *victory* all crowd around the Cross, but no one can get all the pieces fitted together, any more than they can fit together the pieces in the other events of the Gospel story. We affirm these events and the dogmas that define them; we confess them, we believe them, we bow to them, we preach them, and we sing of them. But we cannot *explain* them.

This, surely, is at least part of the glory of Christian Faith: it speeds like a light between two poles, the one pole being the plain events in the Gospel story, the other being the great mysteries evinced in the events. For Christians, the very act of contemplating the events and the mysteries is nourishing and gladdening. For two thousand years now, peasants and sages have focused on the few simple events of the Gospel in their meditations; but no one has come near to exhausting it.

The Cross, as much as any other item in the Gospel story, has been a fountainhead of Christian contemplation. It is sometimes helpful for us in our meditations to reach away from our own time, or our own tradition, in order to get a fresh glimpse of familiar things. We may do this with some profit in connection with the Cross.

For example, there is an Anglo-Saxon poem celebrating the Cross in terms we might not have thought of. It is called *The Dream of the Rood,* and the earliest version of the poem is carved in runes on the eighteen-foot stone cross in the chancel of the church in Ruthwell, Dumfriesshire, in

Scotland. This version dates probably from the seventh century A.D. The poetry of that era tends to have battle and heroic deeds for its subject matter, so it is not strange to find that this poem speaks of the Cross in heroic terms. The poet tells us that he dreamed a dream:

> ... Me-seemed I saw
> A wondrous Tree   towering in air,
> Most shining of crosses   compassed with light ...
> I gazed on the Rood   arrayed in glory,
> Shining in beauty   and gilded with gold
> The cross of the Saviour   beset with gems.[1]

But through this splendor there "outgleamed a token / Of the ancient evil of sinful men": the Cross is wet and stained with blood. As the dreamer dreams on, the Cross speaks to him and tells him of its own experience of having borne the young Warrior in his battle with evil. This is the Cross itself speaking:

> Then I saw the King   of all mankind
> In brave mood hasting   to mount upon me. ...
> Then the young Warrior,   God, the All-Wielder,
> Put off His raiment,   steadfast and strong;
> With lordly mood   in the sight of many
> He mounted the Cross   to redeem mankind.

This notion of Christ as the young Warrior entering the battle in our behalf is one that occurs again and again in Old and Middle English literature. The best-known instance of it is in the fourteenth-century poem called *The Vision of*

[1] *The Dream of the Rood*, in *An Anthology of Old English Poetry*, trans. Charles W. Kennedy (New York: Oxford University Press, 1960), 144ff. All quotations from *The Dream of the Rood* are from this translation.

William concerning Piers the Ploughman, written, most scholars think, by one William Langland. It is an immense work in every way. In the course of the poem, there is a description of Christ's Passion, the harrowing of hell, and the Resurrection. Here, in a modern prose translation, is how the poet visualizes Jesus coming to Jerusalem and the Cross:

> A man came riding along barefoot on an ass, unarmed and without spurs. He looked like the Good Samaritan—or was it Piers the Ploughman? He was young and lusty, like a squire coming to be dubbed knight and receive his golden spurs and cut-away shoes. Then Faith, who was standing at a window, cried out, "See! The Son of David!"—like a herald proclaiming a knight who comes to the tournament.... So I asked Faith the meaning of all this stir— "Who was going to joust in Jerusalem?" "Jesus," he said, "to win back Piers' fruit, which the Devil has claimed." "Is Piers in this city?" I asked. He looked at me keenly and answered, "Jesus, out of chivalry, will joust in Piers' coat-of'arms, and wear His Helmet and mail, Human Nature; He will ride in Piers' doublet, that no one here may know Him as Almighty God. For whatever blows He receives, they cannot wound Him in His divine nature.[2]

This is an image of Christ's work on the Cross that is admittedly difficult to suit to the imagination of modern people whose picture of battle is conditioned by napalm and thermonuclear considerations. But the image itself has protohistoric warrant in the promise in Eden of the One who would bruise the head of the serpent and himself be wounded (a picture of close-quarters combat seems inevitable). Here, perhaps, is a case in point of our need to keep alive ancient

[2] William Langland, *Piers the Ploughman*, trans. J. F. Goodridge (Baltimore: Penguin Books, 1964), 256–57.

imagery, no matter what changes the passing of centuries makes in our culture and our outlook. To take a corollary example, Christians would insist that, no matter how "relevant" or "irrelevant" it may appear to modern imagination, the Gospel story must include a *cross*, even though crucifixion is a total irrelevancy now, since *we* take *our* socially unadjusted people and put them on couches, not crosses, and ask them to tell us about their mothers. But no Christian would feel comfortable with the effort to update Christian imagery by substituting small silver couches on necklaces for the traditional silver cross.

The point is, the ancient story with its exact imagery must continue to be told. If you change the imagery, you change the substance. The same would be true of the Eucharistic Feast—we can't substitute spinach and Coke for bread and wine; or again, of the image of Christ as Shepherd—the substitute picture of him as friendly corner cop, for ghetto children, say, who know nothing of sheep and fields: this will not quite serve. And in our case here of Christ as the young champion entering the lists for us: modern battle imagery of espionage, frogmen, and supersonic pilots may incline us to leave any combat imagery of the Cross to one side, since it does not fit our pictures of modern warfare. But the argument here is that, on the contrary, we must keep alive not only the old *story*, but old *forms* of the story, that help us to visualize what it was all about. Christ as knight seems consonant with the significance of the story: Christ as frogman does not.

Again, the jewels and gold that deck the Cross in *The Dream of the Rood* signify, not fatuous opulence or idolatry, but rather the same thing signified by the woman's costly jar of spikenard: the effort of human imagination to give visible, tangible shape to its awareness of immense worth. When it comes to this sort of thing, we cannot, like Judas, raise "practical" questions such as how much it costs, or whether it is realistic or not. Of course it is not realistic, and no one for a moment supposes that the Cross was anything other than a ghastly, rough-hewn, splintery affair clumsily knocked together. But just as we hail the Cross in high song and anthem (there was no singing on Golgotha that Friday), so we may deck it with gold, both acts testifying to the infinitely precious nature of that which the Cross, all unknown to Caiaphas or Pilate, signifies.

In the poem, the Cross continues to speak:

> Now you may learn,   O man beloved,
> The bitter sorrows   that I have borne,
> The work of caitiffs....
>
> On me a while   God's Son once suffered;
> Now I tower under heaven   in glory attired
> With healing for all   that hold me in awe....
>
> Lo! The Lord of glory
> The Warden of Heaven,   above all wood
> Has glorified me   as Almighty God
> Has honored His Mother,   even Mary herself,
> Over all womankind   in the eyes of men.
>
> (ll. 81–95)

Here we come upon another notion rich in devotional significance for Christians: the idea that, just as God took the plain maiden Mary and, by making her a participant with him in the mystery of the Incarnation, raised her to a unique place so that she was highly favored among women, to be called blessed by all generations, so *mutatis mutandis*, the humble stuff, wood, by "participating" in the mystery of the Atonement, has been raised to a unique glory. It is as though we are imagining a tremendous procession in heaven, say, after the final consummation of all things, when every

creature—men, beasts, stars, angels, seas, mountains, the lot—
comes past the witness stands thronged with the redeemed,
and the heralds cry out as each one passes, "Here is the
Maid Mary! Hail her as the one chosen to bear the Incarnate Word!" and then "Here comes Water! Hail it as the
chosen sign of new birth!" and "Here is Wood! Chosen to
bear the body of the Son of God in his travail! Hail! Hail
all wood, highly favored!"

Fanciful? Of course. But how *do* we propose to think of
these things? We have all sung the Christmas carol about
the friendly beasts: perhaps there is a truth in that way of
imagining things that escapes all our sober calculating.

And, lest we think that this sort of thing may detract
from the glory and adoration due to God alone, we must
remember that such things as *crowns*, and "praise and honor
and glory", are promised to the faithful. What does that
mean? Whatever it means, it will all be offered up to God
in one tremendous offering, with the whole multitude "casting down their golden crowns around the glassy sea".

Almost a thousand years after *The Dream of the Rood* was
written, a poet much closer to us in sensibility as well as in
time, spoke similarly of the Cross. The dear and noble George
Herbert, trying to find some mode of song adequate to
answer to the grace he had experienced, wrote this:

> Awake my lute, and struggle for thy part
>   With all thy art
> The crosse taught all wood to resound his name,
>   Who bore the same.
> His stretched sinews taught all strings, what key
> Is best to celebrate this most high day.[3]

---

[3] George Herbert, "Easter", in *The Works of George Herbert*, ed. F. E. Hutch-
inson (Oxford: Oxford University Press, 1972), 41.

Here the poet pursues the extraordinary idea of a synonymity between the Cross and a musical instrument: both of them are made of wood, both "resound His name", and both have sinews stretched across them. This is illogical in the extreme, of course, and stands at a polar opposite from expository prose, but it may participate in the same sort of thing we find in the Psalms, where the only language appropriate to the high and bright realities of Zion is poetry, with all of its high and bright absurdities. Poetry, psalmody, hymnody—we reach for these modes when our meditations have exhausted expository prose.

There is in the Church an ancient ceremony for Good Friday that goes back to fourth-century Syrian usage, in which the faithful are hailed with "*Ecce lignum Crucis in quo salus mundi pependit*" (Behold the wood of the Cross on which hung the Savior of the world). Here the idea is not that Christians worship wood: rather, it is that our whole consciousness (touch and sight and smell as well as hearing and thinking) is called into the act of worship, and that hence our physical faculties may be appropriately pressed into service (we are not angels). This, of course, is why Christians often bow their heads or kneel when they pray: these muscular movements of neck and knee joints might seem to be wholly unrelated to the business of adoring the Deity, but somehow, being the flesh-and-blood creatures we are, we find that we are helped thereby. Hence also such things as hymn tunes or incense: our ears and noses are not written off as unworthy or irrelevant.

In this Good Friday ceremony, the hymn "Crux fidelis" is sung. It is a peculiar hymn for sensible and logical people to sing, but again, as with the language of the Psalms, it bespeaks paradoxes and high reaches of vision that elude common sense and logic. Here are the words:

> Faithful Cross, above all other,
> One and only noble tree,
> None in foliage, none in blossom,
> None in fruit thy peer may be.
> Sweetest wood and sweetest iron,
> Sweetest weight is hung on thee.[4]

A well-intentioned humanitarian bystander might well huff and puff over the savagery of these sentiments: "*Sweetest* wood! *Sweetest* iron! You Christians are barbarian—celebrating the instruments of torture that wracked and pierced your own prophet!" And the faithful can only answer that the Christian mysteries are full of rich and staggering paradoxes, and that in the case of the Cross, the eye of faith sees the worst thing that ever happened (deicide) to be the best thing that ever happened (salvation), and the most appalling instrument of torture to be the very thing to which we cling for our refuge and joy. A similar paradox is uttered in the ancient formula "*O felix culpa Adae*" (O happy fault of Adam), the idea being, not that we laud sin, but that that sin became the occasion for the greatest thing of all (Grace) to manifest itself.

The same idea is at work in one of the Orthodox liturgies for the Elevation of the Precious Cross of the Lord. At the vigil, these chants are sung:

> The Cross, being set up, doth command every created being to sing the most pure Passion of him who was lifted up thereon. For having upon the same slain him who had slain us, he endowed with life those who were slain, and adorned

[4] This translation of Venantius Fortunatus' hymn (part of the "Pange Lingua") was made by John Mason Neale and published in 1861. Reprinted in *Hymns Ancient and Modern*, Standard Edition (London: William Clowes and Sons, 1916), hymn no. 97.

them and vouchsafed that they might dwell in heaven. . . .
O come, all ye nations, let us adore the blessed Tree, through
which the righteousness eternal hath come to pass: for he
who beguiled our forefather Adam with the tree is himself
beguiled by the Cross, and he who, like a tyrant, did lord it
over that which the King had fashioned, falleth, being overthrown by a downfall strange. The poison of the serpent is
washed away by the blood of God, and the curse of just
condemnation is abolished, in that the Righteous One hath
been condemned by unrighteous judgment: for it was meet
that the tree should be healed by the Tree, and that by the
passion of the Passionless One upon the Tree, the passions
of the condemned one should be destroyed.[5]

Perhaps as we approach Holy Week this year, our efforts to
contemplate the mysteries of our redemption in the Passion and crucifixion of the Lord may be helped by some of
these ancient forms that Christian meditation on the Cross
have taken.

[5] *Service Book of the Holy Orthodox Catholic Apostolic Church*, ed. I. F. Hap-
good (Brooklyn, N.Y.: Syrian Antiochian Orthodox Archdiocese of New
York, 1965), 167.

WHAT IS A SACRAMENT?

Part I

The notion of sacrament has not been a lively one in Evangelical Protestant imagination over the centuries since the Reformation. The historical reasons for this are clear enough: it was the great burden of the Reformers to take the mysteries of the Faith, which had in the late Middle Ages especially been almost entirely located for popular imagination in external forms such as Masses, pilgrimages, shrines, and sacred objects, and to plant these mysteries once more in the place insisted upon by the prophets and apostles as the only proper locale for them—namely, the heart of man.

A drastic and clean sweep, surely, was necessary. The Faith is, precisely, a matter of *faith*, and this is a matter of the heart. It will do you no good to trek to Santiago de Compostela, or to the shrine of Blessed Thomas at Canterbury, or even to the Holy Sepulchre itself. What is needed is a pilgrimage of the heart, from unrighteousness to purity. Again, your money and your beads will have not the slightest effect on your soul's account (and you may be sure there is no tally being kept in any such place as Purgatory). What is needed is repentance, which means only one thing in the Gospel, namely, a turning away from sin and the pursuit of

Originally published in a slightly different form as "The Idea of Sacrament: An Approach", in *The Reformed Journal* (February 1979): 9–13. Reprinted with permission.

holiness from your heart. This alone will put you in the way of salvation. And again, nothing at all is achieved by your simply being under the roof where a Latin Mass is being said. What is needed is not miracles of chemistry up there on the stone slab, full as it is of dead relics, but rather the miracle whereby your own heart becomes the altar on which sacrifices of righteousness are offered in faith to God. All these external acts and objects, far from being helpful, are positively destructive. They nullify the very evangel of grace itself.

The cleavage between these two ways of perceiving how the mysteries of the Faith are to be applied to the soul of man was a stark and abysmal one, and for almost half a millennium now it has remained a great gulf fixed, at least in popular Christian imagination, In the last thirty years, of course, the theologians and liturgiologists and ecumenical emissaries have, in the course of their painstaking work, discovered that it is not a gulf that cannot be bridged: indeed, they have constructed the anchor-work and pinnings for very long spans to be thrown across this gulf, it appears. And ordinary lay Christians on both edges of the chasm have been startled, especially in services where the various "charisms" are manifest, to discover fellow believers and brothers among those whom they had been taught were their worst enemies. But five hundred years' worth of rhetoric, suspicion, and even bloodshed cannot be wafted away in one or two or three decades of good will.

But of course it is not all mere hot-headedness, ignorance, and prejudice. It is not just zealots and partisans who keep enmities, or at least vastly differing views, alive. Even the most patient, wise, and saintly soul can see that a simple matter like whether to put your pulpit or your altar at the center of focus is no mere stubborn bit of social custom. It is a question that reaches all the way to the root, not only of the Christian apprehension of the Gospel, but of man's imagination itself. Given strongly held presuppositions, it becomes almost a matter to fight over.

Sage and holy souls on both sides of the question are able to articulate, with inexpugnable lucidity and consistency, just why they see things the way they do. Is the Bread up there Christ's Body or is it not? Yes. No. Well ... is it salutary for my soul that I hear the promise of Christ's forgiveness made audible through the larynx of another mortal man? or is it confusion? Yes. No. Well ... is the Gospel adequately guarded and enshrined forever in the pages of the Bible, or is Scripture itself entrusted to the Church which is Christ's presence on earth? Yes. No. Well ...

We cannot simply assert here that View A is orthodox and View B thereby heterodox. Our task is to try to describe in the least inflammatory way possible just how it comes about, for example, that Christians who believe utterly the Epistle to the Hebrews, with its insistence on one priesthood and one altar in the heavenlies, nonetheless seem to have a multitudinous priesthood and innumerable altars here on earth. The difficult point for Evangelical imagination to grasp here is that this view is held, not by a Christendom that rejects the Epistle, but by one which passionately espouses its teaching.

The question from which all these differences arise might be variously phrased. What is a sacrament? What is sacramentalism? Is it necessary? Inevitable? Optional? Is it mere frill? Does it represent a muddling and adulterating of the pure Gospel of faith? Is Evangelical Protestantism the richer or the poorer for having preached a religion virtually devoid of any reference to sacrament as such? Is Catholic Christendom unfaithful to the Gospel by having decked the dominical and apostolic teaching with sacramentalism? Perhaps the best place to begin is to attempt a definition.

Sacramentalism is the Christian understanding that the physical is potentially the vehicle of the spiritual. A sacrament is both what it appears superficially to be and also a mode under which something beyond its ingredients is made real and present to us. For a sacramentalist, then, a sacrament is more than a souvenir or a memento, helping to jog the memory with a picture of something. The physical components of the sacrament (bread, wine, water) stand, as it were, on the interface between what we can see and what we cannot. They do, of course, remind us of something that we are trying to recall and witness to, but beyond this function, they make that something real to us only in a mystery.

In a mystery. There, perhaps, is the key. There are no propositions that can quite compass the transaction that occurs in sacrament. Here we are brought up to that frontier where propositions tend to get muddled and die away. No one—no Father, Doctor, or council—has ever found the phraseology and vocabulary adequate to define exactly what is going on in the sacraments.

Here lies one great difficulty that the Evangelical imagination has with the notion of sacrament: Protestantism (and with it, then, Evangelicalism) is strongly propositionalist, from its doctrine of Scripture alone, on through to its practice of theology and preaching, to its piety, which is characterized by such verbal exercises as Bible study and testimony. The notion that the greatest mysteries of the Faith will never quite yield themselves to our efforts to articulate them, which is course affirmed by Protestant imagination, nevertheless finds itself crowded into a corner in the effort to articulate Christian vision in satisfactory propositions.

It is not that the sacramentalist is anti-propositionalist. A sacrament makes no sense if there is no idea proposed as to what is going on. It becomes mere talisman or mumbo-jumbo (which it had become for many in the sixteenth century). Orthodoxy can never be maintained by waving wands and thuribles about. Somewhere in there an Athanasius or an Augustine needed to pick up his pen and spell out what is wrong with the wrong view, and why it is that the right view alone is to be held by everyone. But having granted this, any Christian knows that on every single point of the Faith we come eventually to the place where we must say, "It is a mystery. I cannot press my explanation any further than this." Creation, Fall, redemption—who is equal to these topics?

It makes sense, then, that at the very center of our activity as the Church, we find actions that involve us visibly and unmistakably with the mystery of the Gospel, namely, baptism and the Eucharist, commanded by the Lord and obeyed ceaselessly ever since. How merely physical stuff can have this focal and exalted place in Christian vision stumps us. It is an absurdity. But then, we recall, "merely physical stuff" has exactly this focal and exalted place in every single one of the great events of the Faith, and this is what the sacramentalist seizes upon.

Look at these events: creation, Fall, redemption, Incarnation, Passion, Resurrection, Ascension, Pentecost, and Eucharist. Is there one of them that occurred in a purely "spiritual" realm? The whole drama was played out, to the confusion and outrage of Gnostics, Manicheans, and rationalists of all time, in starkly, embarrassingly physical terms. He *made* something (water and rock and whales), and it all praised him; we botched it by making a grab and trying to call it our own, and everything fell into corruptibility; he planned a rescue and a restoration, and chose a man and a tribe and demanded lamb's blood; then he took on this flesh himself; in the suffering of that flesh he effected the redemption of the world; that flesh came out of the grave, the sign and guarantee to all heaven and hell that victory was won; that flesh ascended into the midmost mysteries of the triune Godhead; the Godhead came down on the tongues and into the flesh of men and, for them, at the center, for as long as history would go on, as Bread and Wine.

The whole scheme was carried forward in heavily carnal terms. Unlike the deities of rationalists and Eastern seers who beckon us all away from the world of water and soil and flesh and blood and bread and wine into the ether of bodilessness, this God returns us to it and it to us in something infinitely richer than escape. It is redemption. The gathering together of all things (all spirits and all flesh) in Christ, says the apostle. Nothing to be swept under the rug.

How, then, is this vision of things to be mediated to us and kept alive in us? Through propositions? Yes, through the Proverbs, the Sermon on the Mount, the apostolic preaching and writing. And through law, where the truth takes on the form not of mere proposition but of command: Get up and help your neighbor get his ox out of the ditch. And through history, where truth takes the form not of mere proposition but of narrative: the God whose name is Yahweh has done this and that for you; remember it. And through Psalm, where truth now takes the form not of mere proposition but of poetry and dance: *Benedicite, omnia opera domini!* Praise him on lute and cymbal! And through prophecy, where truth takes the form of dazzling imagery: Ephraim is a cake not turned; I saw a woman clothed in the sun; dragons and horsemen and falling towers; and through parable, where truth takes the form of vignette: once upon a time there was a woman mopping her floors. And supremely, through enactment, where truth takes the form not of mere proposition but rather of the Word become flesh. All these are ways of understanding what the truth is.

Sacramentalism may be understood, then, as the view that sees a discernible meeting point in appointed physical vehicles between the visible and the invisible realms. Put another way, sacramentalism rejects sheer dualism, if by this we understand that the universe is forever divided utterly between the temporal and the eternal, or the material and the spiritual, or the visible and the invisible, realms. It rejects this much of popular Platonism, that "reality" is located wholly in the spiritual realm, and that the material world is illusion. Hence, it rejects also many of the popularly held teachings of various Eastern religions that speak of an escape *to* reality *away* from the visible world.

Indeed, a true sacramentalism would be unhappy with continual references to the "visible" and "invisible" realms as though they were two different worlds, even though it is aware that this distinction is helpful for our human patterns of thought. For at the foundation of sacramental vision lies the robust affirmation of the whole creation, from seraphim to clams to basalt, as *one good fabric.* There are not two entirely distinct worlds in the creation, the visible and the invisible. God is the Maker of heaven and earth, in one great creative action. He made spirits and he made stones, and they all inhabit one huge world.

It is evil that has introduced the distinction and the enmity. It is after the Fall that you get the corruptible and the incorruptible realms being distinguished. And here especially it must be remembered that corruption applies as much to the spiritual realm as to the material. The devils and damned souls in hell are, precisely, spirits in a state of corruption. Just as good food rots and silver tarnishes and our flesh sickens and decays, all of it because of evil, so the lordliest celestial spirits may rot and tarnish and decay into fiends in hell. It is the same process, the same fabric.

A sacramentalist would suspect that our inability to live in one undivided realm of creation is perhaps one of the disabilities brought upon us by our own sin. Indeed, although there is not a syllable explaining this in the Bible, and certainly no scientific research will ever be able to uncover any data on the point, it may be imagined that a film, as it were, was imposed on our very eyeballs at the Fall, so that we lost the ability to perceive the one whole fabric in which angels and ourselves inhabit a continuous realm. We can no longer *see* very much. We had sown a disjuncture into things by our action (this is ours, and that is God's), and we reaped the harvest in our very eyeballs. We had now to perceive things as divided. Who knows?

But in any event, proceeding from the doctrine of creation as it does, sacramentalism would affirm the oneness of the whole creation, and it would see the material world (that is, as much of the whole fabric as we can descry with our eyes and our lenses) as both real and metaphorical. The material world is understood to be real and not illusory for the reasons just now touched upon. We come now to this world perceived as metaphorical.

This means that, besides being simply itself, as a sort of dead-end, the material world also presents reality to our mortal eyes in a mode suited to these eyes, namely, in visible shapes and textures and colors. It is always signaling to us, so to speak. It is perhaps like a messenger or a herald: the herald is not less a man, or less himself, by virtue of being charged with the duty of announcing someone else.

He is a man who is a herald. Similarly, the visible creation
has this duty, on the sacramentalist view. In its forms and
colors, which are beautiful in themselves like the bright
tabard of the herald, it speaks to us of that which is beyond
itself. Indeed, just as the brightness of the herald's tabard
derives its colors and design directly from the arms of the
king whose emissary the herald is, so the material creation
exhibits the pattern of that which is beyond it.

Another way of putting this, of course, is to say that anyone who cares to look will see played out in the forms and
colors and substance of this world that which is true on all
levels in the universe, visible or invisible, from God on down.
It is not as though this visible world has had an extra job
assigned to it of playacting the truth just for us mortals to
behold, besides getting on with whatever else it is naturally
designed to do. Rather, it is that in this very natural design
of it we find the only pattern there is, exhibited and enacted
under the particular modality of visible matter.

For example, we see in this world seeds sown in prepared soil in springtime, and then nothing happening, and
then shoots, then stalks, then flower, fruit, and harvest. Well,
that is the natural design of things in this world, but it also
happens to be a bright metaphor, in the sense that right
there, in terms of seed and soil and sunlight, we see enacted
that which is true at the top and bottom of everything,
namely, that life proceeds from death, and that only by
something's falling into the ground and dying can we ever,
in any realm, expect a crop. What is true agriculturally is
also true in the highest realm ("he suffered and was buried"), and in every realm in between.

We can see it in politics, for example: in order for a
state to function at all and reap the "harvest" of order and
peace, the various interest groups inhabiting the state must

compromise their special interests, and this compromising is a small form of dying, in that one has to lay one's own case, or part of it, into the ground in order that the crop of peace in the commonwealth may appear. It is visible all through the political fabric, right down to local routines like stop signs and traffic lights (my right to move ahead is "buried" for a moment so that your right may be exercised). Order is the crop proceeding from the sowing of all these little deaths.

And we see the same principle again in the emotional and psychological realms. A child who has been allowed to believe that everything is his for the demanding grows up testy, querulous, and rapacious. We saw this in the generation in the late 1960s who, never having been told by their parents that time, labor, and patience is the price exacted by life for all really worthy things, supposed that by screaming and raging and sitting down on their campuses, they could change the whole order of things and get what they wanted. They knew nothing of grains of wheat falling into the ground and dying and lying silent and dead, perhaps for decades or centuries. No one had ever showed them Flanders Fields or Arnhem, where tens of thousands of mortal seeds lie in silence while the rest of us reap the harvest of whatever peace issued from those sowings. On the other hand, the truly free child is the one who has learned that satisfaction will forever elude the one who grabs, but will come, strangely, to the one who has learned to "bury" self-interest in that odd exchange called sharing. This, of course, is the whole principle of love, which is at the root and pinnacle of everything. Laid-down life. Bliss from self-giving. Harvest from planted seeds. Life from death.

The point here is that all this which is true politically and psychologically and theologically we may see played out for

us any time we care to look at a potato field or a pot of gera-
niums. No other principle has been at work. The physical
world furnishes us with endless metaphors, not by our poking about and extracting occult significances from things but
simply by our observing what is perfectly plainly going on.

So, the sacramentalist (or, surely, any Christian, or indeed
any person who cares to look) sees material things as body-
ing forth their own excellence and beauty, and at the same
time bespeaking significances beyond themselves. The plum-
age of finches and tanagers—does it not present to us a
small case in point of what glory is—*all* glory? The massif
of Mont Blanc—may we not fetch thence some small inkling
of God our rock? The sound of running water, of a winter
wren, or indeed of flutes—do we not in these hear intima-
tions of a greater music spoken of in Psalms and Revelation? The sacramentalist would suppose so.

This, then, is the starting point for sacramentalist vision.
The visible and proximate may be—indeed, is—"full of the
majesty of Thy glory". Things are excellent in themselves
and excellent in their heraldic office. The scheme seems to
run all up and down the fabric, so that when we find it
isolated and pressed into special service at the center of the
Christian mysteries, in the Eucharistic Feast, we are not
scandalized. What did we suppose bread and wine were about
in the first place?

A note of demurral and caution may be sounded here. A
true sacramental vision differs utterly from the diffuse and
pantheistic aspirings of the romantic poets who thought
everything was divine. Sacramentalism, while keenly aware
of the metaphorical, or heraldic, office of material things,
rigorously reserves the specific *sacramental* function to the
occasions when these things are set aside for that function
by the clear and ordered intention of the Church. Traditional Catholic, Orthodox sacramentalism would differ

wholly, then, from the Quaker view, for example, which eliminates special sacramental observances in worship since *all* eating and drinking are held to be "sacramental".

There is a blurring here, the sacramentalist would reply. It is true that all eating and drinking proceed on the same principle as the sacrament, namely, life laid down that others might be nourished, but the Lord did something separate, conscious, significant, and special, on the first Maundy Thursday evening at the Supper, and the Church has always understood that act to have constituted her Lord's example and charge to her to *focus*, in specific acts of worship, what is of course generally true anyway. It would be analogous to the lambs brought to the tabernacle in the Old Testament: *of course* every lamb ever born belonged to God, but it is necessary *for us* that this diffuse truth be focused and enacted by a conscious, costly, physical betokening. A general affirmation of the truth does not seem to be enough.

Here, indeed, there would be a crux between non-sacramentalists and sacramentalists. The former would hold that it is enough to believe the truth in faith since the locale of true religion is in the heart. The latter would hold that, because we are not pure spirits, we mortal men must also *enact* that inner belief in specific, material terms. The giving of alms, for example—it is not enough to say to the pauper, Depart, be warmed and fed. Or the giving of a kiss to our beloved: it is not enough to insist that they *believe* that we love them. Or the conscious setting aside of this loaf and this cup from among thousands of loaves and cups. We need to have what we affirm physically vouchsafed to us. We are not disembodied spirits— mere intellects and wills. We have lips and tongues and stomachs, and these are not despised nor huddled into a corner in the scheme of redemption. This Bread and this Wine has been given to us. Angels, presumably, do not require it just this way; but we mortals do.

WHAT IS A SACRAMENT?

Part II

Besides the idea that the world is both real and metaphorical, there is another principle at work for the sacramentalist. *Enactment*, or ceremony, is very much of the essence. A sacramentalist would urge that he is not fetching some occult or arcane notion from afar and imposing it on things, but is merely proceeding on plain principles that are there for anyone to see.

The principle of enactment is certainly at work in baptism and Eucharist, when we "act out" what we believe to be true. Not only are we not doing something peculiar here, we are in fact carrying to its ultimate point of significance a phenomenon that is absolutely central to man's universal practice in every tribe, culture, and civilization from the beginning of myth and history to the present. It is this: that we mortal men are ritual creatures. We are forever "acting out" things.

Take greetings, for example: there is hardly a culture anywhere that does not have some ritual convention for greeting people. It may be a handshake, a bow, a nod, or whatever, but the principle is always there. We act out with physical gestures (grasping hands, bending the waist,

Originally published in a slightly different form as "Imagination, Rites, and Mystery: Why Did Christ Institute Sacraments?", in *The Reformed Journal* (March 1979): 15–19. Reprinted with permission.

nodding) something that is invisibly at work in the situation. We wish to signal the ideas of welcome and peace and friendship, so, rather than going through a long discourse on the idea, we do something physical. We are ritual creatures. We take the significance, and let a conventional, physical ritual carry it.

Similarly with eating. The business of eating is nothing more, at least from the pragmatic view, than the transfer of energy from point A (the peapod or the rasher of bacon) to point B (my bloodstream) so that I can keep going. The progress of technology has devised enormously efficient means for streamlining this transfer (bottles of glucose, tubes, and needles), but no tribe or society has adopted these streamlined methods for lunch or dinner. Why not? Why do we all follow the laborious and circuitous route of fixing and cooking and garnishing ... to say nothing of setting tables with folded napkins and cutlery, china, and crystal?

It is because we are ritual creatures. These routine functions somehow seem to us to imply more than mere utility. To try to bespeak our sense of this further significance in things, we deck them. We festoon them. We set them about with ritual, even if the ritual is nothing more than folding a paper napkin or holding the door open for a lady—physical things and acts carrying great burdens of significance.

Any religious person is familiar with this sort of thing. Many Christians bow their heads to say grace or kneel down to say their prayers or lower their voices in church buildings. What is this all about? Is it not once more our human habit of registering in a physical way some significance that seems to be there and that we want to acknowledge?

Now it is worth noting that when we mortals come up to the great, intractable mysteries of human life (birth, sex, and death), we ritualize our responses to them, too. Each of these big events represents "nothing more" than a biological event, and a very routine one at that. Yet Hottentots and Saxons, Slavs and Polynesians, New Yorkers and Samoans deck these events elaborately. We ritualize our responses to them.

Consider birth. In our own culture the decking tends to run along white, yellow, pink, and blue lines, with bows, ruffles, silver spoons, and pretty blankets as the tokens. Horses don't bother with this; yet they have the same experience biologically, foaling away merrily just as we do. What is the trouble with us that we add all these extras? Clearly we are creatures such that the mere obstetrics of the event will not cover the topic for us. Something has happened, and we must do something beautiful about it, something beyond the forceps and thermometers and diapers and charts. Those are the accoutrements of obstetrics and pediatrics, but these bows and frills and christenings we concoct are the index of something even deeper in our humanity.

And sex. The approach of a man to a woman is again "simply" a biological event, and a time-worn one at that. Nothing unusual. But all of us set this approach about with very high hedges. (At least we did: the present Western experiment in "free" sexual congress arises from time to time in history, and nothing lasting is ever built on it.) We festoon it all solemnly. Whether this takes the form of puberty dances or shared milkshakes or taboos, leading up to a feast or a nuptial Mass in Chartres, the phenomenon is the same, namely, the marking by ritual tokens of significance in the event.

And death. When we have filled in our medical reports and made our sociological analyses of the dynamics of dying and have staved off corruption with embalming fluid and copper vaults, we set it all about with long palls, drawn hearses, and sung requiems (or whatever). We *do* something about these events, and that something is inevitably ritual.

There is an odd paradox here (and one which appears important to sacramentalist vision), namely, that when we come to the most serious events of all in man's existence, we find that we have somehow moved beyond all of our techniques and measures and methods, and that we must in fact *play*. For that is what ritual, or ceremony, really is. It is a form of playacting. We are doing what children do with their dolls' houses and toy trucks: we are saying, *let this represent that*. With children it is, *let this doll represent Mummy or Queen Eleanor*, or *let this Dinky Toy be my Mack truck*. With the adults it is, *let this gowned procession represent the bride's approach to her lord*, or *let this rite bespeak our honor to the dead person*.

Ceremony, ritual, enactment: these forms of "play" touch on the sources of what we human creatures are.

But there is more. A sacramentalist would suspect that all this ritualizing and decking is not simply a question of our taking inert data and festooning them all arbitrarily, thereby expressing some interior, purely fanciful feelings on our part about these data—feelings that have no connection with external reality. Quite the contrary: the sacramentalist would urge that the ritualizing with which we deck these events is the quintessentially human mode of perceiving and marking the truth about them.

The events are not being forced by us into some Procrustean bed of ritual: rather, man's imagination perceives something real, and something that the eyes of clams or horses can't perceive. It sees a pattern of significance, a web, so to speak, binding together all the diffuse data of the world and of our experience; by setting these data in a formal

context of ritual, ceremony, and enactment, it attempts, not
to impose an arbitrary and fanciful pattern *on* the data, but
rather to elicit, in obedience to what is there, this marvelous interconnectedness among things.

From this deeply human awareness of pattern and interconnectedness among things, everything that marks human
life as human arises: all poetry, music, courtesy, architecture, all grace and ceremony and costume—everything, in
a word, that distinguishes our life from that of chimpan-
zees. It is, of course, the principle of metaphor that is at
work here. B may symbolize A for us, not because we reach
wildly about and seize B arbitrarily, but rather because there
is at work in B this much of what we perceive to be also at
work in A.

We perceive, for example, not an arbitrary but an *appropriate* connection between high ceilings and kings. Why?
Because in both there is a notion of exaltedness. The high
ceiling answers to this high prince. We fashion something
in realm B (architecture) that both answers to and enhances
what we see in realm A (politics). Does it falsify things?
No. If someone urges that tunnels and crawling are especially appropriate to kings, then all mankind would have to
reply that we need to erase everything and start all over
again, recasting the entire known universe.

The same would be true for all such correspondences.
Unless we are prepared to jettison everything we know of man,
God, and the world and call all our perceptions into doubt
(as some philosophers reject the validity of rational thought,
thereby ending the philosophical process), we must proceed
along the lines that seem to be here around us and that are
answered to by everything that we know, including, for Christians, revelation itself. Gold and not offal is the right metaphor for glory; white and not black is the right metaphor for
purity; peak and not slough is the right metaphor for joy; eagle

and not pterodactyl is the right metaphor for splendor; lamb and not crocodile is right for innocence.

Two observations about metaphor (and hence about sacrament) ought to be made at this point. First, we may find two very different images for a single truth we are trying to come at, but this does not controvert the point that there must be some "real" connection between the two terms in the metaphor. For example, we may speak of Christ as king or servant. Is that a confusion or does it mean that any metaphor will do?

Neither. In the first place we find that the notion of Christ is such that the metaphor "king" will catch *this much* about him, but that the metaphor "servant" catches *this other*, which is also true about him. His kingship, for example, is not to be compared to that of Nebuchadnezzar or Genghis Khan, except in its absoluteness and splendor. We want to introduce the further notion of servant at some point in order to get the whole picture right. Again, we may speak of him as lion and lamb, priest and victim, husband and brother. Is it all a jumble, forcing us to the conclusion that any metaphor will then do?

No. In the second place, we may not speak of Christ as thug or snake or butcher. That would do violence to the idea in question. Now it may be observed here that, while the word *thug* implies evil in itself, and hence is wholly and obviously inappropriate, the words *snake* and *butcher* are not like this. There is nothing wrong with snakes and butchers. Snakes are part of the creation, and they must lead their lives and obey their nature just as field mice and chickadees do. Likewise butchers: many of them are saints and heroes.

But we may not speak of *Christ* as snake or butcher, not because of any inherent flaw in these two creatures, but rather because the thing that becomes operative in the metaphor arouses a confusion. It would ask more of us than may be asked if we picture Christ as a snake—even if we do grant that snakes are a lovely part of creation—since snakes glide along on their bellies, and there is nothing about Christ that is clarified for our imaginations by such a picture. Similarly the butcher: we may speak of both Christ and that butcher as men, or as workmen, or as husbands, etc. But we do not speak of Christ as butcher since the word implies slaughter and chopping and shedding blood, and that is not part of Christ's office. The butcher's office is good and praiseworthy, but it does not furnish us with a useful, or indeed a possible, picture of Christ's office.

The second observation about metaphor is that it is preeminently via the metaphorical mode, so to speak, that this "interconnectedness" among things may be perceived. It is difficult to satisfy us by other means—by logic, for example, or chemistry. To be sure, a syllogism can display for us the process whereby we move from, say, lamb to Christ: lambs look and act harmless; Christ (at least in his sacrificial role) looked and acted harmless; therefore lambs and Christ are to that extent similar. So far so good. But that leaves the data inert, so to speak. We do not hang syllogisms on the wall, or hail them in epic and carol. Our humanity wants to paint, with van Eyck, *The Adoration of the Mystic Lamb*, or wants to sing "At the Lamb's High Feast We Sing". (Now in so far as there is a kind of religion that says we ought *not* to follow van Eyck, or sing, and that we ought to restrict our apprehension of these things to verbal propositions, then the sacramentalist would admittedly belong to a very different outlook. The effort being pursued in this essay is to persuade these who may doubt it that sacramentalism is "nothing more" than the gathering of all that makes us human into joyous obedience to what nature and the Gospel both ring out to us always and everywhere.)

Logic, then. It teaches us, and it certainly harmonizes with what we see metaphorically, but it does not entirely compass the business for us. Similarly with chemistry. The straight chemical designation for gold (Au) and its position in the periodic table of the elements, with its valence and so forth, do not very readily yield data useful to us in deciding that gold is an appropriate metaphor for glory, as opposed, say, to zinc. We can't wring from chemistry any easily visible connection between gold and glory. Zinc is as legitimate and secure a part of the table as is gold. It would be difficult to insist on gold's special place as metaphor by means of what we can establish by this method.[1]

The point being urged here is that the faculty perceiving the appropriateness of one thing serving as a metaphor for another is man's imagination. The metaphor is presented to imagination, and assented to by imagination. And something true seems to have been articulated.

It becomes clear at this point that imagination, far from being a matter of foolishness, and the conjuring up of what cannot possibly be true, is the mode of perception that may lie closest to the truth of our humanness. Angels and seraphim do not *need* imagination presumably, since it is said that they behold reality directly, and animals do not *have* imagination as far as we can tell; but we men perceive reality, unlike angels, mediated through a thousand oblique angles and colors in the prism of creation, and we forever try, unlike animals, to descry a pattern by relating all the angles and colors to each other.

---

[1] Who is to say that this is not possible, though. The periodic table itself may be a thrilling cryptogram, bursting and sagging with data all rushing straight to the *Te Deum*. But once more, we mortals are creatures such that, sooner or later, we want to lift the gold off the chart and make a crown out of it; if we have been wrong and foolish to have done so, then we shall have to erase everything and begin over again.

For the sacramentalist, this is all enormously important. It is to this sort of creature—to us—that the sacraments have been presented. Our Lord did not call them sacraments, of course: that is our name for them. But he commanded water, and bread and wine—not for angels, and not for the beasts, but for us.

There may appear to be an anomaly here. The whole point of the Gospel was that external observances now be planted in the heart, and that what had hitherto been a matter of physical gestures and material tokens now move beyond that superficial level into the inner person. A sacrificial spirit now, not just a pennyworth of alms. Purity of heart, not just ceremonial washing. Real justice, not merely sabbath observance. Faith first and faith last. If this is so, then how can our Lord have tied things down once more to material objects? Why did he not insist that the whole locale of his Gospel be in the heart? Or rather, since he did insist on this, why did he then blur it by introducing these few external things?

There have been, since the sixteenth century, three responses in Christendom to this apparent crux. On the one hand is the view that the water of baptism and the bread and wine of the Eucharist are to be understood entirely spiritually and hence that Christians need not include in their piety or church order any special sacramental observances. Faith, not baptism, is what saves us. The communion of the heart, not of bread and wine, is what nourishes us. Hence we will dispense with any such observances at all. There are a few groups (the Quakers and the Salvation Army, among others) that espouse this view.

At one remove from this would be the view that these physical tokens, while proper—even necessary, since they were commanded by the Lord—have no significance beyond that of underscoring as it were what is real and true enough without them. Baptism, for example, does not *do* anything for a person other than declare to all and sundry what has already been effected by grace and grasped by faith. No real transaction occurs. This is a widespread view in many churches.

On the other hand is the view commonly called sacramentalism, in which, in a mystery, something real does occur with the application of the water of baptism, and with the partaking of the Bread and Wine. The line between this and the former view is not necessarily to be drawn along the Protestant-Catholic frontier, since the Reformers themselves were fiercely divided over exactly how we should understand what is going on. Calvin taught what might be called a high view of sacrament; Luther and Zwingli quarreled bitterly over the point at Marburg; and the sixteenth-century Anglicans held all manner of views, themselves changing over the decades of turmoil. So that we are not speaking here of simple sectarian lines.

The questions are rife, of course. The commonest fear about sacramentalism from the non-sacramentalists is contained in the phrase *ex opere operato*, the fear that the sacraments may be believed to be magic, having some automatic and inevitable efficacy all by themselves, and that a person can be saved, for example, by being plunged into water or can ingest a bit of grace automatically by eating a wafer, wholly apart from any question of faith.

Although this is, unhappily, a widely held view among poorly taught Christians in sacramentalist churches, it is not the true teaching of sacramentalism. A sacramentalism that teaches any doctrine other than the Pauline doctrine of salvation by grace through faith is heterodox. (The Council of Trent, itself perhaps the most extreme example of Western sacramentalism, is clear on this point in its statement on justification by faith.) A sacramentalist would see the "efficacy" of the sacraments to be hinted at in the analogy of sunlight: sunlight is in itself strong and health-giving and efficacious, but of course we can shut it out by drawing the blinds. The sunlight must be *received* by us, so to speak, for it to do its work in us. Similarly (and any analogy for a mystery like this is full of flaws), the sacraments will not work magically on us, penetrating any carapace of sin or unbelief we have around us. They are strong and efficacious to do their work, but it is on the living hearts of men that they work, not on stocks and stones. We *can* nullify them if we will, just as we can grow pallid and wan by refusing the strong light of the sun.

The problems come when we try to understand exactly the sense in which the sacraments operate. And obviously this essay will not settle what Fathers, councils, Doctors, Reformers, and Anabaptists have not been able to settle to everyone's satisfaction. It must be strongly urged, however, that a robust sacramentalism in no way calls in question the Pauline doctrine of salvation by grace through faith. The sacramentalist would try to explain, in answer to a question on this point, that it is the same Lord who charged his Apostle with the Gospel of grace who also commanded water and bread and wine—physical transactions, apparently central enough to the mysteries of the Gospel that they be reiterated as command both by the Lord and by his apostles. Preach and baptize. That is how men are to be saved. Do this in remembrance of me, and when you do, I will give my very Body and Blood to you.

The sacramentalist would not be prepared to "spiritual-ize" these commands and promises. Just as all the mysteries of revelation and redemption have been mediated to us in starkly physical terms, so these. It is not for nothing that the Gospel unfolds itself this way. We may not be able to compass it intellectually, but then which of the mysteries

can we thus compass? The Lord's commands and promises
are not idle nor arbitrary, surely: he did not merely cast
about for some handy and helpful reminder of the mysteries and alight on water and bread and wine. Surely (says the
sacramentalist) these tokens themselves stand on that interface between what we can see and what we cannot, spec-
ified and hallowed by the Lord himself.

We run the risk of trivializing our Lord's express commands if we relegate them to a purely ancillary or even
peripheral place in our church order and teaching. The mystery of regeneration presented to us in baptism—have we
quite understood why the Lord insisted on this physical rite?
And the great eucharistic mysteries, in which common stuff
that we bring is received and given back to us, according
to the Lord's promise, as his Body and Blood—surely this is
no peripheral thing? Surely we have here the great paradigms of the Gospel, given to us and enjoined on us, flesh-
and-blood creatures that we are, by the Word Incarnate.

In the sacraments of the Church, we find focused, articulated, set forth, and mediated to us, in obedience to the
Lord's example and command, the great mysteries of creation, Fall, and redemption. The creation is one holy fabric. Our sin has rent and despoiled it, making things
"secular". In the sacraments we find things returned to their
rightful use and place, that is to say, redeemed.[2]

Further, in the sacraments, the Church proceeds on three
great principles that are manifestly woven into the texture

[2] In Eden no special baptism or Eucharist was necessary, presumably, since
nothing needed to be refocused, never having been blurred. No special setting apart of things for God—no "hallowing"—needed to occur since we
still had the clarity of vision that saw truly and saw that everything was
God's. We saw perfectly clearly that all was gift, and hence we offered all
back in the oblation of thanksgiving. No washing was needed since all was
pure. No blood was asked since nothing needed ransoming. Now it is different.

of the creation and of our humanness. First, the material
world is metaphorical. That is, it speaks of the oneness and
wholeness of creation in the visible, plastic terms that our
mortality can grasp (we having forfeited our ability to experience this seamlessness). Second, enactment lies very close
to the root of our peculiar humanness. That is, we mortal
creatures come at reality ceremonially. (I am not speaking
particularly of "High Mass" here: a paper napkin folded on
the breakfast table, or a saltine and paper cup of wine—
these are all we need for our rituals.) And, third, it is this
very enacting that elicits a *real*, not a fanciful, connection
between things. It is an especially clear mode of perception. Things come at us in a blur and a tumble generally,
and in the sacraments things are focused and set in harmonious order; not just water, or bread and wine, but our
whole existence. We enact our redemption here.

For modern Evangelical churches in the West, it may be
part of the Lord's answer to their prayers for renewal that
they consider most earnestly just what the Lord was doing
in giving us these rites that we call sacraments. Do Evangelical piety, teaching, and church order really stand in the
deepest, richest, and most ancient stream of Christian vision,
or do they represent, in this area at least, an unwitting
strangling of some of the flow?

SAINT JOSEPH

We honor Saint Joseph today. Saint Joseph, her most chaste spouse, we say in the Divine Praises at Benediction.

We know almost nothing at all about him. Indeed, if it is a question of obscurity, we would have to search amongst the annals of the Cornish saints to find someone equally unknown.

And yet Saint Joseph is in the forefront, in some way, of any heavenly roster. But how? He sailed no ark like Noah, nor bearded Pharaoh like Moses, nor slew his ten thousands like David, nor prepared the way of the Lord like John the Baptist, nor became the great Apostle to the Gentiles like Saint Paul, nor the Prince of the Apostles like Saint Peter. He founded no order, like Francis, Dominic, or Ignatius; nor did he help shape the very teaching of the Church herself like Athanasius, Anselm, Bonaventure, or Thomas. He did not have a golden tongue like Saint John Chrysostom, nor a golden pen like John Henry Newman. He never ruled the apostolic see like a Gregory, a Boniface, or a Leo. He left no sweet hymn, like Bernard of Clairvaux, no mystical writing like Teresa or John of the Cross, and no godly counsel like Francis de Sales.

And yet he is there, at the center, somehow. No account of the mystery of our redemption is a true account that

Lecture given in a slightly different form at the [Episcopal] Church of All Saints Ashmont, Boston, Feast of St. Joseph, March 19, 1995.

omits this figure. No picture of the Nativity, the Presenta-
tion, or the Finding in the Temple is complete without
him. And we find, attached to his name in Sacred Scripture, one of the noblest attributions ever to be gained by
one of us mortals: he was a just man, says the Gospel.

We wish we knew all that that meant. How was this justice formed in this unknown figure? What had he learned
during the years of his utterly anonymous childhood and
youth, that fitted him, in the eyes of heaven, to be the
guardian of the Virgin Mother of God? What a daunting
vocation. Sailing the ark, or bearding Pharaoh, suddenly
dwindle, we feel, if we compare those tasks with the one
asked of Joseph. The woman to whom you are betrothed is
going to have a child. The child is already conceived, actually: hence you know that it is not yours. But fear not. Fear
not!

How is a man supposed to receive a word like that?
"Joseph, thou son of David, fear not to take unto thee Mary
thy wife: for that which is conceived in her is of the Holy
Ghost" (Mt 1:20, KJV). This is a daunting announcement.
It is all very well for heaven to break through like this, if
you are living in the time of the patriarchs and prophets,
when fire fell here, and mountains smoked there, and seas
and rivers parted to let you through. But remember that
Joseph was living at a time, like our own, when such things
did not happen. There had been no prophet for four hundred years. One day followed another, year after year, century after weary century, and good and holy souls had to
get on with it as best they could, going to the synagogue,
offering their prayers and vows to the Most High, and trying to stick to the path of righteousness. A man like Joseph
would have had no more expectation of a divine visitation
like this than would you or I today.

And suddenly this vocation. You are to take the young woman Mary as your wife: but she—she has been singled out for a vocation that is unimaginable. She is the woman spoken of in the protoevangelium in Genesis, whose Seed will bruise the serpent's head. She is the Second Eve. She is to be the Theotokos. She will be hailed by the Church for all time as "beyond compare more glorious than the seraphim".

But, you will protest here—surely Joseph scarcely grasped all this at that point? No. Of course not. But the angel did say, "And she shall bring forth a son, and thou shalt call his name Jesus: for he shall save his people from their sins."

Even here, we may well suppose that Joseph did not, all in a moment, make the connection between his angelic dream and the immemorial longing in Israel for their Messiah. But Scripture gives us no light at all on this intriguing question as to just how much the parents of our Lord grasped about this son in their household. A whole hectic and saccharine legendary has grown up about the Virgin and Saint Joseph and the home at Nazareth, but if you have ever read any of those tales, you will, I think, have found yourself profoundly unedified. The whole business lurches over into the worst sort of vaporizing and bathos. We do well to stick with what Matthew and Luke have given us.

And I think that, without leaving the text at all, we may descry two things about Saint Joseph that will supply us with fruitful matter to ponder in connection with our own vocation as Christians.

First, it would seem that he was asked to take up a responsibility the main burden of which was that he stand aside, as it were, and remain in faithful attendance, while God did something important with somebody else. The great drama, of course, occurs with the Mother and the Son at center stage. This man, this spouse, does not have one single line in the script. (The Mother herself has very few, but that is another speech.) What do you suppose Joseph thought about and prayed about as the drama unfolded? Certainly it must have become clear to him fairly quickly that he was to be in faithful attendance on this that God was doing in and through the woman. In one sense Joseph was intimately associated with the drama, but in another, he was shut out. Protect Mary; maintain the household; keep bread on the table; be father to this boy as best you can (which, I may say, suggests an interesting point to us: to what extent was it Joseph's fidelity in being a good father that introduced Jesus to the whole idea of Father, which, of course, became virtually the central theme of his whole message? Questions like this remain opaque to us, since they stand on that frontier where our Lord's humanity met his deity, and even the Church councils staggered here). But surely you and I may be encouraged when we reflect that Saint Joseph, patron of the universal Church, had a vocation that kept him always out of the limelight. It required that he be content to attend on something immense that God seemed to be doing in someone else.

And this brings up the second point. Obscurity. No klieg lights, ever. No accolades. No testimonial dinners, or talk shows, or excitement. Ever. Sheer, unrelieved obscurity. Joseph and his household were very, very low in the social and economic pecking order. They were not The Beautiful People, nor did they have a rich and famous lifestyle. Obscurity. Silence. Routine. Sameness. Day in and day out. Year after year. Nobody knows when Joseph died, of course: Mary may have been widowed early on. But for whatever his allotted span of time was, Joseph exists for us all, it seems to me, as the very icon of the faithful servant of God. Obscurity, yes, but obscurity is not a category in the precincts of heaven. Fidelity is.

This is hard for us mortals to live with, sometimes. So much else seems so attractive. Surely just a bit of celebrity would spice things up, or a dash of wealth, or influence, or some exciting connections, or some great success that would set us apart—even a little bit apart—from the trampling herd.

Well—there is the icon of Saint Joseph for us to contemplate, and in front of which we may want to pour out some prayers from the depths of our being. What, I may ask, is the particular obscurity the angel of God has assigned to me as the specific realm in which I may win through to sainthood? If I keep Saint Joseph in my vision, I will have a most encouraging model.

CATHOLIC SPIRITUALITY

My guess is that a great clutter of bric-a-brac swims into your imagination when you hear of Catholic spirituality: rosaries, holy water stoups, crucifixes, little plastic Saint Christophers for your dashboard, and laminated holy cards depicting pastel-tinted saints with their eyes cast soulfully up into the ozone, not to mention all the polychrome statues and banks of candles flickering in little red glass cups (there are even electric candles that have a bogus flicker).

My guess is also that I am addressing at least three groups of people all stirred in together here in this assembly. The biggest group of you would locate yourselves in that wing of Protestantism known as Evangelicalism and will have been brought up in Evangelical households. A second group will tell us, "I was a Catholic until I was fifteen, then I met Jesus", or "I was Catholic until I was seventeen, then I became a Christian." A third group of you are Roman Catholic even as we speak and may possibly have discovered that some of your colleagues here are very far from satisfied that your Catholicism qualifies you as a Christian. There may also be a fourth group, namely, those of you who are trying to shuck off whatever remnants of the Christian religion are still clinging to you so that you can get on with your own agenda.

Lecture given at Gordon College, June 1995.

Let me see if I can throw any light on this topic of Catholic spirituality so that the whole array of us may grasp things in a fairly clear light.

As you know, all of us do what we do for reasons that have roots in our history and culture. Some Jews, for example, wear great fur hats and long black coats and white stockings. You need to inquire into their history before you decide that they have unstylish taste. Calvinists put the pulpit at the center of focus in their churches: they have passionate reasons for adopting this architectural arrangement. Evangelicals sing a certain kind of gospel song, or praise song, which finds its roots in modern American culture. I am speaking, of course, of tradition. To be human at all is to be deeply rooted in tradition. We would all agree that there are bad traditions and good traditions: suttee in India, I suppose, and the shackling of slaves would be bad traditions, whereas taking off one's hat in a church and standing up when a woman comes into the room would be good traditions. To say that something is traditional leaves open the question as to whether it ought to be changed. If it is frivolous, or brutish, or misbegotten, then we would all agree that change is indicated.

There is no such thing, as you know, as nontraditional Christianity. What we do when we meet with other believers for worship, and the sequence we follow, and the very phrases and vocabulary that crop up—these did not spring straight from the pages of the New Testament yesterday. John Wesley, or General William Booth, or Menno Simons, or John Calvin, or Martin Luther, or J. N. Darby, or John Wimber, or D. L. Moody, or Roger Williams, or A. J. Gordon, or Ignatius of Antioch, or Clement of Rome, or Justin Martyr, or Gregory I—these gentlemen stand there between you and the morning of Pentecost in Jerusalem two thousand years ago.

Even if you strive mightily for spontaneity in your worship, for example, you find two things: first, there is an ancient tradition of efforts at spontaneity in worship—it is called Montanism—and secondly, you discover that your spontaneity very quickly jells into half a dozen or so phrases and gestures. We are all human, forsooth, and we can no more shuck off tradition than we can shuck off these bodies of ours.

As our forerunners in the ancient Faith moved out from that dazzling Pentecostal morning into the long haul of history, we find that the touchstone for their life together, and for their prayer, and for their worship, was apostolic. Christianity was not just a higgledy-piggledy aggregate of independent believers and groups scattered across Samaria and Asia Minor. You had to be in obedient, visible, organic communion with the apostles themselves. Then, as the decades rolled on and Peter and John and James and the others died, you found yourself under the authority of the men on whom they had laid their hands. These men were overseers, or pastors: *bishop* is the word that came into play very quickly. If you were a Christian, you said, "Polycarp is my bishop", or "Ignatius is my bishop." There was no such thing in the Church to which you and I owe our faith—there was no such thing as an independent, or individualistic, Christian.

Naturally, zealous types popped up out of the weeds every hour on the half hour, so to speak, saying, "Hi, guys: I'm starting me a church over here", or "I've got a word from the Lord", or "The Holy Ghost has revealed thus and such to me." These men were called heresiarchs by the Christians (there were some women, too).

Things were very strict, actually: if you doubt this, look at Saint Paul's Epistles or eavesdrop on the Council in Jerusalem, which the apostles convened to decide what you were supposed to do about certain matters of conscience. The Christians were not left organizing workshops and symposia to hash over issues: the apostles told you what to do and what to believe. This news may make you skittish, but all of us, Baptist, O.P.C., Coptic, R.C., or Grace Chapel, have to agree that that was the way the apostles did things, for good or ill. If we attempt a different scheme, we do so under the titanic gaze of that great cloud of witnesses who, says the Book of Hebrews, are watching us as we stumble along through our fragment of history.

To be a believer at all in those early days was to look on yourself, not so much as a private individual who had accepted the Lord Jesus Christ as your personal Savior, but rather as one who had joined himself to this entity called the Church. If, say, you were a Christian shopkeeper in Antioch, and I, your pagan neighbor, having watched you and your fellow believers for a couple of years, came to you and said, "Um, I think I'd like to become a Christian", you would not say to me, "Oh! Great! Here's John 3:16. We can just bow our heads here, and you can repeat this prayer after me, and then you'll be a Christian." No. You would say to me, "Ah. You want to be a Christian, do you? Well—I'll introduce you to our bishop, Ignatius, and he will turn you over to some of the Christians for instruction for about a year, and you will be allowed to sit in on our worship (but you'll have to leave when we get to the Lord's Supper every week), and then, next year the bishop will baptize you, and then you'll be a Christian."

If this sounds peculiar to us modern American believers, our attitude toward it is an index of how far we have removed ourselves from the disciplines and traditions of the very men to whom we owe our faith. And incidentally here, that ancient scheme may be what lies at the bottom of the confusion Evangelicals sometimes encounter when they ask some Roman Catholic if he is "saved" or "born again". Most Catholics will mutter and hem and haw, and possibly croak out, "No—I'm a Catholic." In so doing, he is groping for an identity that goes back to apostolic times. That word *catholic* came into play within a few decades after Pentecost. To be catholic was to be identified with Peter and John and Paul, and with Ignatius and Clement and Polycarp, and with that odd crowd in the Roman Empire who worshipped God and his servant Jesus (this is how they often phrased it). It was a profoundly corporate identity. Individualism had not taken control in those centuries, and, interestingly enough, it was at that time that what we see today as Roman Catholic piety began to form itself.

Which brings up a point: earnest Christian believers often speak of "going back to the Book of Acts", or of taking their cues from the New Testament alone, as though they were saying something trenchant. What they miss, of course, is that the infant Church did not take her cues from the New Testament (there was none), and secondly, that in this New Testament you can't find a blueprint for Christan worship (Acts 2:42 lists four ingredients of their meetings together, but does not tell us how they arranged things). And thirdly, of course, to insist too shrilly on a rigorous adherence to the letter of Acts 2:42 is to suggest that the seed which the Holy Ghost planted was a poor seed and never grew. A Roman Catholic sees the growth of the Church, and of her worship, not as a matter of naughty medieval popes Scotch-taping accretions onto the Church's worship until finally you get an extravaganza called a High Mass, but rather as the organic budding and flowering and fruit-bearing of a tree from a healthy seed—a tree big enough for all the birds of heaven to roost in, to borrow the Gospel phrase. So that, when you point out to a Catholic that his worship, the Mass, scarcely looks like those huddled gatherings in the Upper Room and so forth, he will be thinking of the habit that acorns have of growing into enormous oaks, which of course don't look like acorns at all.

This brings us to another point which I might be able to help with here. On this matter of the Mass, or the liturgy, as the apostolic Church called her worship, we blunder into something that might surprise you. When you go to the very, very earliest documents in the Church, you find that corporate worship had taken on a highly specific form. They met, not for a sermon mainly, nor for fellowship mainly, nor primarily for teaching, nor singing, nor anything else at all except the Eucharist. The Lord's Table, in other words. That, from the beginning, was what they meant by worship. They would have been stumped to find Christians two thousand years later gathering for corporate worship on the Lord's Day without celebrating the Eucharist.

And not only this: their worship did not take any old form. They knew nothing at all of spontaneity. Like the Lord Jesus, who had grown up in the synagogue, and like all the people of God right back to Moses and before, they would have known that, when you come together on a regular, recurring, long-term basis to offer the sacrifice of adoration at the Sapphire Throne, you need a form. For the form sets you free from the shallow puddle of your own ad hoc resources of the moment and draws you into the dignity, nobility, and splendor attending the angelic worship of the Most High, and for which you and I yearn with fathomless yearning. For we mortals are, of course, ceremonial creatures. Hurrah for spontaneity in its place, but when we come to the great, central, profound mysteries that undergird our mortal life—birth, marriage, worship, and death—then we reach for a form. A ceremony. Every tribe, culture, society, and civilization has known this.

Why do we ceremonialize that which matters the most to us? Why do you brides dress up that way and walk so slowly down the aisle? Why do they drive the hearse so slowly? Why do you put those candles onto that birthday cake?

Because, you and I would protest, the ceremony, far from obscuring the event and far from cluttering things up, lo and behold, brings home to us the full weight of significance. Oh, to be sure, obstetrics and gynecology are to be praised for their assistance in getting our babies launched, but when we come to what it means—that a new person has appeared on the scene—ah, then, we need to go deeper than the obstetrics can carry us, and the only way we can do that is by means of ceremony. All Jews and all Orthodox and Roman Catholic and Anglican Christians count on this; and all Muslims and Hindus, and indeed people of every tribe and culture, will testify to this. So, if you tax a Roman Catholic friend about why Catholics stick with a rigid form for worship, he will not quite grasp what you are urging on him. Surely, he would want to know, you don't seriously suppose that spontaneity is what we want when we come, as the holy people of God, week after week, century after century, to offer the sacrifice of adoration at the Sapphire Throne?

It may also be helpful here if I explain that not only the structure of the Mass itself—the first part, called the Synaxis, which contains all the scriptural readings, and the sermon and the creed and the prayers, and the second part, called the Anaphora, with the Great Thanksgiving and the Communion itself—that not only this structure, but also the very words themselves, go back to the first and second centuries. It is a tremendously moving thing, believe me, to read the texts of what those early Christians said and did when they gathered, and then to hear those same words in the liturgy in your local parish from Sunday to Sunday. A glorious and unbroken continuity unfurls itself: you know that you are linked with the apostles, the Fathers, the martyrs, the bishops and confessors, and the whole company of the faithful from Pentecost to our own day. A Roman Catholic has a difficult time grasping why Christians would wish to set this ancient liturgy on one side in favor of a modern blueprint.

But my guess is that by this time some of you may be murmuring, "Well—it's all very well, the noble antiquity of which you speak. But come: all these Irish plumbers and Sicilian pasta-cooks and Cuban taxi drivers—am I to believe that they are swept into such dizzy heights every time they go to Mass?"

A legitimate question. Touché. And the answer, of course, is no—no more than your average Hebrew saw the glory of God every time the Levites blew the trumpets, nor than your average Presbyterian lawyer or Episcopalian CEO or Gordon College undergraduate, sees that glory when the organ, or the guitars, strike up the opening hymn. We mortals don't do very well with this business of worship. Where was your mind—where was mine—during the singing of the hymn a few minutes ago? Alas. But all of us, Baptist, Pentecostal, or Catholic, would reach for Saint Augustine's maxim *abusus non tollit usus*, if some nonreligious friend of ours suggested that we ought to abandon our worship practices since most of the time our minds are wandering anyway. "The abuse of a thing does not take away its proper use." We don't throw in the towel on chapel at Gordon

because people's minds wander or they read a magazine in
their laps. We soldier on, keeping the gate of the tabernacle open, so to speak, so that good and holy souls may
come and offer their offerings, and so that others of us,
finding ourselves in these precincts, may perhaps be roused
to our duties toward the Divine Majesty.

Let me touch on one other point about Roman Catholic
worship and piety that, I think, constitutes a scandal to Protestant Christians. It is this business of the physical. Catholics kneel, and bow, and cross themselves. Some even strike
their breast during the Agnus Dei ("Lamb of God"). And
there is often incense. The celebrant wears elaborate vestments. There are candles, and holy water, and bread and
wine. It is not at all the Geneva or Zurich or Edinburgh
pattern of things. Isn't it all, really, pagan?

Well, yes, if you mean that pagans use incense and bow
and light candles. But the minute we say that we know we
are in trouble, since pagans also gather for worship, and
pray, and listen to teaching, just as we Christians do. And
pagans kneel, the way many of you do at your bedside.
Clearly we can't adopt the rule that says, If the pagans do
it, we Christians mustn't. The point is, we men bow, and
kneel, and gather, and lift up holy hands. The rub comes
when you ask which deity is being invoked. If it is Baal or
Osiris, then you have paganism. If it is the God and Father
of our Lord Jesus Christ, then you have Christian worship.

But again—hasn't the New Testament put an end to all
ceremony? Isn't worship a matter strictly of the inner man
now?

Well, yes, if you mean that the Father seeks those who
will worship him in spirit and in truth. But of course, that's
not a New Testament innovation: the prophets were forever
harrying Israel about the same thing. And John Knox and

Jonathan Edwards and Søren Kierkegaard harried the Protestants about their farcical and empty worship rituals. Catholics have no corner on this difficulty.

So—granting that it is always difficult for us mortals to bring
together and keep together the outward form (the singing
in Gordon chapel of "Crown Him with Many Crowns", say)
and the inner reality (my heart actually aspiring thus to crown
the mystic Lamb)—granting this severe difficulty, shouldn't
we pare things down to a stark minimum so that the danger
of mere mumbo-jumbo is diminished?

Possibly so. On the other hand, of course, you and I are
not Gnostics. We are not Manicheans. Those were the people who wanted religion to be a matter of our flying off
into a vacuous and disembodied ether, jettisoning these
embarrassing flesh-and-blood bodies of ours, with all of the
sneezing and wheezing they bring along. All of those high-
minded, nineteenth-century Bostonians like Ralph Waldo
Emerson and Bronson Alcott and William Ellery Channing, were quasi-Manicheans. They wanted Christianity to
be fumigated and cerebral. Sit in your New England church
on a wooden pew and think about God. But please—no
smells and bells. Please.

You and I would answer Emerson and company by pointing out that Christianity, far from being the religion merely
of the Book, like Islam, is profoundly fleshly. But after
the altars and lambs and heifers and burned fat of the Old
Testament, we get spiritual: right? Wrong. There is a
conceiving—of a babe in the womb of a young girl. There
is parturition, and circumcision. There is water to wine at
a wedding. And there is your salvation and mine, wrought,
not by edicts handed down from the heavens, but by thorns
and splinters and nails and gashes. But then we get
spiritual—right? Wrong again. A body, out of the sepulchre.

And worse yet—that body—our human flesh, taken up at
the Ascension into the midmost mysteries of the Holy
Trinity. When's the last time you heard a sermon on the
implications of the Ascension? And then, of course, not
just a book, but Bread and Wine, given to us, day by day,
for as long as history lasts. A very physical religion we
belong to.

This is what is bespoken in the Roman Mass. The Mass
is sacramental worship, as they say: that is, the physical is
understood as being the nexus between the seen and the
unseen; between time and eternity; just as it was on the
altars of Israel, and in the flesh of the Incarnate Son of
God, and on the Cross, and in the Resurrection and the
Ascension. And you and I are more than souls, or intellects. Jesus Christ has saved the whole man, kneecaps,
eardrums, nostrils, and all: hence Christians kneel to pray,
and play guitars in their worship, and bring incense. It is
good for my heart that my knees touch the floor. It is good
for my soul that my neck muscles bend a bit when I say
grace at lunch. These physical things belong to the seamless personhood that is me. Emerson had it all wrong.

I might wind this up here by mentioning one item that
is as sticky as any of the items on the list of questions that
good Evangelicals have about Roman Catholic piety. I mean
the Rosary.

If anything on earth looks like the vain repetition the
Bible warns us against, it would certainly be the Rosary. It
entails seemingly endless repetitions of the Hail Mary. That
can't possibly be "prayer", surely?

Let me see if I can help you see at least the reason Catholics appreciate the Rosary. First, we all know how terribly
difficult it is to fix our minds in Christian meditation. If
you have attempted it yourself, you know that your worst

enemy is wandering thoughts. You also know that you very quickly run out of things to say when you are pondering one of the Gospel mysteries (and surely if one is a serious Christian one will have as part of one's daily exercises just such meditating and pondering). The Rosary supplies us with a way of tarrying (that is the key word, actually) in a systematic and progressive way, in the presence of all the great events of our salvation, in the company of the one who was most receptive to the Lord, namely, the Virgin Mary, who said, you will remember, "Behold the handmaid of the Lord: be it done unto me according to Thy word." Alas—that is what you and I, in our father Adam and our mother Eve did not say in Eden; and it is one way of summing up this whole process of growth in the Christian life we have embarked on. If only I can learn, increasingly, to say, from my heart, "Be it done unto me according to Thy word."

The Rosary presents us with fifteen of the Gospel events—the Annunciation, the Visitation, the Nativity, the Crucifixion, the Resurrection, and so forth—and, by giving us a sort of refrain to murmur as we place ourselves *in conspectu Dei* at each scene—the way charismatics will murmur "Jesus! Jesus!" or the way we Evangelicals repeat "Alleluia!" or "Crown him! crown him!" in a hymn—by giving us a quiet refrain to keep on our tongues as we tarry, it helps us to stay in place. The words are like ball bearings, so to speak. They assist our poor scattered faculties to stay in line. And of course, the "Hail Mary" is biblical: we are simply repeating Gabriel's salutation to this woman—we are one of the many generations who want to call her blessed, as she herself sang in the Magnificat. For of course she was the one of us who was taken most intimately into the whole drama of redemption: the patriarchs and prophets and kings and apostles all bore witness to the Word: Mary bore the Word. She is the fulfillment of Genesis 3:15. Insofar as we increasingly unite our own aspirations with hers, we move closer and closer into intimate union with the Lord. "Behold the handmaid of the Lord": if only I can learn to say that, in a thousand situations all day long when irritation, or resentment, or lust, or impatience surge up in me. "Be it done unto me according to Thy word." It is a wonderful frame of mind for a Christian to aspire to. The Rosary, day by day, presents to us those events upon which our souls ought to be habitually dwelling and helps us to tarry in those Gospel precincts.

My time is up. I have scarcely touched on this matter of the Virgin Mary and have said nothing of the Pope, or of prayers to the saints, and Purgatory, and so many other things that seem an outrage to ardent Evangelical imagination. As a form of shorthand, I may simply say that every single one of these notions and practices is profoundly centered on Jesus Christ who, says the Roman Catholic Church, echoing Saint Paul, is "the one mediator between God and man".

There are gigantic matters that we could talk about. For my part, I want to say a most fervent and heartfelt thanks to Gordon College for having me here today. All my memories of my fifteen years on the faculty here are good memories. God bless and prosper Gordon College, say I.

ON BRAZEN HEAVENS

For about a year now I have been witness to a drama that is all too familiar to us mortal men. Someone finds he has cancer; the medical treadmill begins, with its implacable log of defeat; hope is marshaled, begins the march, is rebuffed at every juncture, flags, rouses, flags again, and is finally quietly mustered out.

And meanwhile, because the people in the drama are Christian believers, everyone is dragged into the maelstrom that marks the place where our experience eddies into the sea of the divine will. The whole question of prayer gapes open.

The promises are raked over. And over and over. "Is the primary condition enough faith on our part?" "We must scour our own hearts to see that there is no stoppage there—of sin or of unbelief." "We must stand on the promise." "We must claim and such." "We must resist the devil and his weapons of doubt."

And we leap at and pursue any and all reports and records of healings, "Look at what happened to so-and-so!" "Listen to this!" "I've just read this wonderful pamphlet." We know the Gospel accounts by heart. We agree that this work of healing did not cease with the apostolic age. We greet

Originally published in a slightly different form in *Christianity Today* (December 7, 1973): 8–11. Reprinted with permission.

gladly the tales of healing that pour in from all quarters in the Church—no longer only from those groups that have traditionally "specialized" in healing, but from the big, old, classic bodies in Christendom—Rome, Anglicanism, Lutheranism, Presbyterianism, and so forth. "God is doing something in our day", we hear, and we grasp at it eagerly.

And meanwhile the surgery goes on its horrific way, and the radiation burns on, week after grim week; and suffering sets in, and the doctors hedge and dodge into the labyrinthine linoleum-and-stainless-steel bureaucracy of the hospital world, and our hearts sicken, and we try to avert our eyes from the black flag that is fluttering wildly on the horizon, mocking us.

And the questions come stealing over us: "Where is now their God?" "Where is promise of his coming?" "He trusted in God that he would deliver him . . ." and so on. And we know that we are not the first men into whose teeth the Tempter and his ilk have flung those taunts.

We look for some light. We look for some help. Our prayers seem to be vanishing like so many wisps, into the serene ether of the cosmos (or worse, into the plaster of the ceiling). We strain our ears for some word from the Mount of God. A whisper will do, we tell ourselves, since clearly no bolts or thunderings have been activated by our importunity (yes, we have tried that tactic, too: the "non-faith" approach).

But only dead silence. Blank. Nothing. "But Lord, how are we supposed to know if we're on the right track at all if we don't get some confirmation from you—some corroboration—in *any* form, Lord—inner peace maybe, or some verse springing to life for us, or some token. Please let us have some recognizable attestation to what you have said in Your Book." Nothing. Silence. Blank.

Perhaps at this point we try to think back over the experience of the people of God through the millennia. There has been a whole spectrum of experience for them: glorious deliverances, great victories, kingdoms toppled, widows receiving their dead back, men wandering about in sheepskins and goatskins—

"Men wandering about in sheepskins and goatskins? What went wrong there?"

"That's in the record of faith."

"But then surely something went wrong."

"No. It is part of the log of the faithful. That is a list of what happened to the people of faith. It is about how they proved God."

The whole spectrum of experience is there. The widow of Nain got her son back and other mothers didn't. Peter got out of prison and John the Baptist didn't. Elijah whirled up to heaven with fiery horses, and Joseph ended in a coffin in Egypt. Paul healed other people, but was turned down on his own request for healing for himself.

A couple of items in the Gospels seem to me to suggest something for the particular situation described in this article, where deliverance did not, in fact, come, and where apparently the juggernaut of sheer nature went on its grim way with no intervention from heaven.

One is the story of Lazarus, and the other is the Emmaus account. You object immediately: "Ah, but in both those cases it turned out that the dead *were* raised." Well, perhaps there is something there for us nonetheless.

For a start, the people involved in those incidents were followers of Jesus, and they had seen him, presumably, heal dozens of people. Then these followers experienced the utter dashing of all their expectations and hopes by death. God did not, it seemed, act. He who had been declared the Living One and the Giver of Life seemed to have turned his back in this case. What went wrong? What did the household at Bethany *not* do that the widow of Nain had done?

How shall we align it all? Who rates and who doesn't? Whatever it is that we might have chosen to say to them in the
days following their experience of death, we would have
had to come to terms somehow with the bleak fact that
God had done something for others that he had not done
for them.

From the vantage point of two thousand years, we later
believers can, of course, see that there was something wonderful in prospect, and that it emerged within a very few
days in both cases. The stories make sense. They are almost
better than they would have been if the deaths had not
occurred. But of course this line would have been frosty
comfort for Mary and Martha, or for the two en route to
Emmaus, if we had insisted to them, "Well, surely God is
up to something. We'll just have to wait."

And yet what else could we have said? Their experience
at that point was of the utter finality of death, which had
thrown everything they had expected into limbo. For them
there was no walking and leaping and praising God. No
embracing and ecstatic tears of reunion. Only the silence
of shrouds and sepulchres, and then the turning back, not
just to the flat routines of daily life, but to the miserable
duel with the tedious voices pressing in upon their exhausted
imaginations with "Right! *Now* where are you? Tell us about
your faith now! What'd you do wrong?"

The point is that for x number of days, their experience was of defeat. For us, alas, the "x number of days"
may be greatly multiplied. And it is small comfort to us
to be told that the difference, then, between us and, say,
Mary and Martha's experience of Lazarus' death, or of the
two on the road to Emmaus, is only a quantitative difference. "They had to wait four days. You have to wait one,
or five, or seventy years. What's the real difference?" That

is like telling someone on the rack his pain is only quantitatively different from mine with my hangnail. The quantity *is* the difference. But there is, perhaps, at least this much help for us whose experience is that of Mary and Martha and the others, and not that of the widow of Nain and Jairus: the experience of the faithful *has*, in fact, included the experience of utter death. That seems to be part of the pattern, and it would be hard indeed to insist on the death being attributable to some failure of faith on somebody's part.

There is also this to be observed: that it sometimes seems that those on the higher reaches of faith are asked to experience this "absence" of God. For instance, Jesus seemed ready enough to show his authority to chance bystanders, and to the multitudes, but look at his own circle. John the Baptist wasn't let off—he had his head chopped off. James was killed in prison. And the Virgin herself had to go through the horror of seeing her Son tortured. No legions of angels intervened there. There was also Job, of course. And Saint Paul—he had some sort of healing ministry himself, so that handkerchiefs were sent out from him with apparently healing efficacy for *others*, but, irony of ironies, his own prayer for *himself* was "unanswered". He had to slog through life with whatever his "thorn" was. What does this data do to our categories?

But there is more. Turning again to the disclosure of God in Scripture, we seem to see that, in his economy, there is no slippage. Nothing simply disappears. No sparrow falls without his knowing (and, one might think, caring) about it. No hair on anybody's head is without its number. Oh, you say, that's only a metaphor; it's not literal. A metaphor of *what*, then? we might ask. Is the implication there that God *doesn't* keep tabs on things?

And so we begin to think about all our prayers and vigils and fastings and abstinences, and the offices and sacraments of the Church that have gone up to the throne on behalf of the sufferer. They have, apparently, been lost in the blue. They have vanished, as no sparrow, no hair, has ever done. Hey, what about that?

And we know that this is false. It is nonsense. All right then—we prayed, with much faith or with little; we searched ourselves; we fasted; we anointed and laid on hands; we kept vigil. And nothing happened.

Did it not? What angle of vision are we speaking from? Is it not true that again and again in the biblical picture of things, the story has to be allowed to *finish*? Was it not the case with Lazarus' household at Bethany, and with the two en route to Emmaus? And is it not the case with the Whole Story, actually—that it must be allowed to finish, and that this is precisely what the faithful have been watching for since the beginning of time? In the face of suffering and endurance and loss and waiting and death, what is it that has kept the spirits of the faithful from flagging utterly down through the millennia? Is it not the hope of redemption? Is it not the great Finish to the Story—and to all their little stories of wandering about in sheepskins and goatskins as well as to the One Big Story of the whole creation, which is itself groaning and waiting? And is not that Finish called glorious? Does it not entail what amounts to a redoing of all that has gone wrong, and a remaking of all that is ruined, and a finding of all that has been lost in the shuffle, and an unfolding of it all in a blaze of joy and splendor?

A finding of all that is lost? All sparrows, and all petitions and tears and vigils and fastings? Yes, all petitions and tears and vigils and fastings.

"But where *are* they? The thing is over and done with. He is dead. They had no effect."

Hadn't they? How do you know what is piling up in that great treasury kept by the Divine Love to be opened in that Day? How do you know that this death *and* your prayers and tears and fasts will not *together* be suddenly and breath-takingly displayed, before all the faithful, and before angels and archangels, and before kings and widows and prophets, as gems in that display? Oh no, don't speak of things being lost. Say rather that they are hidden—received and accepted and taken up into the secrets of the divine mysteries, to be transformed and multiplied, like everything else we offer to him—loaves and fishes, or mites, or bread and wine—and given back to you and to the one for whom you kept vigil, in the presence of the whole host of men and angels, in a hilarity of glory as unimaginable to you in your vigil as golden wings are to the worm in the chrysalis.

But how does it *work*? We may well ask. How *does* redemption work?

ASCENSION

Today is the day when the Church calls upon us both to recall and to reflect upon the mystery of our Lord's Ascension into heaven.

By referring to this event as a mystery, I am only, of course, employing common Christian terminology. We speak of all the great events attending upon the Incarnation of our Lord as "mysteries", for in these events heaven touches earth somehow. We may say that the events themselves—the Annunciation, the Nativity, the miracles, the Transfiguration, the Passion, and Resurrection—that these events are to be found on the cusp, so to speak, between time and eternity, or at the frontier, if we like that better, that runs between heaven and earth. And certainly we all have experience of this same sort of mystery in the sacraments, which themselves exist on that cusp, or on that frontier. Where are we, for example, at the eucharistic mystery? In Needham or Dedham or Scituate? Well, yes, in a manner of speaking. But we are also, no less literally, in the heavenlies with the angels and archangels and all the company of heaven. It is a mystery—which is one of the meanings of the word *sacrament*, by the way.

But we are speaking of the Ascension. I have long felt that this event is one of the strangest of all the Gospel mysteries.

Lecture given at the [Episcopal] Church of All Saints Ashmont, Boston, Feast of the Ascension, 1996.

For what is it that we are confessing when we repeat in the Creed, "he ascended into heaven"? A scoffer would harry us with raucous questions. "The Ascension, eh? Let's see: you Christians believe, then, that this man, speaking to his friends up on top of a hill, presently began to float upward. Then along comes a convenient cloud so that the marvel is obscured. What, pray, are we to imagine as happening then? Did this decorous upward float pick up speed gradually (after all, it's a long way to heaven)? Did he eventually reach the speed of light? What time of day did he pass Jupiter? Did he keep his sandals so that we are to think of a pair of sandals in the Blessed Trinity now? Or did they drop off at some point? Is this second Person of the Trinity still clad in a tunic or garment purchased in Nazareth or Bethany? And are we to suppose that the Holy Trinity changed as he arrived at the Sapphire Throne, now to include human flesh?"

Naturally we will all be spluttering at our scoffer by this time, trying to get him to cease and desist, and to listen while we attempt to throw some light on this point in the Creed. But what light?

Well, for one thing, the man's questions are misbegotten. To pursue an interrogation like that is to miss entirely the nature of things. It would be akin to bringing up obstetrics and gynecology in the effort to throw light on the Virgin Birth, or to resort to organic chemistry in an attempt to get to the bottom of the question about the Body and Blood at the Mass. This trigonometric, or ballistic, approach to the Ascension may fling itself forever at the rock face of the mystery, but no door will open in response to the assault.

The key to the door is faith. We affirm by faith that Jesus Christ ascended to his Father at the end of his allotted time here on this earth. And to locate our affirmation in the precincts of faith is not to hand things over either to the wild-eyed visionaries who see apparitions in every bush, nor to clergy who have learned doublespeak in seminary, and love to keep the old vocabulary of the Gospel while all the time playing hob with the sober truth to which that vocabulary refers. (You have all heard theologians and clerics speak of "the Easter faith". A harmless-enough sounding phrase, it would seem, except that it cloaks a rank denial. Easter—so this line of thought would run—doesn't imply anything quite so embarrassing as a vacant sepulchre. That happy story is what the primitive Christians came up with as a way of expressing their confidence in the undying spirit of Jesus, etc., etc., etc.)

No, it isn't, say you and I—and all the apostles and confessors and martyrs and Doctors of the Church who have preceded us. Jesus Christ's body arose from Joseph of Arimathea's tomb, and thereby stands or falls the whole Christian Faith. And it is likewise with the Ascension.

We believe that our Lord Jesus Christ did indeed ascend to his Father, carrying our flesh—the flesh he had received from the gift of the Virgin Mary—into the midmost mysteries of the Trinity. Logic fails. Scientific language stammers. Even our imaginations stop short of the scene. We don't know how to visualize things at all, as of the Ascension—not that any of us could have done much better at visualizing the Trinity before the Ascension.

But our reflections on this feast day do not need to linger, perplexed and teased by such imponderables as those of which we have been speaking. The Ascension is an event full of significance for you and me even now as we move along from day to day in our Christian lives.

In raising Christ Jesus, God has raised us with him and made us to sit in heavenly places with him and crowned us as his coheirs. "Heirs of God and joint heirs with Jesus

Christ", says Saint Paul. That is our status. The abyss of death has been bridged, so that when we refer to the doctrine of the communion of the saints, we are not reaching for a vaporous metaphor by which to bolster our melancholy spirits on this long and arduous pilgrimage here on earth. We really do believe that that abyss of death has been bridged, and that we, the Church in pilgrimage, are truly one with those who have gone ahead of us, starting with our Lord himself, Saint Stephen the Protomartyr, and our Lady. We are one, undivided, living, interceding fellowship who share in the priesthood of Jesus before the throne of God. The Church encourages us to pray for those who have gone ahead of us—who knows what schooling they must complete before they are able to bear up under the titanic glory of the Beatific Vision—and the Church assures us that they are praying for us. This is what we invoke in the great Litany at the Easter Vigil—and, it is to be hoped, in our own prayers during the rest of the year. The Ascension of Jesus Christ has made this an actuality, not a fugitive dream or forlorn hope.

And the Ascension quickens our flagging spirits as we tread along during this earthly life. "I go to prepare a place for you," he said, "that where I am, there ye may be also." Better than the Emerald City of Oz, better than Narnia or Rivendell or Lothlorien, better than the Gardens of the Hesperides: "eye hath not seen, nor ear heard, neither have entered into the heart of man, the things which God hath prepared for them that love him." Hurrah. No wonder the Scripture and the liturgy are full of injunctions to us to lift up our hearts. *Sursum corda*. We lift them up to the Lord. He is there, awaiting us, and by his Holy Spirit, he is here accompanying us. Let us hasten, then, to Mount Zion with singing.

RECOGNIZING THE CHURCH

A Personal Pilgrimage and the Discovery of Five Marks of the Church

I was brought up in an Evangelical household. To say this is to say something good.

My father was a layman, not a preacher, but he was a devoted and assiduous, daily student of the Bible. He and my mother exist to this day in my imagination as the very icons of the godly man and woman. It was a wonderful thing—that sage, earnest, transparent, Bible-centered faith. I owe the fact that I am a believer today, and that my whole pilgrimage, steep and tortuous as it has been sometimes, has been *toward* the center, not away from it, to the faith and prayers and example of my father and mother.

I believe that I and my five brothers and sisters, all of whom, now, in our sixties, are Christians who want to follow the Lord wholly, would all testify to this godly influence of our parents. The household was a household suffused with the Bible. We sang hymns—daily—hundreds of them over the years, so that probably all six of us know scores of hymns by heart. We had family prayers twice a day, after breakfast and after supper. Our parents prayed with us at our bedside, the last thing at night. We all went to Sunday School and church regularly.

Originally published in a slightly different form in *Touchstone* (Fall 1997): 17–22. Reprinted with permission.

There is only one agenda in a Fundamentalist Sunday school: the Bible. The Bible day in and day out, year in and year out. Flannelgraph lessons, sword drills, Scripture memory: everything was focused directly on the Bible itself. I am grateful for every minute of this, now, fifty years later. Because of this the whole of Scripture, from Genesis to Revelation, is ringing in my ears all the time. Hundreds of verses, in the language of the King James Version, are there, intact, in my memory. I hope that, if my memory fails and I lose my wits in my old age, perhaps these verses, from so long ago, will remain there and bring me solace.

The Christian believers among whom I grew up were very forthcoming about the Faith. They spoke easily and informally about "the Lord". When you were among them you knew that you were among people of "like precious faith", as Saint Peter phrases it. Many of the guests in our household had been overseas missionaries, some of them interned in concentration camps by the Japanese during World War II. Our ears were full of stories of how God had been faithful in all sorts of human extremities. It would be hard to find a better ambience, I think, than this good and trusty Evangelicalism of my youth.

But I speak as one whose pilgrimage has led him from the world of Protestant Evangelicalism to the Roman Catholic Church. One way or another, all of us whose nurture has been in one of the sectors of Protestantism where the Bible is honored, where the Gospel is preached without dissimulation, and where Jesus Christ is worshipped as God and Savior—all of us desire to be faithful to the ancient Faith that we profess and to be found obedient to the will of God. Certainly such fidelity and obedience have motivated us so far, and we want to be able to give an accounting of ourselves when it comes to our turn at the Divine

Tribunal, for we must all appear before the Judgment Seat of Christ.

Why then, would anyone want to leave such a world? Was not that a rendering of the ancient Faith almost without equal? Surely to leave it would be to go from great plenty out to famine and penury?

Of my own case, I would have to say that I did not want to leave it. Certainly I was restless as a young man, like all young men, and any grass across any fence tended to look very green. I did, out of mere curiosity, draw back from the little church of my parents and my childhood when I returned to my hometown after having graduated from college and put in my time in the army. I visited the local Presbyterian church . . . and the Methodist and the Lutheran and the Episcopalian.

Only this last one held any great attraction for me—I think it was a matter of aesthetics more than any other single factor. The Episcopal liturgy is the most elegant thing in the world, and this is to be attributed to their Prayer Book, which has since been supplanted by a modern translation, but which, in 1960, was still the old Book of Common Prayer, with its matchless Shakespearean prose. Episcopal churches tend to be gothic, with stained glass and cool, dark interiors. Episcopal hymnody is virtually the best in the world, if we are speaking of a rich treasury of hymns drawn from the era of Isaac Watts and Charles Wesley, as well as from ancient Christendom. I was attracted by all of this. There was also a strange note of nostalgia in it, since I knew that my mother had been "saved" out of Episcopalianism into Fundamentalism in about 1915, but that she still retained an undying love for Episcopal hymns and liturgy. Somehow that nostalgia had communicated itself to me.

The next step in my pilgrimage was made easy. I found myself teaching at a boys' school in England, so this put me in the neighborhood of the Church of England. There is a robust Evangelical wing in this old church. So I did not have to "leave" anything. I could have all this and heaven too, so to speak. I was received into the Church of England in 1962 and found myself among the best crowd of all, I thought: Evangelicals who took the liturgy, and the atmosphere, of Anglicanism for granted. I loved it.

When I returned to the United States and married, my wife, who was a wise and holy woman, was fairly quickly received into the Episcopal church—or the Anglican church, as many prefer to call it—and our two children were raised as Anglicans. Fortunately, we found ourselves, both in New York in the early years of our marriage, and then in Massachusetts, in parishes where the Scripture was honored, and the Gospel was preached, and sturdy fellowship was central.

Two questions, I think, spring into the minds of people, when they hear of someone opting into Anglicanism. First, what about the liberalism in these big Protestant denominations? And second, doesn't one have to settle into worship that is dull and lifeless since it is all canned and rote, leaving behind the wonderful spontaneity and freshness that marks the worship in the Evangelical and Pentecostal churches?

On the first question, there is only one answer, and that is yes, one does have to learn to live in a denomination that has very largely given itself over to an extremely liberal interpretation of Scripture and now, alas, of sexual morality. The good and faithful souls in these Protestant denominations suffer over this, of course, and will tell you that they are trying to bear witness in the situation, and that the Church historically has been plagued always with heresy and sin, and that we can't keep splitting and splitting, as we Evangelicals have done, in the interest of doctrinal or moral purity. You end up with an ecclesiastical flea market that way, such people might urge.

On the second question, about canned and rote worship, we come to an immense issue. What is at stake here is the rock-bottom question as to what worship is, and how you do it. Put briefly, the question comes to this: worship is the thing we were created for—to know God, and knowing him, to bless him and adore him forever. This is what the seraphim, and the cherubim, and all the angelic hierarchy do ceaselessly. This is what creation is doing: the Psalms call upon winds and mountains and seas and frosts and hail and sun and stars to worship the Most High. We believe that in some very literal sense the entire creation does, each part of it after its own unique mode, "worship" him. But you and I belong to the species whose dignity entails *leading* the praises of our world.

To worship God is to ascribe worth to him. It is an activity distinct from teaching, and from fellowship, and from witnessing, and from sharing. It is an act, not an experience. We come to church primarily to do something, not to receive something, although of course in the ancient worship of the Church, we do indeed receive God himself, under the sacramental species of Bread and Wine. But our task in worship is to offer the oblation of ourselves and our adoration at the Sapphire Throne.

Obviously this is a daunting and an august task. Fortunately we are not left to our own resources, nor to the whim of the moment, nor even to our own experience. The faithful have been worshipping God since the beginning, and there is help for us. All of us, even those of us who come from the so-called free churches where spontaneity is supposed to be the rule, are accustomed to borrowing secondhand, canned words to assist us in worship. I am speaking of hymns. When we sing "Amazing Grace" or "O, For a Thousand Tongues to Sing", we are borrowing John Newton's and Charles Wesley's words. And we discover that, far from cramping or restricting our worship, these secondhand words bring us up to a level quite unattainable by our own spontaneous efforts. They take us away from ourselves.

That is another crucial point in ritual worship: people who are fellowshipping with each other, and sharing, are, characteristically, facing each other. People who are worshipping are, all together, facing something else, namely, the Sapphire Throne. The liturgy of the Church brings us into these precincts. Our Lord Jesus Christ was accustomed to this kind of worship—indeed, when he joined his parents and fellow Jews in weekly worship, he entered into the ritual. No one had ever heard of spontaneous public worship. The early Church, in great wisdom, realized that this is a principle that goes to the root of the mystery of our being. Spontaneity is a good and precious thing. The Lord loves any lisping, stammering, broken, and halting words we can offer to him, as he loves the buzzing of bumblebees and the braying of donkeys. But when we come together for the particular act of offering our corporate, regular, recurring adoration to him, then we need a form.

During my twenty-three years as an Anglican, I discovered, and gradually became at home in, the world of liturgy, and of sacrament, and of the Church year. But also as I read in theology and Church history and in the tradition of Christian spirituality, I found myself increasingly acutely conscious of a question: But what is the Church?

Every Sunday at the Anglican liturgy I found myself repeating, "I believe in one, holy, catholic, and apostolic Church." These are words from an era that all of us—Roman, Orthodox, Anglican, Protestant, and unaffiliated—must take seriously, since all of us, whether we are pleased to admit it or not, are the direct beneficiaries of the work of the men who hammered out those words

You and I may think, in some of our less reflective moments, that all we need is the Bible and our own wits. *Sola Scriptura*. Just me and my Bible. But that is an impertinent notion. Every Christian in every assembly of believers in this world is incalculably in the debt of the men who succeeded the apostles. For they are the ones who, during those early centuries when the Church was moving from the morning of Pentecost out into the long haul of history, fought and thought and worked and wrote and died, so that "the faith once for all delivered to the saints" might indeed be handed on. Heresiarchs popped up out of the weeds left, right, and center, and all of them believed in the "verbal inspiration" of Scripture. It was the Church, in her bishops and councils, that preserved the Faith from the errors of the heresiarchs and other zealots, and that shepherded the faithful along in The Way, as it was called.

You and I, insofar as we are familiar with modern Protestantism, and, a fortiori, with Evangelicalism and Pentecostalism, are familiar with a state of affairs that would have been unimaginable to our Fathers in the Faith in those early days. I am referring to the oddity, that, even though we all say we believe in the final and fixed truth of divine revelation, we are nevertheless all at odds when it comes to deciding just what that truth is.

Oh, to be sure, we all agree on the so-called fundamentals of the Gospel—but of course those fundamentals have been articulated and distilled for us by the Church that wrote the creeds. The Mormons and the Jehovah's Witnesses and the Modernists all toil away at the pages of the Bible, but you and I would say they are not getting the right things *out* of that Bible. Why do we say that? Because, whether we acknowledge it or not, our "orthodox" understanding of the Bible has been articulated for us by *the Church*. All sorts of notions, for example, have cropped up about the Trinity, about the mystery of our Lord's divine and human nature, and so forth. The reason you and I are not Nestorians nor Eutychians nor Apollinarians nor Docetists nor Arians nor Montanists is that the Church guarded and interpreted and taught the Bible, and we, the faithful, have had a reliable and apostolic voice in the Church that says, "*This* is what Holy Scripture is to be understood as teaching; and *that* which you hear Eutyches or Sabellius teaching from the Bible, is not to be believed."

But I was speaking of the question that began to force its way into my mind during those years: What is the Church? What may have appeared as a digression just now, when I referred to the men who worked so hard to preserve the Faith, and the bishops and councils who settled upon the right understanding of revelation, was not a digression at all. When I heard myself repeating the words from the Nicene Creed at the liturgy, "I believe in one, holy, catholic, and apostolic Church", I was, of course, saying words that are not directly from any one text in the Bible, and yet that have been spoken in all of Christendom for a millennium and a half now and in some sense constitute a plumb line for us.

The Creed is not Scripture; that is true. But then all of us, whether we come from groups that repeat the Creed or not, would agree, "Oh yes, indeed; that is the Faith which we all profess." Some would add, "But of course, we get it straight out of the Bible. We don't need any creed." The great difficulty here is that Eutyches and Sabellius and Arius got *their* notions straight out of the Bible as well. Who will arbitrate these things for us? Who will speak with authority to us faithful, all of us rushing about flapping the pages of our well-thumbed New Testaments, locked in shrill contests over the two natures of Christ, or baptism, or the Lord's Supper, or the mystery of predestination?

This question formed itself in the following way for me, a twentieth-century Christian: Who will arbitrate for us between Luther and Calvin? Or between Luther and Zwingli, both appealing loudly to Scripture, and each with a view of the Lord's Table that categorically excludes the other's view? And who will arbitrate for us between John Wesley and George Whitefield—that is, between Arminius and Calvin? Or between J. N. Darby (he thought he had found *the* biblical pattern for Christian gathering, and the Plymouth Brethren to this day adhere to his teaching)—and *all* the denominations? Or between the dispensationalists and the Calvinists on the question of eschatology?

A piquant version of this situation presented itself to us loosely affiliated Evangelicals, with all of our independent seminaries and Grace chapels and Moody churches, and so forth. When a crucial issue arises—say, what we should teach about sexuality—who will speak to us with a finally authoritative voice? The best we can do is to get *Christianity Today* to run a symposium, with one article by J. I. Packer plumping for traditional morality and one article by one of our lesbian feminist Evangelicals (there are some) showing that we have all been wrong for the entire 3,500 years since Sinai, and that what the Bible really teaches is that indeed homosexuals may enjoy a fully expressed sexual life. The trouble here is that J. I. Packer has no more authority than our lesbian friend, so the message to the faithful is "Take your pick."

This is not, whatever else we wish to say about it, a picture of things that would be recognizable to the apostles, nor to the generations that followed them. The faithful, in those early centuries, were certainly aware of a great Babel of voices among the Christians, teaching this and teaching that, on every conceivable point of revelation. But the faithful were also aware that there was a body that could speak into the chaos and declare, with serene and final authority, what the Faith that had been taught by the apostles was. Clearly we Evangelicals had been living in a scheme of things altogether unrecognizable to the apostles and the Fathers of the Church.

"I believe in one, holy, catholic, and apostolic Church", I found myself saying in the Creed. What Church? What is the Church? What was the Church in the minds of the men who framed that Creed? Clearly it was not the donnybrook that the world sees nowadays, with literally thousands of groups, big and small, all clamoring, and all claiming to be, in some sense, the Church.

As an Anglican I became aware that I, as an individual believer, stood in a very long and august lineage of the faithful, stretching back to the apostles and Fathers. The picture had changed for me: it was no longer primarily me, my Bible, and Jesus (although heaven knows that is not altogether a bad picture: the only question is, is it the whole picture?). Looming for me, as an Anglican, was "the Faith", ancient, serene, undimmed, true. And that Faith somehow could not be split apart from "the Church". But then, what was the Church?

I realized that, one way or another, I had to come to terms with the Church in all of her antiquity, her authority, her unity, her liturgy, and her sacraments. Those five marks, or aspects, of the Church are matters that all of us,

I think, would find to be eluding us in the free churches. I speak as a Roman Catholic, for that is where my own pilgrimage has brought me in my quest for this Church in all of her antiquity, authority, unity, liturgy, and sacraments. Let me touch on each of these briefly.

First, the *antiquity* of the Church confronts me. As an Evangelical, I discovered while I was in college that it was possible to dismiss the entire Church as having gone off the rails by about A.D. 95. That is, we, with our open Bibles, knew better than old Ignatius or Polycarp or Clement, who had been taught by the apostles themselves—we knew better than they, just what the Church is, and what she should look like. Never mind that our worship services would have been unrecognizable to them, or that our church government would have been equally unrecognizable, or the vocabulary in which we spoke of the Christian life would have been equally unrecognizable. We were right, and the Fathers were wrong. That settled the matter.

The trouble here was that what these wrong-headed men wrote—about God, about our Lord Jesus Christ, about his Church, about the Christian's walk and warfare—was so titanic, and so rich, and so luminous, that their error seemed infinitely truer and more glorious than my truth. I gradually felt that it was I, not they, who was under surveillance. The "glorious company of the apostles, the noble army of martyrs, and the holy Church throughout all the world" (to quote the ancient hymn, the *Te Deum*) judge me, not I them. Ignatius, Polycarp, Clement, Justin, Irenaeus, Cyprian, Cyril, Basil, the Gregorys, Augustine, Ambrose, Hilary, Benedict—it is under the gaze of this senate that I find myself standing. Alas. How tawdry, how otiose, how flimsy, how embarrassing seem the arguments that I had been prepared, so gaily, to put forward against the crushing radiance of these men's confession. The Church is here, in all of her antiquity, judging me.

Second, the Church in her *authority* confronts me. That strange authority to bind and loose that our Lord bestowed on his disciples has not evaporated from the Church—or so the Church has believed from the beginning. If you will read the story of those decades that followed Pentecost, and especially that followed upon the death of the apostles, you will discover that the unction to teach and to preside in the Church that passed from the apostles to the bishops was understood to be an apostolic unction. I, for example, could not start up out of the bulrushes and say, "Hi, everybody! The Lord has led me to be a bishop! I'm starting me a church over here." The whole Christian community— bishop, presbyters, deacons, and laity—would have looked solemnly at me and gone about their business.

The Holy Spirit, in those days, did not carry on private transactions with isolated souls, and then announce to the Church that so-and-so had been anointed for this or that ministry. The unction of the Holy Spirit and the authority of the Church to ordain for ministry were not two random enterprises. The Holy Spirit worked in, and through, the Church's ministry and voice. To be sure, he could do what he wanted to do, as he had always done, being God. Under the Old Covenant, we could say that he worked in and through Israel, but of course you find these extra characters like Job and Jethro and the Magi, coming across the stage from outside the Covenant, yet nonetheless undeniably having been in touch with God. God can do what he wants, of course.

But the Church understands herself to be the appointed vessel for God's working, just as the Incarnation was. Her authority is not her own. She arrogates nothing to herself.

Her bishops and patriarchs are the merest custodians, the merest passers-on, we might say, of the deposit of faith. As a Roman Catholic, I am, of course, acutely conscious of this. When someone objects to me, "But who does the Catholic Church think she is, taking this high and mighty line" (about abortion or about sexual morality or about who may or may not come to the Lord's Table), the answer is, "She doesn't think she's anything particular, if you mean that she has set herself up among the wares in the flea market as somehow the best. She has her given task to do—to pass on the teaching given by the apostles, and she has no warrant to change that. She is not taking her cues from the Nielsen ratings, nor from a poll, nor even from a sociological survey as to what people feel comfortable with nowadays. She didn't start the Church, and it's not her Church."

As a free-church Christian, one can, of course, make up one's mind about lots of things. Shall I fast or not? Well, that's for me to decide. Shall I give alms? Again— a matter for my own judgment. Must I go to church? That, certainly, is my own affair. Need I observe this or that feast day in the Church year? I'll make up my own mind. Piety and devotion are matters of one's own tailoring: no one may peer over my shoulder and tell me what to do.

Indeed, no one may do anything of the sort—*if* we are speaking of ourselves as Americans who have constitutional rights. But if we are speaking of ourselves as Christian believers, then there is a touchstone other than the Constitution by which our choices must be tested.

Our Christian ancestors knew nothing of this sprightly individualism when it came to the disciplines of the spiritual life. They fasted on Fridays, and they went to church on Sundays. Some Roman pope did not make these things up. They took shape in the Church, very early; and nobody dreamed of cobbling up a private spirituality. And likewise with all sorts of questions. Shall women be ordained as priests? It is, eventually, not a matter of job description, nor of politics, nor even of common sense or public justice. The question is settled by what the Church understands the priesthood to be—with cogent reasoning given, to be sure. It is not a question to be left interminably open to the public forum for decade after decade of hot debate.

The Church is here, in all of her authority, judging us.

Third, the Church in her *unity* confronts me. This is the most difficult and daunting matter. But one thing eventually became clear: my happy Evangelical view of the Church's "unity" as being nothing more than the worldwide clutter that we had under our general umbrella, was, for good or ill, not what the ancient Church had understood by the word unity. As an Evangelical, I could pick which source of things appealed most to me: Dallas Seminary, Fuller Seminary, John Wimber, Azusa Street, the Peninsula Bible Church, Hudson Taylor, the deeper life as taught at Keswick, Virginia Mollenkott, John Stott, or Sam Shoemaker. And in one sense, variety is doubtless a sign of vigorous life in the Church. But in another sense, of course, it is a disaster. It is disastrous if I invest any of the above with the authority that belongs alone to the Church. But then who shall guide my choices?

Once again, we come back to the picture we have in the ancient Church. Whatever varieties of expression there may have been—in Alexandria as over against Lyons, or in Antioch as over against Rome—nevertheless, when it came to the Faith itself, and also to order and discipline and piety in the Church, no one was left groping, or mulling over the choices in the flea market.

Where we Protestants were pleased to live with a muddle—even with stark contradiction (as in the case of Luther versus Zwingli, for example)—the Church of antiquity was united. No one needed to remain in doubt for long as to what the Christian Church might be, or where she might be found. The Montanists were certainly zealous and earnest and had much to commend them: the difficulty, finally, was that they were *not the Church*. Likewise with the Donatists. God bless them for their fidelity and ardor and purity, but they were *not the Church*. As protracted and difficult as the Arian controversy was, no one needed to remain forever in doubt as to what the Church had settled upon: Athanasius was fighting for the apostolic Faith, *against heresy*. It did not remain an open question forever.

There was one Church, and the Church was one. And this was a discernible, visible, embodied unity, not a loose aggregate of vaguely like-minded believers with their various task forces all across the globe. The bishop of Antioch was not analogous to the general secretary of the World Evangelical Fellowship or the head of the National Association of Evangelicals. He could speak with the full authority of the Church behind him; these latter gentlemen can only speak for their own organization. He was not even analogous to the stated clerk of the Presbyterian Church, nor the presiding bishop of the Episcopalians, neither of whom is understood by his clientele to be speaking in matters of doctrine and morality with an undoubted apostolic authority.

This line of thought could bring us quickly to the point at which various voices today might start bidding for our attention, each one of them with "Hey—*ours* is the apostolic voice—over here!" That is not my task here. I only would want to urge you to test your own understanding of the Church against the Church's ancient understanding of herself as united, as one. What is that unity? It is a matter that has perhaps been answered too superficially and frivolously for the last two hundred years in American Protestantism. The Church in her unity is here, judging us.

Fourth, the *liturgy* of the Church confronts and judges me. That seems like an odd way of putting it: In what sense can anyone say that the liturgy "judges" me? Certainly it does not condemn me, nor pass any sort of explicit judgment on me. But if only by virtue of its extreme antiquity and universality, it constitutes some sort of touchstone for the whole topic of Christian worship.

Often the topic is approached as though it were a matter of taste: John likes fancy worship—smells and bells—and Bill likes simplicity and spontaneity and informality. There's the end of the discussion. And certainly, as I mentioned before, God receives any efforts, however halting and homespun, which anyone offers as worship, just as any father or mother will receive the offering of a limp fistful of dandelions as a bouquet from a tiny child. On the other hand, two considerations might be put forward at this point.

First, what did the Church, from the beginning, understand by worship—that is, by her corporate, regular act of worship? The Book of Acts gives us little light on the precise shape or content of the Christians' gatherings: the apostles' doctrine, fellowship, the breaking of bread, and the prayers are mentioned. Saint Paul's Epistles do not spell out what is to be done. We have to look to other early writings if we are curious about the apostolic Church's worship. And what we find when we do so is the Eucharistic Liturgy. This, apparently, was what they did as worship. If we think we have improved on that pattern, we may wish to submit our innovations for scrutiny to the early Church in order to discover whether our innovations have in fact been improvements.

Which brings us to the second consideration: the content of the Eucharistic Liturgy. From the beginning the Church seems to have followed a given sequence: readings from Scripture (including the Letters from Paul and Peter and John), then prayers, and then the so-called Anaphora— the "offering", or, as it was also called, the Great Thanksgiving. This was the great Eucharistic Prayer, which took on a fairly exact shape at the outset, and which you may still hear if you will listen to the liturgy in any of the ancient churches. Psalmody, canticle, and hymns also came to be included, and certain acclamations like the Kyrie, eleison! The whole presents a shape of such rich perfection that one wonders what exactly is the task of the "coordinators of worship" on the staff of various churches. The worship of the ancient Church is far from being a matter of endless tinkering, experimenting, and innovating. The entire mystery of revelation and redemption is unfurled for us in the Church's liturgy. That liturgy is here in all of its plentitude, majesty, and magnificence, judging us.

Fifth and finally, the *sacraments* of the Church confront me. The word *sacrament* is the Latin word for the Greek *mysterion*, mystery. Indeed, we are in the presence of mystery here, for the sacraments, like the Incarnation itself, constitute physical points at which the eternal touches time, or the unseen touches the seen, or grace touches nature. It is the Gnostics and Manicheans who want a purely disembodied religion.

Judaism, and its fulfillment, Christianity, are heavy with matter. First, at creation itself, where solid matter was spoken into existence by the Word of God. Then redemption, beginning, not with the wave of a spiritual wand, nor mere edicts pronounced from the sky, but rather with skins and blood—the pelts of animals slaughtered by the Lord God to cover our guilty nakedness. Stone altars, blood, fat, scapegoats, incense, gold, acacia wood—the Old Covenant is heavily physical.

Then the New Covenant: we now escape into the purely spiritual and leave the physical behind, right? Wrong. First a pregnancy, then a birth. Obstetrics and gynecology, right at the center of redemption. Fasting in the wilderness, water to wine, a crown of thorns, splinters and nails and blood—our eternal salvation carried out in grotesquely physical terms. Then pure spirituality, right? Wrong. A corpse resuscitated. And not only that—a human body taken up into the midmost mysteries of the eternal Trinity. And Bread and Wine, Body and Blood, pledged and given to the Church, for as long as history lasts. Who has relegated this great gift to the margins of Christian worship and consciousness? By what warrant did men, fifteen hundred years after the Lord's gift of his Body and Blood, decide that this was a mere detail, somewhat embarrassing, and certainly nothing central or crucial—a show-and-tell device at best? O tragedy! O sacrilege! What impoverishment for the faithful!

May God grant, in these latter days, a gigantic ingathering, as it were, when Christians who have loved and served him according to patterns and disciplines and notions quite remote from those of the ancient Church find themselves taking their places once again in the great eucharistic mystery of his one, holy, catholic, and apostolic Church.

THE TOUCHSTONE OF ORTHODOXY

I would like to lodge something in your imagination—a small touchstone, we might say, by which, if you are so disposed, you may test the ideas and slogans and voguish trends that come your way.

Some such touchstone is necessary, I would think, for anyone who is not content to be a mere fool, and who does not want to be in the tragicomic position of waggling along behind every bandwagon that trundles past. And of course you and I find ourselves at a point in history that has a terribly heavy traffic in bandwagons. More of them are coming at us more rapidly and more noisily than, I should think, at any other time since the expulsion from Eden. You can't avoid them. They rumble and blare and lurch, magnified and amplified by every kilowatt and decibel the media can muster. A hundred years ago, or a thousand or ten thousand for that matter, mountebanks and wizards and false prophets had to whip up what following they could on the strength of their own voice and their own tricks. Now every jester has an instant, vast, and utterly credulous audience via the talk shows. The audience is credulous, I say, because they have been schooled in the tradition of moral and intellectual democracy, in which every idea is

Originally published in a slightly different form in *Christianity Today* (January 5, 1979): 12–16. Reprinted with permission.

worth exactly as much as every other idea, and in which we are committed to giving equal time, not just on the air or in the columns of newsprint, but also in our *minds*—equal time, I say, to Isaiah and Beelzebub, for example, or to Saint Thomas Aquinas and Mick Jagger, or the Blessed Virgin and Bella Abzug. We see the talk-show hosts, sitting in vapid amiability while their guests blithely dismantle the entirety of history and myth, and we pick up this frame of mind. We take on an earnest, humorless frame of mind that gravely receives all data as "input", so that we hear one person telling us about the joys of open marriage, and another about what an emancipation it is to find that one is no longer a man or a woman but a person, and still another going on about what a step forward it will be when we learn to address God as "Our Androgyne, which art in Heaven"—we hear all this, and our only response is, "What I hear you saying is . . ." or "I need this input" or "Heavy" or some such trenchant comment.

But this will not do. It is not good enough to receive all data as though it is arriving from some cosmic grist mill, all of it to be ground into your loaf. There is wheat and there is chaff. Distinctions have to be made. There is good stuff and bad stuff. And the only way to sort out the good from the bad is to *discriminate*. There is no question of a moral democracy, any more than there is of a gastronomic democracy. If you eat vegetables, they will do you good; if you eat toadstools, they will kill you. Somebody has to discriminate between the two and tell us which is which. They are not neutral data for our stomachs. Again, there is no moral democracy any more than there is a mathematical democracy. Two plus two equals four, and we may knock our foreheads on the floor and turn purple in the face because this stark datum doesn't grab us right, or we may shout that our math teacher is an uptight traditionalist and pig—we may adopt this line, I say, but "two plus two equals four" remains unthreatened by our tantrum.

We need a touchstone. We need to learn to discriminate. Your big job in life is to learn the discipline of discrimination, if you didn't learn it in school. The moral vision furnishing this touchstone I am speaking about is that of ancient orthodoxy, or, put another way, of catholic orthodoxy. Now some of you may start in your seats when you read that phrase: "catholic orthodoxy"? The man has gotten his messages mixed up: he thinks he is at the Shrine of Our Lady of Loreto, or Saint Perpetua's Seminary, or somewhere. This is an Evangelical audience.

I am aware of this. That is why I say that the moral vision that obtains here is that of catholic orthodoxy, that is, of the dogmatic tradition taught by the apostles, received by the Church, and agreed upon by all orthodox Christians always and everywhere, whether Anabaptist, Reformation, Latin, or Eastern. The Vincentian Canon is a useful way of phrasing it: *quod semper, quod ubique, et quod ab omnibus creditum est*: what has always been believed, everywhere, and by everyone. Any serious and thoughtful Christian is a dogmatist, not in the sense of being pigheaded or ostrichlike, but in the sense of having a lively awareness that he stands in a defined tradition of received teaching that has been articulated by the holy prophets and apostles and handed down through the centuries. It is spelled out in the Bible and guarded and proclaimed by the Church. The Christian vision is a vision of the eternal, that is, of majestic fixities and mysteries that stand in judgment upon our history and our existence. The Word that was Incarnate in the drama played out on the stage of our history was the Word that articulated order out of chaos in the beginning and that will utter the final summing up at the end.

For this reason, the thinking Christian finds himself in a perpetually ambiguous, not to say peculiar, position vis-à-vis his own epoch. He is, let's face it, what the loose-jointed marionettes of contemporaneity call "uptight". That is, he is, in fact, stuck with an attitude that will be sniffing into things and that wants to ask difficult questions—that wants to take a second and a third look at things, to see how they look when you line them up next to the fixed standard. He is not quite at liberty to let it all hang out: indeed, he suspects that letting it all hang out is what you get in nurseries with babies screaming and vomiting, or in mental hospitals, where they have failed to align their actions with accepted patterns, or at drunken orgies where inhibition and reticence are thrown to the winds.

The Christian will be forever asking how this idea or that one *fits*. Fits what? Fits the pattern, says the Christian—the solemn, blissful, austerely and magnificently orchestrated pattern of glory that we call creation, or the Dance. The Christian will be forever testing things in the light of the bright fixities that Christian vision perceives and celebrates.

This is the reason why Christians are not ordinarily found in the van of contemporaneity. The Palm Sunday mob is the same in every century, forever throwing down their garments and their palms at the feet of the new prophet, hailing and exulting in things simply because they seem new and promising. *Innovative* and *creative* and *unstructured* are their favorite words, but of course by Friday this crowd has gotten bored by the creatively unstructured innovations, so they crucify the prophet and chase after fresh ones. (The point in this metaphor here is simply the flighty frame of mind of the mob, which will give Christians pause when they hear loud slogans abroad: the prophet in question here, of course, *was* bringing in something true, but they had no way of discriminating between him and Simon Magus, or any other zealot.)

It is particularly difficult now for Christians to keep their wits about them and their sights unblurred. The sheer tumble and force of novelty that comes at us all makes it nearly impossible to keep clear in one's imagination—or in one's moral vision, shall we say—the fixities arching over the broil of our history and our fashions. Let me mention a few of the items in this tumble as examples of what I mean. We might call them *cults*, since that is what they are, really.

There is the cult, for example, of the self. You have heard people talking about self-affirmation, and self-discovery, and self-acceptance, and self-identity. The great idea is to discover who you are. Fine. But any Christian will listen to this vocabulary with some wariness, since the vision he is already committed to sees a drastic paradox in this matter of the self. The biblical notion seems to be that we get to point A by heading toward point Z: that is, we move toward authentic self-knowledge by abandoning the quest for self-knowledge. Self-knowledge seems to be more or less irrelevant in this vision. Or at least irrelevant while we are en route to where we are going. Then—ah, then—we get the white stone with our real name engraved on it. This is given to the men who overcome, whatever that means. It does not seem to be promised to those who have sought themselves all along the way. I know this sounds like a cavalier oversimplification, and as though I am jettisoning the whole of the behavioral sciences on the strength of one verse in the book of Revelation. That is not quite what I have in mind. The point I am making here is that no Christian can listen with unmixed belief to popular vocabulary about the quest for the self that so ferociously engages our generation.

Again, there is the cult of frankness. "Let's be honest", meaning thereby, "Let's tell it like it is. If you think it, say it. Don't be uptight. Break down the hedges and barriers of convention that obstruct the openness between you and your brother." Fine. Candor is all to the good. But any Christian will also want to know how we propose to guard the shrine that is the other person and will want to know, before he opens up the shrine of himself to others, just who has the warrant to come in here. Just as (says the Christian) there are high hedges that stand between you and me physically, so that I have no warrant to possess your body unless I am your spouse, so there are high hedges between you and me psychologically and emotionally and spiritually, and I have to know what the warrant is to enter the shrine of your personality before I barge in. For this reason, a Christian will distrust the popular idea, so violently dramatized in the more extreme forms of T-group, that we all have a warrant to know everything about you, just as he distrusts the idea of physical orgies. He does not believe that you can suspend the rules, even for one evening's experiment, physically or psychologically. And, I should think the same would apply religiously: a Christian will enter only very cautiously into the forms of religious exercise that call for us all to be putting all our cards on the table all the time. Not everybody has the warrant to *see* your cards, remember.

This notion, surely, is also at work in the contemporary celebration of "open marriage", where the idea is that we will all be very grown up and very sensible, and get beyond being uptight about some old-timey notions of fidelity and monogamy and so forth. Good heavens, we're modern men

and women now and know how to handle a variety of sexual relationships.

No, says the Christian. That ain't the way it is, baby.
That ain't the way it is. And the same notion would be at
work in the current cult of pornography in magazines and
cinema: the idea there is—how emancipated! how modern!
how un-uptight! But the Christian, curmudgeon that he is,
suspects that this whole Dionysian romp is misbegotten, and
that there are places you *can't* enter with impunity. All religions and all tribes and all myths have known that there are
taboos—all of them, that is, except Sodom, Rome in its
decline, and us.

Or, third, there is the cult of liberation. Here the notion
is, declare your autonomy. Proclaim your emancipation.
Smash the chains tradition has shackled you with. Discard
the conventions and taboos written in the holy books and
set about redefining and reforging human existence. If you
listen to the rhetoric of some of the forms of lib in our
own time, you will hear this eager zest to redefine and reforge
everything. Don't give one moment's courtesy to ten thousand years of myth and history: it's all a cynical plot. The
human race has missed the boat entirely, and we will do it
right.

Well, whatever side of the various lib questions you find
yourself on, if you are a thinking Christian and an orthodox one, you will enter into the discussion with solid com-
mitment to the validity of history (since the drama of your
redemption was played out in history), and with a great
skepticism about the chances of the twentieth century coming upon some emancipating truth that escaped, somehow, the attention of the patriarchs, the prophets, the
apostles, the Fathers, and the rest of the train of sages and
witnesses in history. You will need to move carefully and

painstakingly *through* the data, and you will suspect that the distinction assumed in the Bible between man and woman (for example) is perhaps the richest distinction in the whole creation, and that we blur, or deny, that distinction (it is being attempted now) to our own impoverishment. You will bring, in other words, the touchstone of ancient Jewish and Christian vision to bear upon the hasty slogans of your own decade.

Or again, there is the cult of the unstructured, which I have already mentioned in passing. You have no doubt sat on committees whose job was to plan some event. Sooner or later in the discussion some bright soul pipes up, "I know! Let's just have it unstructured! That way everybody will be free to ..." and so forth. But I daresay you have not sat on a committee where anyone ventured to observe in reply to this suggestion, "Fine, but remember that hell is the ultimately unstructured place." The City of God is measured out four-square, with adamantine foundations and jeweled gates, and that is not just an idea from some kooky prophecy chart. It is there, built into the structure of the universe and our existence, and we dismantle things to our peril. Anybody who was not born yesterday knows that it is the structures and the conventions that help us through chaotic and impossible situations and that gather and bear up our flying emotions. Victory parades, music at marriages or funerals, dances of joy, sonnets of love, liturgical processions: Are these not, every one of them, the structured forms that we bring to raw experience and emotion, and that turn out to be the very things we needed to enhance and heighten our capacity to experience and articulate the events? If we were all left standing about vaguely in the face of huge experiences, we would soon enough find ourselves reduced to the feeble level (alarmingly common in our own time, alas)

of "Oh wow" or "Outta sight." That is to real, profound
experience what pabulum is to pâté: just not as good. Think
of the child who has never been taught the simple convention of saying "How do you do?" Every time he has to
encounter an adult, he is thrust back on his unstructured
spontaneity, and that is misery for him and everyone else.
Or again, think of the feeble and flimsy efforts at bonhomie
that go on at get-togethers where nothing is planned. And
what would we do with our nuptial joy without the splendid structure of the wedding ceremony, or with our grief
without the office for the burial of the dead? Our own era
tries, but it is a pitiable spectacle in an arena filled with
myriads from every tribe and civilization who knew better—
who knew that traditional and ceremonial structures and
courtesies and conventions are the very vehicles that bear
us along. Our era thinks they are cages imprisoning us. A
Christian, of course, will have plowed deep into his imagination the solemn and blissful imagery of the tabernacle
and the Apocalypse, and he will suspect that this is something fairly close to the taproot of things. In this sense he is
a radical—a person who wants to go to the root. He declines
to accept the contemporary definition of radical, which
means simply violent or sweeping or utopian.

A fifth cult in our time is the cult of the convenient,
made possible for us by our stunning advances in technology and medicine. We now have immense mysteries dis-
solved for us by a pill or a test-tube, or a quick visit to the
doctor. Contraception, for example, and abortion are avail-
able on easy demand. It's all quite bracing. But any Christian, with his imagination suffused with the ancient biblical
awareness of the awesome thing that human life is, will want
to know just what it is we are manipulating here. Good
heavens—babies made or unmade at the popping of a pill.

I am urging that the Christian will always have a salting of skepticism in his imagination about the brisk modern traffic in these things. If you disagree with the Catholic Church, you had better have weightier arguments against her than simply the argument that the Church's teaching is *inconvenient*. How do you shoot it down from natural theology? It will take more than shouting, "I have a right to my own body!"

A sixth cult in our time is, of course, the much-celebrated new morality. Here the idea is that we now have fresh light on things, and that no prophets or priests are going to tell us what varieties of sexual activity, say, are legitimate, much less with whom we may enjoy these diversions. We make our own choices now. But a Christian is stuck with all these intractable *taboos* again. You can't do this and you can't do that, until you are as pinched and unhappy as Mrs. Grundy. What's the matter with Christians? Can't they *live*?

And I suppose the answer here is, "Nothing more is the matter with them than has been the matter with the Jews and Muslims and Hindus and pagans all down through history who have known perfectly well that the sexual phenomenon was a high and sacred thing, to be surrounded with the most fierce strictures." Queen Victoria did not make up "conventional morality". Neither did the Puritans. Neither did the Catholic Church. Nor the apostles. Nor the rabbis. A Christian suspects that it is all built into the choreography of the great Dance, and that all these tiresome taboos are actually cues and clues, nudging us on toward our authentic bliss and wholeness. Follow the yellow brick road. That way lies the City.

That's the end of my argument. I hope, even if you disagree with me passionately, that you will see my main point, which is that the Christian vision arises from sources, and stretches toward vistas, that are infinitely beyond the power of mere contemporaneity to alter. *We* didn't set the Dance going, and we can't reorchestrate it. We might even, if we are courageous and radical enough, discover that the pattern of that Dance—observed and obeyed so gravely and joyously by the great company of sages, patriarchs, prophets, psalmists, apostles, confessors, and witnesses, and all the ranks of angels and archangels and thrones and dominations and powers, right up to the terrible cherubim and seraphim themselves—that this pattern is the very guarantor of our true bliss and liberty.

EXISTING THINGS:
SELF, SOCIETY, GOD

WHO AM I? WHO AM I?

If someone were vouchsafed in a dream to listen in on two voices and heard the following fragments—"Who am I?" "... my self-concept", "... identity crisis", "... self-awareness"—uttered repeatedly, and then were asked to guess from this little scrap of data, what century he was listening in on, he would not have much trouble deciding. It will probably not have been Aeschylus and Herodotus talking, nor Aquinas and Siger of Brabant, nor even Alexander Pope and Doctor Arbuthnot. His first guess would be, "Those were voices from the twentieth century."

How can he tell? Why would he not guess fifth-century-B.C. Athens, or thirteenth-century Paris, or eighteenth-century London? Because, he would tell us, he was assuming that the voices were typical of their era, and those remarks belong to the twentieth century.

And he will have been correct, of course. No other century or culture of which we have any records has ever been so galvanized by the particular notion underlying those remarks. No Icelandic saga, no Hebrew psalm, no Navajo legend, no Latin georgic, no Russian novel, has anyone talking quite like that.

Originally published in a slightly different form in *Christianity Today* (July 8, 1977): 10–13. Reprinted with permission. [Slightly updated.—ED.]

The point here is, those fragments are straws in an enormous wind. You can tell a great deal about what is occupying people in a given era by listening to what they say. And you do not have to read very far in the annals or poetry, say, of Greece, or the Middle Ages, or the Enlightenment, before you pick up some notions as to what big questions were at work in their imaginations. If you find people consulting oracles, you will conclude (correctly) that they thought it was terribly important to find out what the gods wanted them to do. Again, if you find them confessing their sins to a priest, you will conclude (correctly) that they thought it was terribly important to behave themselves in a way that would bear the scrutiny of some Divine Tribunal. Or again, if you find them briskly dismantling erstwhile superstitions in the name of Reason, you may safely infer that they trust this faculty.

Our own time is especially marked by the tormented pursuit of the question "Who am I?" To say "especially marked" is to understate it: say rather, hagridden or bedeviled. We seek the answer earnestly, assiduously, nay, desperately. There is hardly a single exchange of cocktail-party chat that in its own blithe way does not assume this vast, laborious quest as being the natural occupation of us all. "My dear, my shrink told me . . ." "Oh, she's very insecure." "I have this thing about my self-image." "He's going to take a year off from seminary to try and find himself."

But it is not only in random chat that we hear the news of this pursuit. The whole enterprise of art in our century bears loud witness to it. The sole burden of poetry, theater, cinema, painting, and fiction in our time is that somewhere in there we lost ourselves and hence must grope pathetically for any straw of affirmation that may float by in the dark. From Eliot's *The Waste Land* through the theater of

Ionesco, Pinter, Beckett, and Albee; the films of Buñuel, Truffaut, Robbe-Grillet, and Bergman; the painting of the Dadaists, the Surrealists, and the ilk of Warhol; to the novels of Faulkner, Camus, Vonnegut, and Saul Bellow, we have sent up flares signaling "Help! What are we?" (We hesitate even to make the cautious affirmation implicit in the question "*who* are we?")

What does it all spring from? From two assumptions, really: first, that it is in fact our business to look into this question of our identity; and second, that somewhere in there the quarry has got lost.

To take the second one first: everyone's identity has got lost somewhere. That is the assumption. Who am I? we ask and can find neither an answer nor any sage who can tell us where to look. To be sure, we attempt it: you can stop at a thousand roadside palmists in Florida and find solace; or you can consult the stars in the afternoon paper in the hope that the Archer or the Crab will help; or you can sign in with a guru of one sort or another, or join a group that will nudge you along toward an answer by getting you to sit in a circle with them, or breathe with them, or take off your clothes, or dance with them, or work through your hang-ups with them. People used to be told to go on an ocean voyage when they were at the end of their tether, the notion being not so much that they find out who they were as that they simmer down and let the salt and the spray and the breeze freshen them up. There was a more remote time when people turned for help to soothsayers, priests, or sibyls, since these practitioners are adept at peering into the darkness where the god lurks, and it was the god who knew the answer they wanted. Now we turn to other practitioners who are adept at peering into the darkness where our identity lurks, since that is what we seek rather than the god.

Where was it lost, this thing we pursue with such zeal? Is it not a naked contradiction for us to be asserting that such a thing as our *identity* can even be in doubt? Surely (a visitor from another planet might protest), you can't mean what you're saying—that you aren't sure who you *are!* You're *you*, clearly. What is it you want to know?

Ah, yes, we would have to explain wearily, but there's more to it than that. These shells by means of which we present ourselves to you are mere carapaces. You think this is what we are, but if you were to poke into us a bit you would find that what is in there has only a very tenuous connection with what you see. In fact, we are almost afraid to raise the question, but a horrible doubt flits by now and again as to whether there is anything in there at all. We've tried poking, and whatever it is in there feels more and more like less and less. Most disquieting.

But how, our interlocutor might pursue, did this state of affairs come about? I have never yet met creatures who weren't sure who they *were*. Most creatures aren't especially interested, much less puzzled, by the fact *that* they are, leave alone *who* they are. Dogs appear to have no problems on this level, and nothing we hear of angels indicates anything like it. But here you all are, paralyzed by the question. How did it all come about?

What would we say? It would be extremely difficult to rake back through history and locate the spot where the question *Who am I?* pushed its way to center stage. We could probably find it somewhere after the Renaissance— somewhere in the eighteenth or nineteenth centuries, no doubt—when, having exiled the gods, we had nothing left to contemplate but ourselves.

But whether Adam knew any such curiosity would be impossible to guess, although given the perfectly harmonious nature of Eden, it may be doubted whether any disjuncture at all had been introduced into the blissful wholeness of his being whereby he might have been disposed to ask who he was. A certain distance is necessary between the asker of any question and the thing asked about, so that when we find an entity (a man) asking about himself, we have found an entity with a fissure running through the fabric of his being. An "asking self" stands on one side and peers across the fissure at the "asked-about self". One way of imagining the perfection and integrity of Adam's being is to say that he enjoyed, like God in whose image he had been made, an undivided wholeness (the Persons of the Trinity aren't *divisions*) totally free from any perplexing and paralyzing question about itself. It may further be wondered whether self-consciousness was not introduced at the Fall, when we made a grab for varieties of knowledge that turned out to be too much for us. (Perhaps it was one of the flies in Pandora's box, too.) Whatever may be the truth here, it is most interesting to note that in the picture of Eden in the Bible, there is not one rag of suggestion that Adam's consciousness was ever turned toward himself. Two things are presented to him, neither of them himself. There is the earth, and he is told to subdue it and fill it and rule it and to receive its bounty. And there is Eve. She is brought to him and immediately his attention is focused on this *other*. His eyes look at her, and he bears witness of her in his first recorded words. She is the form of humanness made for the eyes of the man to contemplate, and vice versa. There were no mirrors in Eden, and the myth of Narcissus may suggest something frightening and important about that.

But of course all this is conjecture. We can only make of Eden what we can from the sparse narrative. It is perhaps worth wondering about.

If we look through ancient history, we find that the question "Who art *Thou*?" is much more lively than the question "Who am *I*?" Men seem to be troubled by the gods, who keep addressing them and presenting themselves to them and asking things of them. The Old Testament bears witness to this, too. Who art Thou, Lord? Alas, I am undone, I have seen the Lord. Where shall I hide from Thy presence? I will not let thee go except thou bless me. The main thing seems to be to come to terms, not with oneself but with what is required of one. There is, before very long, a whole Law, imposed by fiat from outside, describing in effect exactly how things will be, and demanding acquiescence on pain of death. Here is what we are to give our attention to. No one is asked for input. No one's convenience or comfort is considered. And there is not a syllable's worth of recognition given to any problems someone might have over discovering who he is.

That makes it sound grim beyond belief, but if we step back and look at the phenomenon of mankind and how salvation came to it, some such picture emerges. It is all very alien to our gentle ways of thinking, and much too peremptory. God ought to have begun on a much more conciliatory note. He ought to have sat down with us and listened to us. We could have rapped with him about our hang-ups. We could have worked through our problems.

But alas, there it all is, this daunting set of absolutes, imposed on us from the top, and not a whisper in there allowing me time or room to discover myself first.

Or is it quite so grim? Put that way, it is daunting indeed. But then it turns out that the Giver of that high Law is no capricious and maleficent deity tormenting his creatures as wanton boys torment flies. He is Elohim, Adonai, El Shaddai, Jehovah-nissi, the God of Abraham, even, it turns out, the God and Father of our Lord Jesus Christ—Jesus Christ who loved to call himself the Son of Man. One of us. Emmanuel.

Ah. Now there is relief. The picture, surely, has changed. The demands will be relaxed. He knows our frame. He was in all points tempted as we are. He is afflicted in all our afflictions. Perhaps he will help us out of our dilemma. Perhaps, being the Word of God, he will speak comfort to us and affirm us in our sorrowful quest for ourselves. What does he say?

Thou shalt love the Lord thy God with all thy heart. Thou shalt love thy neighbor as thyself. Deny yourself. Follow me. Be kind. Be faithful. Blessed are the pure in heart, and the merciful, and those who mourn, and the peace-makers . . .

Yes. Yes of course. All that. But is there a word about my self-image? Can you tell me how to come to terms with myself? After all, I must find out who I am before I can do anything else.

Must you? To him that overcometh will I give a white stone, and in the stone a new name written, which no man knoweth saving he that receiveth it. Your identity, perhaps, is a great treasure, precious beyond your wildest imaginings, kept for you by the great Custodian of souls to be given to you at the Last Day when all things are made whole.

Some such picture as the above would seem to be indicated in the biblical emphasis. There is a curious lack of any suggestion that our business is to find out who we are. And, if we object that we have to work through our problems before we can set about disposing ourselves rightly vis-à-vis God and our neighbor, we find that the language of both Testaments lacks what we might call any "problem-orientation". We are not addressed, either by Yahweh from Sinai, or by the Son of Man from Olivet, as primarily creatures with problems. The cues given in the Law and the prophets and the Gospel and the Epistles seem, oddly enough for us men who live in the epoch of the quest for identity and self-realization, to point us right away from that focus, right away from much attention on ourselves as objects of our curiosity. Even the very injunctions to repent, or to keep our hearts with all diligence, or to examine ourselves, carry no suggestion that this self-examination is by way of discovering something there (myself) that will be the proper object for my attention. It is to be a clearing away of rubble and impediments so that I can get on with the business at hand, which is that I be delivered from all sin and that I discover, lo and behold, my real freedom and personhood not in looking for *it*, but in learning to love God and my neighbor. It takes the combined efforts of the Law, the prophets, the Gospel, and the Epistles, to help me in this enterprise, but there it is.

There is an obvious objection to this hasty line of thought, of course. It would go something like this: surely you aren't going to string together a few maxims from the Bible and set them suddenly over against the entire, gargantuan preoccupation of our whole epoch? After all, this is the era of behavioral sciences. They are the sovereign disciplines in our century. Here we are, this late in history, only now uncovering the whole unhappy complex of things deep in our insides that poison the well for us, and you tell us to drop all that—the whole enterprise— and pick up a few scraps of Scripture and get on with it. That, surely, is bibliomancy. What about the whole burgeoning area of counseling? The industrialized, computerized, management-oriented, profit-obsessed, materialistic, rationalistic modern era has brutalized people; nay, worse, it has depersonalized them wholly and is stamping them out in stereotypes like nuts and bolts from a press, when all the time their humanity cries out piteously for some recognition and attestation and liberation. And you want them to deny themselves. Fie.

This raises at once the question of the sense in which biblical categories are perennially valid. Do Christ's words to us all need to be recast for this new age of ours, so remote from his early, simple world? Or again, should our understanding of his words be revised so that we hear in his apparently peremptory and harsh maxims some entirely fresh note, unheard by the Fathers, the Reformers, the Pietists, and the rest of our predecessors? Or again, is it a false problem altogether: Is there no tension between these biblical suggestions that our great task is certainly not that of finding out who we are and our own earnest pursuit of this very thing?

Sooner or later it comes down, for any one of us, to how we understand these biblical cues for our own health, and how we are going to help the people who come to us struggling with what are called identity crises and other awful burdens laid on them by the cruelties of life. We can't just quote "Deny yourself" at them and wave them away. How shall we bear faithful witness to the biblical vision of liberty and health and wholeness lying in a direction straight away from ourselves (for the motion of Charity is forever outward) and at the same time patiently and mercifully help them along toward some capacity even to begin to perceive, then to grasp, this great and bracing and taxing self-forgetting bliss they were made for?

It is a sticky question. For, as long as the Word of God lasts, there is no alternative vision of bliss possible, nor any new definition of freedom. We have no warrant to suggest alternatives. The saints are the ones who have won through to that glorious state of affairs—despite whatever frightful personal limitations they staggered along under—where giving equals receiving, and self-forgetfulness equals, lo, self-discovery. The white stone is *given*, not sought. If that name engraved on that stone is not our identity, then what is it?

Perhaps it is a question of our realizing two things: first, that like so many other thunderous achievements of modern civilization, this acute self-consciousness and self-scrutiny that has been laid on us by the sciences of the last one hundred years may be a burden beyond our capacity to manage. Our ids may be there, so to speak, but they may be none of our business, just as the fruit in Eden was there but was not healthy for us to chew on.

Secondly, finding ourselves willy-nilly in such a situation, we may be obliged to use tools never before necessary in man's history, the tools of psychological analysis and so forth, to help extricate us from the prison of our own building. But we shall have to remember that they are, precisely, tools, like forceps or scalpels, which may be called in to excise or gouge in order to relieve a terrible condition, but they are not part of the living thing itself: they are not bone and sinew and nerve. Or, to change the metaphor slightly, the scrutiny of ourselves may be like a drug or a purgative, swallowed not as food and nourishment, but in order to assist us as quickly as possible back to *health*, which is that state of affairs in which our own insides are working quietly and efficiently so that we can get on with the job. The Law and the Gospel may be like old prescriptions, stowed on a high shelf from earlier days. Perhaps the medicines they prescribe—confession (with its corollary of forgiveness) and obedience (with its corollary of freedom)—are more useful than we think. If a patient is so debilitated that he cannot swallow even these nostrums, then of course we must help him with all the secondary skills at our disposal. But sooner or later we will be wanting to get him to the point where he can take these, for then he will be en route to health.

But what of the original question, Who am I? The Christian vision would not be able to see it as the crucial question for us mortal men. We seem to have been obliged to affirm a paradox, namely, that we get to Point A (real self-hood) by heading toward Point Z (self-forgetfulness—the sort of thing enjoined on us in the Law and the Gospels). Whoever we are, these identities of ours are in the keeping of a faithful and able Custodian, and they will be given to us one day. Our task now is to participate in the ripening of those identities by following the cues, not by pawing into the safe.

BALLET AND GENDER

When my wife and I lived in New York, we went often to the ballet. Ballet is a highly civilized art form—strange, I am sure, to those who are not versed in this art, like a very dry wine ("Hey, I like strawberry daiquiris much better!" Poor blighter).

One witnesses a paradox in ballet: a paradox that touches exquisitely on the topic we have in hand in these columns, namely, gender, and, a fortiori, husbands and wives.

There are two sexes on stage in classical ballet. One of them is bigger, stronger, and more awesome than the other in the sheer bravura of the leaps he can execute. That is the man. The other is smaller (usually tiny), more fragile, and more awesome than the other in the sheer weightlessness she seems to achieve. That is the woman. They are equal in grace, skill, intelligence, dignity, beauty, and prowess. (Read this last sentence five times out loud.)

The entire evening passes in bliss for the audience; and my own guess would be that not once does the word "equality" present itself to anyone's mind. We are not witnessing a contest: we are drawn into the great mystery embodied in the dignity of the two sexes. The choreography is structured, with perfect punctilio, to exhibit the magnificent reciprocity (not

Originally published in a slightly different form in the Gordon College *Tartan* (Fall 2002). Reprinted with permission.

identity) of the two sexes. No one thinks less of the ballerina that she cannot leap as far as the *danseur*. No one thinks less of the *danseur* that he cannot execute the minutely detailed movements of the ballerina. The two complement (but do not copy) each other.

Another part of the paradox: of course the man is bigger and stronger and can "do" more than the ballerina. *But*—the whole of his masculinity is brought into subjection to one, single, not-to-be-gainsaid task: to set forth for the delight of the whole audience this woman in all of her grace. Of course he is the one who lifts her high above his head (she cannot reciprocate). Of course he steadies her in her pirouettes (likewise, she does not do this for him). The entire joy of the thing is *the reciprocity, which is different.* If someone, in the name of that grim, grey, drab, jejune category so popular in our own pitiful epoch, namely, *equality*, came along and demanded, on pain of a boycott, that the choreographer equalize the roles, the choreographer would shoot himself, the audience would demand their money back, and the dancers would be aghast.

For a person who sees the two sexes as the most exquisite and mysterious duality in a creation already a great chiaroscuro of rich dualities (dawn and dusk; mountain and valley; hot and cold; edelweiss and Everest; sweet and tart), the last thing he wants is to smudge out this elegant distinctiveness in the name of a juridical egalitarianism. My own guess is that, at present, nearly every man who goes by the name Christian is terrified lest he appear to harbor any rag of a notion that the man should be the "head" in the marriage relationship. Poor Saint Paul has been stood on his aching apostolic head over the last thirty years in the agonized effort to make him unsay what he clearly says. Please to remember that current Evangelical exegesis on this topic was developed in the wake of the militant feminist movement. No one had, up until then, ever witnessed such efforts being mooted. What had been, for eons, the source of the greatest ecstasy for us mortals, namely, the fact that we are two sexes, *and not identical*, has become the arena of fury, frustration, desperation, and sullenness.

But what am I leading up to? My opposite number in this present dialogue cites Saint Paul and Genesis. It may be remembered that Saint Paul roots the mystery of the husband's burden of "headship" not in the Fall, but in the creation, and in the great mystery of Christ and the Church. Should I love my wife as Christ loves the Church? That would seem to be my biblical set of marching orders. Should she love me also thusly? Well—Saint Paul drops his great metaphor there, much to the discomfiture of those who try so sedulously to make Holy Scripture mesh with the agenda of contemporaneity. Of course the love she offers to me has for its pattern our Lord's own "*self-donation*", as mine toward her should. But it is no good straining at the obvious, and trying to find a way to tiptoe around Sacred Scripture, and the way it has been understood by the Church for two thousand years, and by the rabbis before that. There is some mystic sense, which can only ennoble both me and my wife, in which I must bow and receive the mantle of "headship" in my household. Am I the boss-man? Nope. Ask anyone who knows my wise, godly, brilliant (*summa cum laude*), tough wife. But does she insist that I not shirk my duty as "head"? *Yes.* But in the more than forty years of our marriage, I have never once uttered the words "Quiet, woman: here's how we're doing it. I'm the head man in this show." And yet I know that, in a mystery, I stand before the Sapphire Throne as, in some sense, the one finally answerable for this family.

There are two equal tragedies that afflict marriage now. The one is the all-too-common situation in which the man (men are usually oafs) bosses his wife about. But the other is equally tragic, namely, that of the man who, terrified of the mystery of his masculinity, refuses to accept this mantle and tries to set up some sort of "fair" or "equal" enterprise (love knows nothing at all of those words: they come from the hellish world of litigation), with "equal" slices of the pie, alas, and all the squinting and calculating and gerrymandering that go along with that gritty effort. My wife is my friend, yes: but in the mystery of creation, she is infinitely, infinitely more than that. She is woman and I am not. She is the one who has given me my masculinity—not by trying to ape men (what a sad travesty that is), but by being gloriously woman.

One last metaphor: in traditional ballroom dancing, the man leads. Is this because he is a better dancer? Or is he better looking? Or is he just a superior being? No, no, a thousand times no, we would all shout. Then what? Anyone who knows the joys of ballroom dancing knows that the entire being of the woman cries out to be thus "led", and that the entire frame of mind of the good man in dancing is: "Look everyone! Look at this woman! She is the glory of this dance. You are wasting your time looking at me."

TO BEAR MY FATHER'S NAME

An Awesome Honor

As I sit at my desk writing, a number of eyes gaze down on me. They look out from several icons, three pictures of John Henry Newman and a small ceramic figure of Saint Edward the Confessor.

This is all very august and alarming, this cloud of witnesses. I sometimes fancy that they are saying to me, "What are you doing?" or more narrowly, "What are you thinking?" or worst of all, "What are you?"

But ranged around the alcove where my desk sits is a frieze that is more alarming yet. In it are five huge photographs, and the gentlemen who look down on me from them are my father, his father, his uncle, and his two grandfathers.

Now it would all be very well if the interest here were merely genealogical; it is heady to point to power and glory in one's forebears, but I do not belong to one of the families that can do much of that; there are no Cabots or Lodges or Winthrops there. So it is not a gallery of the noble and renowned under whose eyes I sit.

Or rather, not the renowned. But not noble? On two accountings at least I ought to reconsider that. First, being a Christian, I stand under the authority of the divine law

Originally published in a slightly different form in *Christianity Today* (June 6, 1980): 16–19. Reprinted with permission.

that enjoins us to honor our fathers and mothers. That may seem an oddity, indeed sheer mindlessness, in this era of orgiastic self-analysis, which eagerly and remorselessly begins by rooting one's own "problems" in one's parents' short-comings, thereby dismantling any honor supposed to attach to them. But for any serious Jew or Christian, a most sol-emn interdict lies across this path (see Ex. 20:12). Whoever it may be who bears the responsibility for pointing out a man's faults, it is not his son.

But also on a second accounting, I rescind the hasty com-ment that these fathers who look down on me are not among the noble. Oh, to be sure, you will not find them in Debrett (the list of peers). But their names and achievements are in a higher register, one kept with complete faithfulness by angels—at least so one might gather from the visions of Saint John the Divine.

What achievements? And in what way am I, middle-aged myself, obliged to pay honor to my fathers under this ancient and divine command?

No doubt a man may do this in any number of ways. Four occur to me: I can remember them; I can give thanks for them; I can follow their example; and I can speak of them, especially to my children.

Once more one feels obliged to protest rather awk-wardly here, since the whole enterprise is so embarrass-ingly anachronistic. How is an activity like this to be kept alive when the thing that is dinned at us all with dazzling and deafening iteration, by every kilowatt and decibel avail-able, is that we cut loose? To be authentically ourselves (we are told), we must not only declare our independence from whatever is past: we must positively disavow it. Whatever our fathers espoused or embodied is to be avoided like the pestilence. We must be "now" people (the adverb has, alas, apparently been dragooned into service as an adjective by the breathless zealots of contemporaneity. Alas for the poor word; alas for English syntax; alas for the sensibility that can spawn horrors like this).

But how shall I remember my fathers? Two of the five gentlemen looking down on me from above my desk I do not remember at all: they are the two great-grandfathers. Of these two, I know almost nothing of my father's paternal grandfather except that I bear the surname he passed on to his posterity. But that is a heavy thing. What is a name? What is a good name? It is rather to be chosen than great riches.

What makes a name good? As far as the history books go, it would seem to be a matter of the bearer having exhibited some great valor or intrepidity or integrity or service to mankind. For most of us, the only throng witnessing what we are making of our name will be not the jostling multitude with klieg lights and video cameras, but only the host of saints and angels; but when you come down to it, that is as venerable a company as any we will find in the Royal Enclosure at Ascot, or even in the audience at the Oscar presentations.

So, what duty do I owe to this man of whom I know next to nothing, this man with the high stiff collar and the thoroughly "manly" profile (that was a Victorian word, since rejected by more timorous generations), and the eyes in which you seem to see great gentleness and great reticence dancing oddly with great wit and humor—an amusing and fugitive business that I can see looking out at me now, more than a hundred years later, from the eyes of my brothers and sisters and *their* children.

I know more about the other great-grandfather, Henry Clay Trumbull. His eyes twinkle quite unabashedly, and an

immense beard cascades down his chest. He was a chaplain
in the Union Army during the Civil War, and he seems to
have had a hand in bringing the Sunday school movement
to America during the nineteenth century. Christians who
trace their religious lineage back through mainstream
Evangelicalism to good Fundamentalism (the Moody-
Wheaton-Dallas-Columbia Bible College–Scofield Bible–
Sunday School Times connection, so to speak) know his name,
if they are old enough. He was "illustrious" (another nice
old word), and people looked to him for strong leadership
and faithful teaching, which he gave.

He died some decades before I was born, but he existed
for me not only in photographs in family houses but also in
the stories kept vigorously alive in the family by the for-
midable array of *grand-dame* great-aunts, all of whom were
his daughters and all of whom seemed to be looking at you
through lorgnettes, even though they weren't. The main
thing about this family seems to have been its explosive
violence, which was always saved in the nick of time by
merriment. Do not imagine bitter shouting matches such
as you might see in TV soap operas: rather, there would be
loud and frenzied bursts of polysyllabic frustration, vexation, or rage, going off like a Roman candle, and, like a
Roman candle, dissipating in a shower of coruscating
harmlessness.

Once, for example, when my father's father was courting
the young lady who was to become his wife (my grand-
mother, that is), he heard a stentorian bellow from upstairs.
Hastening up in the greatest anxiety, and expecting the apocalyptic worst, he found my great-grandfather (his father-
in-law-to-be) dancing in rage in his study, demanding to
know *why* books always fell to the *left* when they flopped
over in the shelves. This sort of thing has furnished generations' worth of hilarity at family gatherings for us, not

least because we all see this very volatile elixir boiling through our own veins. But it may be that same elixir, purified and made holy, that made this man so energetic and uncompromising a champion of godliness.

My father's father, Philip Howard, Sr., I knew until he died when I was 11. He was terribly infirm, having had at least one severe stroke before I was born, and he was almost blind into the bargain. So my recollection of him is of his shuffling about, being cared for with infinite solicitude by my aunt, his daughter. Even to my young eyes, there was a tragic irony in seeing a napkin being tucked at dinner under the chin of this man whom the Christian world seemed to think, and whom I knew, was a great and noble man.

When he laughed, though, I saw decades of hearty male camaraderie, and of his beloved hiking and fly-fishing in the mountains of New Hampshire, all coming out in their sheer, hardy good health and vigor. He seemed to move in an almost palpable aura of what I can only describe as the particular sanctity one associates with the orthodox past of Philadelphia Presbyterianism: gentlemanly, civilized, gracious, urbane, sober, and merry.

It is a brand of churchmanship that does not exist in our own time as far as I know, but I am glad to have seen it. My grandfather knew intimately all the early Fundamentalists, in the days when there was no stigma other than orthodoxy attached to that word. It was only later that it came to be associated with the rather hectic, tawdry, and semi-Manichean piety for which it seems to be blamed nowadays.

The fourth picture above my desk is of my father's uncle, Charles Gallaudet Trumbull. He was the one son in the huge family of daughters over which my great-grandfather reigned. I remember seeing him once or twice in my infancy, but my main impression of him is from family stories, the earliest of which is of his smashing, as a small boy, a closet door to splinters.

One of his sisters had locked him in with the pledge that she would let him out the instant she heard his cry for release. The catch was that, once she had him locked in, she proceeded to run shrieking about the house with her ears stopped up so that she could not hear him, thus technically keeping her word. (They were taught a fierce standard of truthfulness in that family.)

It may be pointed out that his bursting with such violence from this entombment is to be attributed to a terrible plague of claustrophobia that gripped, and still grips, the entire family. I and my daughter still eye tight places nervously. This great-uncle became famous in the sector of American Christendom of which I am speaking on a twofold accounting. For one thing, he was instrumental in importing from England the so-called Keswick teaching, which also went under the name of the "victorious life". His two pamphlets, *The Life That Wins* and *The Perils of the Victorious Life*, were influential beyond all calculating in the life of early twentieth-century American Evangelical piety. Second, he was for many years the editor of *The Sunday School Times*.

But this needs a paragraph to itself, since that journal is indistinguishable from, and indeed almost synonymous with, four of the five men of whom I am speaking (the only one not included being my father's paternal grandfather, a physician whose interests did not lie along these lines). *The Sunday School Times* began in the mid-nineteenth century and lasted just over a century. During its heyday it enjoyed an eminence probably unknown by any journal nowadays.

It had a reputation for absolute integrity and trustworthiness, and for editorial purity, and for wise and sober Christian common sense that would be as out of date now as the statesmanship of Lord Palmerston.

My great-grandfather was the first editor, his son (my great-uncle) was the second, and my father the third (rather like Henry I, II, and III, whose reigns seemed to span century after century). My grandfather, Philip E. Howard, Sr., was president of the company. It was a dynastic affair to be sure, but no dynasty was ever less "dynastic": there was nothing imperious or megalomaniacal about any of these men, strong though they were. I really do think that I have been given some glimpse of what is meant by that odd scriptural comment about Moses—the giant Moses—being *meek*, since I have known men like that—my forebears.

Which brings me to the last of the five, my father, Philip E. Howard, Jr. He was, I think, the meekest man I have ever known. Not the weakest: the meekest. There had been funneled down to him all these generations of orthodoxy and conviction and integrity, plus a passionate love for the outdoors and a wry humor. I suppose almost everything I think about God and the world and existence—especially about contemporary existence—has been shaped by my inheritance, and most especially by my father.

I don't think he was aware of doing any particular "shaping" other than passing on faithfully, as thousands of generations of godly fathers have done since Abraham, the counsel of God. Or to put it another way: the thing that was supreme in his mind, taking precedence even over his responsibility as editor of *The Sunday School Times*, which weighed on him cruelly, was raising his six children to love and serve God.

As it happens, he accomplished this—we are all past middle-age now, and all remain within the pale of conservative orthodoxy, which is no credit to us: there is a heritage to which we are accountable. But not for one minute of his life would he have predicted success on this front. He prayed most earnestly for all of us at least twice a day, but first during his morning prayers. These began at five o'clock and included one to two hours of Bible study, Scripture memory work, some systematic reading in Matthew Henry's *Commentary* (a seventeenth-century work), and then prayer. He prayed for his responsibilities, his friends, missions, Christians all over the world, and then his family.

We all knew we were prayed for by name. Once in a while if I happened to have tiptoed downstairs early and his study door was open, I could see him kneeling at the chair in his study with a blue afghan over his shoulders. I do not know what images young boys form of their fathers these days, but I for one cannot be grateful enough for this one.

I am sure that a good deal of his influence on his children came in the form of his own tastes and inclinations. To the eye of the 1980s, he would look austere and distinguished, although he never thought of himself as either. He wore dark blue or gray, wool, three-piece suits, dark ties with tiny dots or designs in them, and long, black, silk socks. He thought of himself as ungainly and would regale the family with tales of his pratfalls and maladroitness. Social situations made him uneasy: he became edgy in the neighborhood of loud, back-slapping male bonhomie or too much female burbling.

He loved to sit down at the piano like a great spider and play his favorite hymns, which ranged from William Cowper and Isaac Watts to "Praise Him! Praise Him!" or "All the Way My Savior Leads Me". His soul turned to ashes in the presence of any sort of religious tomfoolery such as the high jinks of cheap preachers and the treacly words and worse melodies of the "choruses" that dominated Fundamentalist piety in the forties (my earliest recollections). We never heard him scoff or rail at anyone's piety, but we knew that a great deal of what was abroad agonized him. And yet he remained absolutely faithful to the embattled minority of conservative Protestants known as Fundamentalists who struggled and lived for biblical fidelity in those very dark days of the Modernist ascendency. I myself would guess that one reason none of his six children has ever been inclined to leave the Faith is that we had nothing to despise or rebel against in what we saw in our father (and, I may say, in our mother).

He loved very simple pleasures, too. The days of our upbringing were the decades of depression and war, so there was not much chance for luxury and waste in any event, but the simplicity of his tastes and preferences had a purity and integrity about them that was exquisite. He was an amateur ornithologist, so we all grew up in a world in which black-capped chickadees, winter wrens, tufted titmice, and hermit thrushes were important inhabitants, and you cannot go far astray with that crowd. He could imitate the songs of these birds almost perfectly, and if there are any residual and remote echoes of Eden left in our poor world, it must be these songs. Here again, his influence on our imaginations was not something he calculated.

Early in these brief reminiscences I mentioned four ways in which a man might pay honor to his fathers. In these comments I have touched on the first and the last of these ways, namely, remembering my fathers and speaking of them. As for the second and third, those I must try to do myself, day by day. Insofar as I give thanks for these men, it is a salutary discipline for my own soul, for it is an offering enjoined on me by the Most High, and all such offerings come back to the offerer multiplied a thousandfold.

The real rub comes in the third item: following their example. Alas. What a farce for me even to presume to place myself in this lineage. Ah—but that is not a matter of choice. My fathers, like everyone else's fathers, are part of the given data, like the century in which one is born or the color of one's hair. Well, then, heaven help me to follow their example well enough so that thirty years from now, if my own son has pictures like these five over his desk, he may not be ashamed to add a sixth.

THE YOKE OF FATHERHOOD

Suddenly, after ten thousand years of myth and history, we find ourselves floundering in a marsh. The footing upon which our forebears proceeded through life has fallen away, and we are awash in the fen.

What marsh? What fen? What footing?

The footing, surely, would have been the whole set of suppositions that lay underneath the ordinary business of man's life for all tribes, all cultures, and all civilizations, Oriental, African, Occidental, or Oceanic, for as many eons as we can uncover. One of these suppositions, and one that appears to have been vastly widespread, was that mankind appears under the splendid and dual modality of male and female, and that this is good. It took no special perspicacity to see this: any savage, any peasant, any coolie, proceeded on this assumption, along with the sages, seers, and saints. All young men and women becoming aware of each other, all bridegrooms approaching their brides, all husbands and wives coupling fruitfully, all fathers and mothers united in rearing their sons and daughters so that they in their turn might enter this wonderful Dance—they all thought, if they thought about it at all, that the distinction was there, and given, and clear, and rich.

Originally published in a slightly different form in *Christianity Today* (June 23, 1978): 10–14. Reprinted with permission.

But suddenly we are told that it has all been a mistake. The distinction that has appeared to everyone as such a bright fixity, and that has nourished all song and story, and has gilded all human ordinariness with bliss, and from which has sprung all manner of valor and charity and nobility and joy—this distinction is cultural only. It is superficial. It is irrelevant. Nay, it is pernicious. We are *persons*, not men and women. Pray don't chain us down to these heavy and embarrassing fleshy categories. There is an entity "me" that has nothing to do with the costume under which I am obliged to masquerade. I (a man, alas) am indistinguishable from you (a woman, alas). You and I have nothing to gather from our anatomy. Our bodies furnish no cues to anything more far-reaching than necessary biology. Some mechanism, of course, had to be devised for multiplying the race, and this seems to be how the pieces fell. But let's leave it at that.

This is not a straw man (or straw person, shall we say) that I have conjured. I never could have thought it up. But it has been offered to us in the last half-decade, and it is called the androgynous ideal; it underlies a great deal of the public debate on the topic of sexuality now. It is sometimes even urged by religious people that Jesus was a sort of crypto-androgyne, the idea being that he was mild and could weep and therefore does not fit society's stereotypes as to what maleness means.

But surely Christian vision would see all this as Gnostic? That is, there have always been efforts to disengage earthly existence from the prison of flesh, and to fly to the heavenly ether where we are liberated into real and eternal life, unhampered by these bodies. Eastern religions, mystery cults, and all forms of Gnosticism and Manicheanism offer this as the desideratum. But early in the game, the Church condemned the whole effort as heterodox. She did this because she espoused the doctrine of the Incarnation. This is the worst possible scandal. God is a spirit. It is too mortifying that he should appear in human flesh, not just in a charade, but really, truly united to that flesh, taking our nature to himself and *becoming* man. All the gods, at one time or another, popped down in human form (usually it was to satisfy their concupiscent desire for some nymph or shepherd boy). But only the God of Israel can be called Emmanuel. "When Thou tookest upon Thee to deliver man, Thou didst not abhor the Virgin's womb", says the *Te Deum*. That's getting clinical.

Indeed, all the great acts in the drama of redemption proceed in grossly carnal terms. Creation (he *made* these things—these pebbles and flatworms and radishes); Covenant (you had to lug stones and build altars, and knife your best lamb in the throat); Incarnation (he did not abhor the Virgin's womb); Passion (the drama gets down to pieces of timber and gashes); Resurrection (oh-oh—just when we thought the flesh had been overthrown, out it comes again); Ascension (this is too much: that flesh taken into the midmost mysteries of the triune Godhead forever); Eucharist and baptism (things—physical things—at the center of Christian vision and practice for as long as time lasts).

Clearly, Christians are stuck with a whole scheme of things that invests matter with enormous significance. Nay, that is putting it too mildly. It is more than a question of attaching some adventitious meaning to matter, thus turning everything physical into symbols or some such. Is it not, rather, that the Christian vision would see the creation as one, whole, seamless fabric, with everything from seraphim to jellyfish to shale participating in one good order? The distinction between the visible and the invisible, or matter and spirit, is an unhappy, post-Fall distinction, a fissure in the fabric, introduced by us when we made our grab in Eden and doomed ourselves to live thereafter in a divided world. The disjuncture is of our making, and we must live with it. No doubt our very eyeballs were affected at the Fall, so that we can no longer see things as undivided. But Christian vision would have a prior notion of a realm in which there is a lovely harmony at work entailing all things, so that the very external shapes and forms of things bespeak what they *are*.

But what does this have to do with fatherhood?

Would it not be that, over against the current effort to redefine sexuality entirely, and hence to reshuffle the roles that have attached to male and female, and thus to realign family life in brand-new patterns—would it not be that Christians will want to pause in front of three huge data before they join this brisk effort?

First, universal wisdom. If all tribes and cultures, and all sages and poets, have seen something a certain way, and it has appeared to them, not as horrid but as blissful, even a cause for celebration, then surely any reflective person will hesitate before agreeing to recast the whole picture under the pistol of one decade's debate?

Second, nature: the stark biology of the matter attests to what all poetry, myth, and ceremony have celebrated, namely, that the male, bearing that particular aspect of the *imago Dei* disclosed in male stature and anatomy, enacts somehow a role of initiator and seeker. The sexual imagery is too vivid to need comment here. And we may also guess, in this connection, that the reason the poets and philosophers and mathematicians and composers and conquerors and chairmen have been mostly men has been not so much because of a diabolically successful plot to keep women at their brooms, as because the male of the species is bedeviled with an odd awareness of being on the perimeter of things somehow and must seek the center. Hence he has tried, fiercely, sorrowfully, desperately, to bring some order out of chaos—in poetry, philosophy, music, conquest. Whereas the woman, bearing the image of God under the species of womb and breasts, is already there at the center of the operation. She does not need to go anywhere, as it were. Perhaps old jests about women's intuition were not wholly misbegotten. If this is all wildly fanciful, and too embarrassingly folklorish, we may at least wonder whether, when we meet protohistoric and universal *types* (man as father, lord, initiator, protector, and woman as mother, lady, receiver, and nourisher), we have come upon, not stereotypes, but *arche*types.

Third, Scripture. The Bible assumes sexual differentiation in its language. It is fervently urged now, of course, that the revelation came to us during patriarchal centuries, and that the language is thus culturally conditioned. God as King and Father, and Jesus as Son and Bridegroom—this is all ancient Mediterranean and really ought to be seen for what it is. The difficulty here is the old difficulty about image and thing. When you change the imagery, you change the thing. Jesus as kind corner cop rather than shepherd, for example, since ghetto kids don't know about sheep. It is a plausible and well-intentioned effort, but loses something. We may need to tell city kids about sheep somewhere in there. Or the image of the Cross: we don't crucify the misfits in our society now, we hurry them to analysts' couches. Hence, in the effort to update Christian imagery, we ought to substitute tiny silver couches on the chains around our necks, since the Cross is a wholly outmoded symbol. But surely something has got lost here? Or God as King: we don't have kings in modern secular democracies, so perhaps we ought to begin speaking of him in more contemporary, and thus more gripping, terms—as Chairperson of the ad hoc caucus, perhaps. (There would be a squeak trying to huddle all those syllables into, say, Handel's acclamation of God as "King of Kings", where he set the music up for only three syllables; but we can surely manage this.)

The point here is that Christians suspect that biblical language and imagery judge us, and not vice versa. It spreads and arches over all of history, like the Christos Pantocrator looming gigantically over Orthodox church interiors. If the Psalms sing about dragons and great deeps praising the Lord, we are not altogether prepared to jettison the picture when the Loch Ness expedition fails to rouse the monster. If we hear of morning stars singing, we want to hold onto the picture somehow, as a clue and glimpse of dazzling realities beyond the reach of our radio antennae that don't seem to be catching that song. If Revelation is full of the imagery of crowns and scepters and horses, we hesitate before substituting fedoras, attaché cases, and flying saucers. If the apostolic writings are full of pictures of husband as "head" and wife as "body" (pictures drawn by the Apostle, not from the Curse, as is frequently urged now, but from the twofold source of creation and the eschatological mystery of Christ and his Spouse), then we will want to know what on earth that may mean before we replace it all with our sociology texts.

It is for some such reasons as the above that I find myself unprepared to espouse the new castings of family life so briskly urged upon us now. If I may transpose into a first-person key here, I may list the notions that seem essential to me in my experience of fatherhood.

First, it is not *my* experience in any case. Or rather, it is, but it is mine only in the sense that I have stepped into a mystery that has been here since the beginning. All fathers have stepped into it, whether they are aborigines, tsars, or bank clerks. For all of them, there has been the great mystery of entering (literally) into the knowledge of the other, and of finding that knowledge to be both ecstatic and fruitful. This other creature, this third party, issues from the mystic (and very carnal) union of the two who bear the two antiphonal modes of the divine image.

What does it all mean? What on earth is all this plumbing and obstetrics about? Is it not the enactment, under the species of male and female anatomy, of what is true, namely, that we are made for each other, and that our wholeness is to be found in thus uniting, and, further, that this wholeness turns out to be, not a solitude, but fruitful? The very biology attests to the theological mystery: I, a man, am made for the other—but not just any other. I am made for the other who is also the image of God, but *not me*. Not a mirror image of myself. (Hence, whatever may be being said now in behalf of homosexual union, one will want to have this Edenic picture at the bottom of his imagination, in which the Adam and the Eve—me and my wife, now, ten thousand generations later—enact the mystery of mankind in which the image of God, under the dual modality of man and woman, appears in its wholeness.)

My experience of fatherhood, then, is not mine. It depends upon my being united with a woman, my lady and wife, as all fathers have been united. (Promiscuity, and hence the fathering of "fatherless" children, is nobody's ideal.)

Secondly, my experience of fatherhood is unfair. It is unfair because it absolutely cuts me off from ever being a mother. Here is a whole, rich aspect of being human that I, because of my anatomy, am cut off from. I shall never, never know the experience of bearing a child in my body. I shall never suckle an infant. I may dandle my babies, and change their diapers, and bathe them, and rock them to sleep, and kiss and fondle and love them (and I love all that)—but I have not carried them in my womb and nursed them at my breast. It is unfair. My wife has entered into mysteries that I cannot quite share. I may stand next to her at the delivery table (I did), but it is she and not I who is physically experiencing parturition.

But no. It is only some testy, crabbed, pinched, and mercenary frame of mind that will complain thus. It will be the frame of mind that is forever demanding equal time and equal shares and equal slices of the pie. Dear heaven! My wife got the *whole* pie of motherhood. Where's the equality in this universe? Where's the justice? I'm a second-class citizen! I protest! I demand ...

No. No, no, no, say all lovers, and all mothers and fathers since Eden. What are you talking about? These mysteries of love, and of fruitfulness, and of birth and fatherhood and motherhood, know nothing at all of your calculating, political, committee-model language. Of *course* your wife got the whole pie, and she got it for one reason and one reason only, and that the worst possible reason: she is a woman. You are utterly discriminated against on the basis of your sex alone. You are cut off from the absolutely central human thing, if this is how you insist on seeing it.

So I am bidden to retreat from my headlong protestations of equality, as Peter was hushed up with his chattering on the Mount of Transfiguration, and to look again at the splendor unveiled.

I, like all husbands, have been united with a woman who brings as her great gift to me that aspect of the image of God that completes me. And I offer to her the only gift I can offer, my very limitation, namely, my manhood, which is that aspect of the divine image made to complete her, and which I bear. She was made to be a mother. Her egg and womb await the fructifying seed. I was made to be a father. My loins offer that seed to the only matrix that will receive and vivify it. She was made to be a mother. Her breasts and arms await the infant who will find nourishment and comfort there. And I? What gift may I bring now? What role may I play in this unfolding drama? Have I only a bit part in the first scene, never to reappear until the curtain call?

It would not seem so. The image I bear, of maleness, and the role I enact, of husband and father, are deeper and more far-reaching than the single act of procreation. That forms part of my role, of course. But then?

Then I am still husband and father. It is my appointed gift, or burden, or yoke, to *be* husband and father, precisely because I am a man, it would seem. With respect to my wife, I am instructed by the Apostle to be "head". Not boss: head. The Apostle gives me my cue here by referring to the headship of the divine Bridegroom vis-à-vis his spouse. It is a headship brought as gift, not wielded as club, and offered—"submitted", if you will—*to* her, *for* her, in obedience to the divine choreography, so to speak. I did not think it up.

What is this headship, if it is not "boss-hood"? Here again, I must take my cues from the Apostle, nay, from the Lord himself: it seems to have something to do with answerability before God. Somehow I am the one who stands before the Most High as the one responsible for this family. Responsible all by myself? Surely not, since I am made one with my spouse here. And yet, just as the one, single act of procreation distributed itself between the two of us for one single end, so here there is no question of exchanging roles, any more than there is of Christ, in the interest of his spouse's health and freedom, stepping aside and saying, "Right. Now we adopt the round-table model." What can it mean? I am not sure *what* it means, any more than I can unscramble and plot out the mystery of the Eucharist. But I obey, and in obeying, move perhaps slowly but nonetheless farther and farther, toward the place where I will be vouchsafed to see what it all means.

And with respect to my children? It means that I bear the yoke of fatherhood. Again, I did not make up the terms of this task. And I am unable, for reasons I have listed above, to assign it all to a dark plot, or to society's stereotypes. I passionately believe that this ancient office is rooted in all the divine mysteries, and unfurled in creation, and enjoined upon me and all fathers for as long as time lasts. Nothing new—but nothing outdated either.

I and my wife and our children live now, as everyone does, under the heady mythology of change. Our epoch is in the process of changing the terms of everything, not just politics, ecology, economics, and technology. Genetics, sexuality, morality—it is all to be redone. This mythology has a wide and eager hearing in the Evangelical church, and very convincing voices plump for it. It frequently entails a delicate rewriting of the Bible, in the name of "biblical" radicalism. I would be one of those who are not prepared to whisk away the picture of family structures, say, as that has been understood by the prophets and Fathers and the whole Church, for all of history. No matter what the world is into which I usher my children, I will want them to have experienced a realm in which love and authority are synonymous, and where liberty and obedience are synonymous, and where something of what is true in the eternal realm is made present and visible in ordinary, flesh-and-blood family relationships. Unlike the Freudians, I do not believe that we have projected mankind's experience of fatherhood onto the cosmos and come up with the notion of God the Father. On the contrary, I believe that the Father has given us a little toehold into something of that eternal Fatherhood by giving to us the experience of fatherhood ourselves. I stand—frightening thought—*in loco Dei* for the moment toward my children.

This is dangerous language. It is dangerous on at least two counts. First, it may lead me to suppose that I *am* God, or can replace God, for my children, and this is false. Secondly, it may make it sound as though, if a man believes this, he has a guarantee of success in raising his children. Here I must earnestly and hastily demur: my children, at the time of this writing, are seven and ten. The acid test is still to come. God in heaven alone knows how I'm doing in this role. I will write no books or articles on successful fatherhood—at least not until I am ninety, and both my children have turned out to be aging saints and have raised their own crop of mature saints. Any time before that is too soon.

But how shall I understand this role of being, so to speak, in the place of God for my children? Is it not that I must understand that, just as great mysteries are both cloaked and revealed in the very imagery of maleness that I and every man bear, so in this household in which I find myself, the ancient role of father is appointed to me, as the ancient role of mother is appointed to my wife, and that we must do our best to learn our cues and lines and to enact our roles as the playwright intended? How, for example, shall my children ever grasp the odd notion that it is love and not caprice or tyranny that demands obedience unless they discover this paradox at home? I want them to be familiar with this paradox so that they will already be familiar with the God whose love (not whose tyranny) makes high demands on us. And how shall they know that obedience and freedom are synonymous unless they are taught the steps in this strange dance at home? They will grow up in a world that thinks these ideas are outrageous and brutalizing and that insists that the way toward freedom and authenticity lies in declaring our total independence of authority and in forging our own morality. How will anyone explain to them about the God "whose service is perfect freedom" if I have not somehow tried not only to teach them this, but to *be* this for them?

I may fail. But that will be, precisely, my failure. Perhaps I may step altogether aside here and point in a more sure direction. I point to my own father. He was a man oppressed with great burdens and limitations (he thought), and he suffered intensely over a sense of his own unworthiness. But to six children, all of them now aging, and all on the side of the angels, he stood, decade after decade, as an image of the Father. He loved us greatly, and he asked (and got) our obedience. The household was by no means a participatory democracy. That would have been a shabby betrayal. Obedience was nonnegotiable. Things ran on schedule. Order was of the essence. But lest this sound impossibly grim and Edwardian, it was also the most hilarious household I have ever encountered. We spent a good deal of our time laughing our heads off, mostly at each other. But the bedrock upon which the hilarious liberty was grounded was that we had a father who, in obedience to the ancient rubric, shouldered his yoke of fatherhood, with all that that has implied of primacy and headship, and carried it for the sake of his family, and a mother who understood in her innermost being what the great charge to our mother Eve was—to be a helpmeet for this man. I am sure that our vision of God is to be attributed very heavily to our experience of love and authority embodied in our parents; and I would think that our vision of Christ and his Church is to be attributed very heavily to what we witnessed of this man and this woman enacting year after year before our eyes the corresponding (not interchangeable) roles of husband and wife.

FAMILY WORSHIP

In the household where I grew up outside of Philadelphia, going to church (*and* Sunday school, as it happens—we were Protestant Fundamentalists) was as natural and inevitable as eating dinner together. Actually, that last phrase about dinner may not be as helpful as I originally thought: I realize that nowadays, in the 1990s, it may be a rare family that really does, seven nights a week, sit down around a table that has been set, with the father presiding at one end and the mother at the other.

My childhood occurred in the 1930s and '40s when, despite the Depression and the War, domestic life had not flown into fragments, as has happened since. Back then, things like dinner and going to church—and also family prayers twice a day—were as regular as the ticking of the clock. And they were quintessentially family propositions. No one was at liberty to absent himself—barring, of course, some genuinely legitimate reason like the flu, or "grippe" as we used to call it.

Such a routine might well sound grim to families—and perhaps particularly to the young—nowadays. Golly! (one might think): that sounds like Massachusetts Bay Colony to me! No thanks!

Originally published in a slightly different form in *Lay Witness* (June 1998): 4–5. Reprinted with permission.

There is an intriguing paradox here, however. A helter-skelter household may have a certain kind of "freedom" about it, in the sense that no one is held to any sort of routine and regular responsibility, and everyone can fly in and out, grabbing a slice of microwaved pizza or one of those thick drinks in the graphically appealing bottles by way of a meal. But the immemorial testimony of mankind is virtually unanimous: order and routine are, oddly enough, *liberating*. The rules become guardians of true freedom.

I was immensely impressed at a large theme park several years ago: rather than leaving the throngs to crowd around the entrances to the various amusements, jostling and shoving for position, they had set up iron fences that snaked back and forth and kept us all in line. No one needed to fret and protest, "Hey! They're cutting line up there!" The fences gave us all the freedom to relax and enjoy.

But what are we leading up to? In a word, we're leading up to the topic of going to Mass together—of looking on the Church's liturgy as a profoundly important family occasion, not to be taken lightly. It is not for nothing that Vatican II and the Holy Father speak of the family household as "the domestic church". For it is (or should be) in the day-to-day routines and intimacies of family life that we all have the chance to learn charity, or to "grow up into Christ" (cf. Eph 4:15).

To many, such a line of thought will sound idealistic, not to say farfetched. But if we reflect briefly, we will agree that indeed there are few better opportunities in life for us to learn the simple, yet mountainous, lessons of love. Why mountainous? Because, as anyone who has tried it will testify, some of the simplest requirements of love are the hardest—as hard, we might say, as making it up that last bone-wearying mile to the summit. For example, what about just refraining from tossing off the remark that will *so* neatly cut someone off at the ankles? Not easy. Or what about returning generosity and good humor for some insult? Or keeping a steady temper and good cheer when a thousand irritating trivialities have conspired to drive us up the wall? Not easy.

This discussion may seem somewhat afield from our topic of going to Mass together as a family. But there is a connection—or more than a mere connection: we could say it is all of a piece. Living a truly Catholic life cannot really be parceled out into bits and pieces: the Rosary here, Mass there, a novena now and again, CCD, a retreat, and so forth. There is only one agenda for the Christian, and that is, as we mentioned above, to be configured to Christ. The Church is the place where this occurs—and by "the Church" we mean our private prayers as well as public occasions like the liturgy, since it is as members of one another as well as of Christ that we live.

For centuries, the notion of families assisting at Mass together was generally taken for granted. "Assisting at" is actually the traditional word, rather than "hearing" Mass, or "going to" Mass. We are not an audience: we are *congregatio*, brought together by the Holy Spirit, as the Holy Father stresses in his apostolic letter *Tertio Millennio Adveniente* (TMA). Referring to the Vatican II document *Lumen Gentium*, he says, "the unity of the Body of Christ is founded on the activity of the Spirit, guaranteed by the apostolic ministry and sustained by mutual love" (TMA, no. 47).

There we have, in brief form, a hint of the whole picture. The Holy Spirit is indeed the One who brings us together, and 1998 is the year designated by the Holy Father to mark especially the ministry of the Spirit as we move toward the Great Jubilee of the Year 2000. If we have a keen sense that it is the Holy Spirit no less in our families than in our parishes who unites us to each other and to Christ, we will see the seamlessness, so to speak, of the "domestic church" and the parish. The latter, of course, is the local epiphany of the universal Church.

And the Mass is the central act in the Church. *If, in our busy, even frenetic, world of the late twentieth century, Catholics could recover the notion of the liturgy as "family worship", great benefits would be gained.* There simply is no better teacher of the Faith than the liturgy!

The liturgy is actually an unfurling of the entire Gospel. At each celebration of the Mass, God's whole saving revelation of himself is opened up before us. It may be the case that, in many families, the parents find themselves somewhat uncertain as to how to go about passing along the fullness of the Faith to their children. It is not unusual, of course, for parents to hope, vaguely, that CCD will somehow take care of the matter. And certainly we are all profoundly grateful for the faithful and hard-working volunteers who, year after year, give their time to teaching in the parish.

But we also know that it is often the case that, if what is taught in the parish is not undergirded and affirmed and energized by the way the Faith is held and practiced at home, there can occur a certain "slippage". How many Catholic young people look on confirmation as a sort of graduation from churchgoing? And from how many people do we hear the words, "I was brought up Catholic, but ..."?

Thinking back on my own Protestant background, I am absolutely sure that the long-term effects of finding myself in the pew week after week, year after year, with both of my parents there, and all the siblings—that these effects are incalculable. The family solidarity constituted a firm foundation for the lively faith that led me eventually into the ancient Roman Catholic Church.

Catholics, of course, are particularly fortunate, in that their "worship service" does not take the form of a meeting, as is the case with Protestantism. Catholic worship is an enactment that calls for the whole person to participate, physically as well as spiritually. (Outsiders wonder what all the up and down, genuflecting, bowing, kneeling, and crossing of themselves on the part of the worshippers is all about.) Catholic parents can, little by little, one item at a time, explain simply to their children what this or that act signifies and thus, over a period of time, draw their children into intelligent, believing participation.

For example, parents can explain that the sign of the cross is a most solemn business, for by it we signify in a bodily way what we wish to be the case in the inner man. Namely, we place our whole being—intellect, affections, and actions—willingly under the Cross of Jesus Christ, who invites us to enter into the great mystery of his own self-giving on our behalf, learning what it means to give ourselves for others ("self-donation" is the term the Holy Father often uses).

Or the holy water font. Is it just an offhand act we hurry through as we come, distracted, into the church? It should remind us of the water of our baptism, whereby we were "buried with Christ" and risen with him to newness of life. Or genuflecting. It is easily done, and therefore often thoughtlessly done. But what an opportunity to impress on our children that, like the seraphim themselves, we bow the knee in the presence of the Most High—who is, in fact, present here, in the tabernacle. What a chance to introduce the whole idea of majesty, holiness, glory, and exaltedness into the imagination of our children, who certainly are not encouraged along these lines with the fare they are offered on, say, MTV.

The *Confiteor*. Acknowledging that we are sinners will strike our nonreligious contemporaries as an exceedingly unhealthy opener for worship. Heavens! We ought to affirm and assert ourselves, and not grovel in this way. But Catholics know that it is not groveling: it is the true and healthy stance of the creature before the Creator and Redeemer. It glories in the joy of forgiveness. It exults in the stark truth: we have failed. But God receives us anyway. It is yet another chance to initiate our children, naturally and simply, into what the Good News is all about.

As anyone can see, we could run on to many pages with a line of thought like this. But let us at least say that the Mass is a glorious opportunity for catechesis in the best setting of all—the family.

NOTES UPON HEARING HANDEL'S
CORONATION ANTHEMS

On October 11, 1727, George II was crowned in Westminster Abbey King of England. He was a Hanoverian king, to be sure—a turn of history that has always vexed Jacobeans. But king he was, for good or ill. As things turned out, he was good enough, if rather dull, which seems to be a stubborn quality to be found in Germanic monarchs. Queen Elizabeth II, fortunately, has plenty of Stuart and Tudor, not to say Plantagenet, blood in her, which is probably why she is so good.

In any event, George II was crowned king. But that is only the proximate cause of these remarks. As it happens, another George (Frideric Handel) wrote a set of anthems for the coronation. Anyone who is familiar with these splendid choral works will agree that when it comes to music that bespeaks *pomp*, in the best sense of that word, and sheer exultation, the *Coronation Anthems* are in the front rank.

And, before we go another sentence, it may be apposite here, lest any reader who has been maimed by modernity be put off by the word *pomp*, to quote the best lines ever written on the topic. They occur in C. S. Lewis' *Preface to Paradise Lost*; Lewis is speaking of the Middle English word *solempne*:

> The *Solempne* is the festal which is also the stately and the ceremonial, the proper occasion for *pomp*—and the very

fact that *pompous* is now used only in a bad sense measures the degree to which we have lost the old idea of "solemnity". To recover it you must think of a court ball, or a coronation, or a victory march, as these things appear to people who *enjoy* them; in an age when every one puts on his oldest clothes to be happy in, you re-awake the simpler state of mind in which people put on gold and scarlet to be happy in. Above all, you must be rid of the hideous idea, fruit of a widespread inferiority complex, that pomp, on the proper occasions, has any connexion with vanity or self-conceit. A celebrant approaching the altar, a princess led out by a king to dance a minuet, ... a major-domo preceding the boar's head at a Christmas feast—all these wear unusual clothes and move with calculated dignity. This does not mean that they are vain, but that they are obedient; they are obeying the *hoc age* which presides over every solemnity.[1]

That is a long quotation. But who will carp? (Readers who might like to savor an equally delightful apologia for *ritual* may go on to page 21 of the same slim paperback.) The point is that not only in the music, but also in the text, of Handel's anthems, we find a level, nay, a whole genus, of jubilation, that is opaque and incomprehensible to our own epoch.

The text is entirely taken from Sacred Scripture. Oddly, the verses from the Psalms are almost direct quotes from the Coverdale, that is to say, the Book of Common Prayer, version of the Psalms. Why there are smallish variations in wording, I am not Scripture scholar enough to know. It made perfect sense, of course, for Handel to use the BCP wording, since that is what was sung in the Church of

[1] C. S. Lewis, *A Preface to Paradise Lost* (Oxford: Oxford University Press, 1970), 17.

England until the 1970s. The Authorized Version was reserved for all other occasions when Scripture was used, either liturgically or personally.

But the thing that can only strike a modern man as, at best quaint, and at worst, terrible politics, is the unabashed *joy* over *the person of the king himself*. Every sentiment has for its burden the notion that the king is rightly to be exalted, and that every conceivable bliss and luxury is to be his, and that no tribute from us mortals nor blessing from the King of Kings, is unfitting in these royal precincts. I myself am at a disadvantage here, since, espousing as I do all of these sentiments, it is difficult for me to make some sense out of them for my contemporaries. There is a shadow of this ethos still hovering faintly over London. There is at least *something* about the Queen herself that makes even the most cro-magnon paparazzo mind his manners (or perhaps not: I may be whistling in the dark here). Elderly spinsters in villages like Agatha Christie's Saint Mary Mead certainly love the Queen (as I do); and I expect Tony Blair is on his best behavior when he goes to the Palace for his weekly report to Her Majesty (does the PM still do that?), Labourite though he may be. But let us face things: the notion of *majesty* at all will draw only snickers or ribaldry in most quarters now. The Prince of Wales has not helped things here—although his somewhat rackety way of life brings us directly back to the central point, oddly.

Very, very few monarchs in the history of the world have measured up to the pure and fervent wish on the part of the populace that they should be supremely fortunate, happy, blessed, honored, exalted, and adored—the wish that is at work in every line of Handel's text. (It is no use trying to convey anything of the music in mere print here. Go buy the David Willcocks King's College EMI CD. Anyway, you

know Handel's *Messiah*, so you know what he could do
with pomp: "Worthy is the Lamb . . . ", and so forth.) If we
were to hunt about for a monarch who fulfilled the sentiments at work in these lines, we would be a long time at
the task. Some Byzantine emperor, maybe? John Tzetzes?
Michael Palaeologus? Constantine VII Porphyrogenitus? At
least that last one's name ought to qualify him. But alas: the
court of Byzantium was a cloaca of murder, intrigue, and—
yes—Byzantine perfidiousness. Well, then—any of the khans
or sultans or pharaohs? From what we know of how they
could (and would) have everyone's skin pulled off slowly at
the smallest whim, we would all stop short of offering the
ovations to them we find in Handel's texts (which, lest any
reader be wondering, will be forthcoming below). What
about the Caesars? No. Too bloody, most of them. Well,
what about some Christian kings? The tsars? The trouble
here is that everyone from Ivan the Terrible to poor Nicholas
II disappoints us somehow. Frederick Barbarossa? Charles
V? Henry V? Philip II? Elizabeth I? In every case, we find
ourselves checked over something. Well again, what about
some saints who were kings and queens? Elizabeth of Hun-
gary? Louis IX? The pickings are slim. We wish Charlemagne measured up, or Clovis. But again, we find ourselves
suspecting that too narrow a scrutiny of the palace records
would betray some ghastly backstage jiggery-pokery that
would flatten our zeal to offer such anthems even to these
monarchs.

Actually, one of the greatest joys of my boyhood was
hearing the choirboys in Westminster Abbey in 1953 burst
forth with "Zadok the Priest and Nathan the Prophet,
anointed Solomon King. And all the people rejoic'd and
said: God save the King, long live the King, may the King
live for ever! Amen, Alleluia!" It was entirely beside the

point that it was a queen who was being crowned. A monarch is a monarch, and "prince" is a word as fitting for a woman as for a man, if you know your royal history. And all of us on that day (I was next to my radio in the U.S.A., not in the Abbey: my ducal credentials are shaky even if I do share a family name with the Premier Peer of the Realm) were caught up into a reality that transcended both the cold drizzle in London, and the aftermath of the War, and the fact that this was only a powerless constitutional monarch being crowned in any event.

Reality? Reality? Surely . . . ? Yes, reality. And that brings us to the whole point. What is this region in which the people's joy is somehow gathered up, fulfilled, and crowned, in the glory of their monarch? It is *terra incognita* to modern man. We are democrats. I'm as good as you are. The queen gets catarrh the same as I do. What's so special about her? For an American, who has not even any residual imagery to keep this vision of things before his eyes, the difficulty is insuperable. Alleluia! to Jimmy Carter? To Bill Clinton? Spare us.

And, on that level, the objections are all too sadly true. George II himself was a very long chalk from measuring up to the exaltation of Handel's texts. Listen to some excerpts: "Glory and great worship hast thou laid upon him. . . . Let thy hand be strengthened, and thy right hand be exalted. . . . Kings' daughters were among thy honourable women. Upon thy right hand did stand the Queen in vesture of gold, and the King shall have pleasure in thy beauty." One of my favorite choruses is, "My heart is inditing of a good matter; I speak of the things which I have made unto the King." Here is the poet, or the craftsman, who has made something beautiful; and it is to the king that he wishes to speak of it. The best that my hand can achieve—perhaps the Majesty of England will take some small pleasure in it. I hope so. That would crown all of my labor with joy. Oh—fancy bringing joy to the Prince.

And with this we begin to see where it all comes from, and where it all it leads. There is, of course, only one King who can properly and fully and justly receive all of this adulation and good will. We know that. But—in spite of all politics and intrigues and the failures and wickedness of kings who are, like the rest of us, miserable offenders—in spite of all that—*there is something salutary in the frame of mind that has kept alive the notion that majesty is in the cards, and that it is very meet, right, and our bounden duty, to extol that majesty.* The human crowned head is the icon of majesty: gold leaf peeling, the whole thing blotted, chipped, encrusted with the discolorations of age, but nonetheless the icon.

This is all irrelevant, nonsense, and even mephitic, to your democratic outlook. But any Christian is stuck with the notion that majesty, and not the ad hoc caucus of the whole, is at the bottom (or top) of things. The iconography has vanished from the modern map in most places (God save some rag of the truth in England anyway). But we may at least hear Handel's *Coronation Anthems* as bespeaking a reality that will endure when all congresses, parliaments, dails, diets, and politburos, have crumbled, and we may, perhaps, keep alive in our inner vision the clarity that can at least see the iconography in this imperfect world.

And one last note. The joy and sheer exultation that we find in Handel's text, and, a fortiori, in ten thousand years' worth of the common people dancing and rejoicing over their kings, is a hint at the quality of true Joy. Again, from the Christian point of view, true Joy is to be found in my forgetting myself altogether, and in the spectacle of majesty out there. In a democracy, there is precious little to admire. It is all too workaday and grubby, and there is no imagery to keep alive the mystery that should attend even human high office. People like Stalin and Mao and others whose power lay wholly in slaughter, and craven and venal and pusillanimous politicians, have spoiled the picture for us all. But a populace that can wait all night in the rain merely to see the crowned head passing in the great golden state coach, has at least a toehold in something that is True.

CHRISTIAN STUDIES

Anachronism or Salvation?

Some time ago my wife and I were talking, as we tend to do from time to time. I remember only the following fragment from our conversation, but, judging from this fragment, the conversation must have been about doom and one thing and another, which conversations with me tend to be about. I remember saying to her that the thing I fear most in life is chaos: the breakdown of order, so that we are reduced to everyone screaming and clawing each other's eyes out in grocery stores, scrabbling for the last dirty celery leaves in the corner and the last wrinkled potato, and, finally, the last bits of chewing gum and ersatz butterscotch topping—anything to fend off starvation. Then starvation itself—especially for one's children. Lines of refugees, slogging along country roads, pushing wheelbarrows and rickshaws piled high with saucepans, rocking chairs, stuffed animals, and quilts (why do refugees always have so many *quilts*, I am always asking myself). I have been looking and looking at pictures of refugees all my life—Belgians and Poles and Estonians when I was a little boy, then later Koreans and Pakistanis and Nigerians, then Somalis, then Vietnamese and Cambodians and Laotians,

Originally this lecture, given at Hillsdale College in Autumn 1980, was published in a slightly different form as "Christian Studies: Anachronism or Salvation?" in *Imprimis* 10, no. 2 (February 1981): 1–6. © 1981 by Hillsdale College. Reprinted with permission.

now Cubans. In these pictures there are always bedrolls and quilts everywhere. Why? Come to think of it, I suppose the reason is obvious, isn't it? What does life come down to, when we have been dispossessed? If we can only have a saucepan with, pray God, something to put *in* it and a place to lay our heads, like the foxes in their holes. That is the last ditch. After that, you sit on the ground, hollow-eyed and ghostlike, and wait for death.

Anyway, I was visualizing all of this as a sort of final horror. When my wife got a chance to say something, she, because she is wise and because she is good, and because she is a woman and therefore sees more clearly than I do, said that the thing she fears most in her imagination is having our children taken away forcibly and taught things that are monstrous and grotesque: Marxist doctrines of man, for example, and cruelty and cynicism, or the bitter, harsh, and sordid vision of life proclaimed so fiercely by prophets like Jane Fonda, Germaine Greer, and the Department of Health, Education, and Welfare.

When she said this I realized that she had in fact touched on something that was, if possible, more frightening than the visions of horror I had conjured. But in what sense was it more frightening? After all, one can imagine one's children, lined up outside the commune dormitory in neat grey tunics, hair brushed, cheeks scrubbed, singing in a great chorus, "Onward and upward with *liberté, egalité, fraternité*", and, on cue from the matron in her tunic and epaulettes, raising their fists in the air with a shout of victorious scorn for God, mother, apple pie, and the Boy Scouts. What emancipation! They would be healthy, busy, and disciplined. Who could wish for more?

But Christ and all his holy angels defend us from the advent of this state of affairs.

Now at this point you may be murmuring to yourself or your neighbor, "What is going on? The man has got his cues wrong. He has pulled out the wrong speech. We asked him to make us a speech at the inauguration of an Institute for Christian Studies, and here we are two minutes into the thing, head over heels in wheelbarrows, proletarian communes, and paranoia. Come. Someone signal the chairman. We cannot go on like this."

But if you will hold off your signal to the chairman for a moment, I will try to explain why I have conjured these pictures. My reason is this: better hands than mine, including names familiar to this audience, such as Malcolm Muggeridge, Erik von Kuehnelt-Leddihn, George Roche, William F. Buckley, and Russell Kirk, have given us astute analyses of what has happened in Western society in the last two hundred years, and what we may expect in the coming apocalyptic decades. I myself am a teacher and a father, and I very often find my mind running along lines that are coterminous with our concerns here today.

Why inaugurate an Institute for Christian Studies? Why indeed? Are there not seminaries, Bible institutes, and Sunday schools aplenty to do this job? Well, yes, there are numberless enterprises of that ilk. But where shall we find an institute in which the bold study of unabashed orthodox Christian tradition, including Scripture, history, theology, and the arts, is pursued in close proximity to the wider enterprise of Western thought, history, science, and humane letters? What I am describing is, of course, the notion upon which all of Western education was founded, from the school of Alcuin at the court of Charlemagne, right on through the foundations at Paris, Padua, Salamanca, Oxford, and Cambridge, to Harvard and Yale. The difficulty now is that it is hard to find very clear and lively evidence in the curricula of these venerable institutions of the original notion.

Rather than speaking generally and theoretically in my comments here, since I am neither a theologian nor a historian, I thought I might, with your permission, cast my remarks in the form of a series of concerns that present themselves to me—to me as a teacher in an institution of liberal learning and as the father of children who are approaching their years of higher education.

What is it, finally, that I want my students, and my children, to know? Why does it matter so much to me that I be given the chance to teach them? Why do I recoil at the idea of their being handed over to the government for the shaping of their vision?

The answer is that I believe what Saint Augustine and the Venerable Bede and Saint Thomas Aquinas and Saint Thomas More and Erasmus and Pascal and Cardinal Newman believed, that sanctity is the state toward which all educational enterprises ought to assist us, under grace.

Sanctity? How did we get here so fast? Who is talking about sanctity?

But, on the Christian view, if it is not sanctity toward which we must move, on pain of our lives, then what is it? I may press the question on myself as well as on my students and my children: What do I think I want? Where am I headed?

There are numbers of answers, of course, and modern education beckons us in various directions. Money for example, or more euphemistically, prosperity. This is one obvious good, and which of us does not find this irresistible? Money does so many things. It opens exciting doors. It will help me get to know the people I need to get to know, and it will help me get the house I want, and the style of life I want, and it will educate my children and above all give me at least some security. With inflation and unemployment and peril of one sort and another looming upon us so frighteningly now, who is going to say that money is not an enormously attractive buffer between us and the ragged edge? It would seem to be one of the eminently legitimate motives for one's getting educated. After all, the best positions are open only to the best educated.

Or, secondly, fame. If plain money seems a bit crass, then there is this, the desire for which is the last infirmity of noble minds. The idea of being widely respected and sought after by all sorts of fascinating people and of being thought to be a fascinating person by everyone is wholly attractive. Who would not like to hear the phone ring and find out that it is NBC or *Time* magazine on the line wanting us for a prime-time talk show or a cover story? Why, the very thought of it makes us start preening and looking in the mirror.

Or the beautiful life. Since life is so harrying and ambiguous these days, one may as well try to make it as amusing and dazzling as one can while it lasts. Eat, drink, and be merry, for tomorrow comes the crash or the bomb or the lab report with the dreaded news. The wish to have a bit of fun and to kick up one's heels on the brink of the abyss is not, of course, entirely pernicious. God defend us from the gaunt people who will spoil every jollity and every festivity by walking about with placards announcing the Trump of Doom. (After all, the Teacher whom we particularly acknowledged in an Institute for Christian Studies assisted himself in the merriment at Cana of Galilee by setting the party up to six fresh kegs after everyone had drunk quite enough, surely.)

Or just plain security, stability, and peace, heaven knows this is attractive. With the walls crumbling about our ears, and the economy collapsing, and oil disappearing, and energy and environment emerging as apocalyptic problems, and violence washing up to our very doorsteps—perhaps our greatest wish is for mere peace and security. One begins to appreciate once again some of those robust litanies they used to say in church, beseeching the protection of heaven against one threat or another. "From the fury of the Norsemen, good Lord deliver us", implored the Anglo-Saxons, and we might gloss this for our own purposes to read, "From the fury of the Persians". Or "From ghoulies and ghosties and long-leggity beasties, and things that go bump in the night, good Lord, deliver us", prayed the Cornishmen, and we might add, ". . . things that go bump in the night *or* the day, like nuclear meltdown or muggers' blackjacks landing on our skulls".

Security, then, is a thing most earnestly to be longed for at any time in the history of mankind, and certainly in these days. Hence it might well siphon our attention away from the only thing (sanctity) that matters in the view of the Christian sages and Doctors. Let us by all means bolt and bar the doors against contingency and peril. The irony here, of course, is that there are no bolts or bars that will hold that door against the final interloper, Death.

But it seems a bit much to regale us with the spectre of Death during a speech at the Inaugural of an Institute for Christian Studies. After all, this is a time of beginning, not of ending. But is not this the point? Will not such an institute endeavor to keep alive in its very curriculum such titanic considerations as the Four Last Things that loom so large in Christian tradition and that a feebler post-Enlightenment academia huddles so successfully under the rug? At least two poets would not consider it odd that Death be mentioned on an occasion such as this. Dante would not blink an eye, and T. S. Eliot would no doubt murmur, "In my end is my beginning." If it is objected that this is a macabre note to strike, we may remember one of the salutary notions that kept the Fathers and the Doctors and the philosophers and divines hard at their work century after century. Some went so far as to have a skull grinning at them from a shelf as they worked over their books and parchments. *Memento mori* was the idea. All serious scholarship, and certainly all Christian scholarship by definition, must have as its subject matter what we might call The Important Things. Many items bid for a place in this august curriculum, and money, fame, amusement, and security are strong bidders. But Death is the arbiter who, once for all, will sort out the bidders and hand the prize to Sanctity. If nothing else will get our attention, Death will. I heard an undergraduate not long ago say in an offhand way, "I'm not into the Christian thing this week." Well, lady, I thought to myself, then you had better send up a prayer to Zeus or Wotan, since you are going to need all the help you can get when the Fates get around to snipping the thread of your story."

My favorite set of last words are those of a medieval pope. "Wait! Wait!" he cried out on his deathbed. Who of us will not feel like saying that? (Just give me a bit more time to get my act together.) The students who land in my office during the ninth week of term wondering whether there might not be some arrangements we could make since somehow the preceding nine weeks seem to have gone by without their having thought much about the term paper that is due the next day and the examination next week—are we not all like this? I must confess that when I find myself in this scene I usually find my imagination traveling forward to the time when it is my turn to be haled up in front of the Divine Tribunal by Saint Michael the Archangel. Wait. Wait.

But this would seem to be straying from our topic. But once again, an Institute for Christian Studies will have as at least part of its mandate the keeping alive of the ancient tradition in which there arched over the whole enterprise of man's life, including the academic, the firmament of the Ineffable. Creation. Evil. Redemption. Incarnation. Judgment. Felicity. Sanctity. Grace. These words named the huge realities pondered by the men who founded Western institutions of learning. Does the curriculum of the modern university include all this? If not, is it the richer for the omission?

But to return to my earlier question as to what it is that I would like my children and my students to know, or better yet, to be, as a result of their education.

For one thing, I would like them to be awake. There are a number of stupefying things about, however. The sheer force and noise under which we live batters and stuns us into imbecility and torpor. We may test this at any point. Pause, at any random moment of any day, inside or outside, and list the noises that you hear. If there is not a jet plane going overhead, there will be a truck going past. If the television is not going, there will be the roar of the interstate. If you are in a university dormitory you will hear someone's stereo pouring out noise at a shattering decibel level, or if you are in a supermarket you will hear worse, namely, the saccharine and treacly lullaby of Muzak. I spend my summers in a place that, short of sheer wilderness, is as rural as you can get east of the Dakotas. I have counted the following noises that are native to this pastoral countryside where I go: trucks—gravel trucks, oil trucks, and the pick-up trucks of all the local handymen; hot rods, popping and slamming up and down the roads; dirt bikes; chain saws; bulldozers; small aircraft; and worst of all, Air Force jets that maneuver directly over Sugar Hill, New Hampshire, every day starting at exactly 10:40 A.M., stretching a deafening canopy of sound from horizon to horizon. And that is the *country*. What shall we say of the cities and suburbs where, besides living with far more noise than that, people never turn off the television and the stereo?

I myself have wondered whether television is not a twentieth-century variation on the theme of what we did in the Garden of Eden when we made a grab for a kind of knowledge that we were not made for and that hence turned out to be crushing. It killed us. We were not made to bear the knowledge of good and evil: only gods can bear that and live. We thought we could shoulder it, and it killed us. I wonder if television is not our own special technological variation on this theme. For what does it do? It pours avalanches of data at us with a force and speed that can only destroy us psychologically, morally, emotionally, and spiritually. We mortal creatures were not made to bear the instant, vivid, and gigantic spectacle of chaos and suffering and strife in every corner of the world. If we think we can, then we are guilty of the sin that we were guilty of originally, namely, thinking that we can be as gods. The Greeks called it *hubris*. Saint Francis himself could not bear the spectacle, not because his heart did not have enough charity in it, but because he would have known that the poor and the lepers and the hungry he had as his neighbors were a load heavy enough for any mortal charity to bear.

Do I mean, then, that we shut our eyes and our compassion and lock ourselves away from the suffering of the world? Surely not. But the *spectacle* of universal suffering and chaos pouring into affluent American living rooms hour upon hour every day, year after year, can have only the negative effect of getting us *accustomed* to the spectacle. We get calloused. Our threshold of "shockability" goes up and up until we are blasé. The thing that we thought was consciousness-raising turns out to be consciousness-blunting. We turn out to be spectators, like Romans at the arena.

Worse than this, of course, is the *bogus* violence that comes at us in what is called entertainment, where we are glutted still further with violence dished up for its own amusement value: people being blown to bits, guns blazing, knives flashing, cars careening, and marriages breaking down and breaking down on thousands upon thousands of tedious soap-opera afternoons. And, topping all this up, the neanderthal throb of acid, punk, and funk rock, blatting and yelling in our ears, stunning and cudgeling our sensibilities until they are flat, flat, flat. Does it surprise you, then, that high school students sit in class paralyzed by boredom? That nothing is "relevant" except powerful kicks? How would you go about flagging down their jaded attention with such hot topics as sanctity, grace, courtesy, charity, and all the other accoutrements of civilized life assumed by the Western tradition to be indispensable? How will we keep alive ears that are able to hear Mozart or Shakespeare, or eyes that can see Vermeer or Fra Angelico? How shall I keep alive in my students some rag of grace and agility and tenderness—some quality of being awake to the texture and fragility of life; some capacity to adore what is adorable, and to extol what is praiseworthy, and to recognize nobility, perfection, virtue, and beauty wherever it appears—in a Brandenburg Concerto, or in a Mother Teresa, or even in some Golden Retriever wagging his great plume of a tail at us—or even in someone's bending to pick up a gum wrapper thrown down on campus by one of the barbarians who has not learned what civility, much less sanctity, is?

For another thing, I would like my children and my students to know what courtesy and grace are, and to introduce them to this, I will have to introduce them not only to the ancient Western tradition, but to the particular Christian tradition. It is easy enough to see how impossible a task this is nowadays simply by looking at our own reaction to the words themselves. Courtesy? Grace? The very words make us wince. We think of nineteenth-century ladies' finishing schools, and pinkies extended over bone-china cups of Darjeeling tea, and pursed lips being dabbed demurely with lace hankies. What on earth have courtesy and grace to do with anything in this hey-hey, hang-loose era we live in now?

Well, they have something to do with something, I suspect. And that something must be the old worn-out notion of *charity*—a notion that no Jew and no Christian can give the back of his hand to, no matter what era he lives in, since charity was commanded, described, and spelled out in the Law at Sinai, and taught in the Sermon on the Mount, and incarnated and enacted for an example for us forever and ever when the Most High came to visit us.

But what is it supposed to look like now? This is a different epoch, and vastly different demands are going to be made on our graduates. Surely we cannot expect them to be bowing and salaaming their way through life? No; surely not. But will they be truly educated if they have not seen what it meant to honor the other person, and to be kind and generous, even in the smallest exchanges of ordinary life? What was moral theology about? What were all the books, written with such earnestness by the Renaissance Christian humanists, spelling out what the virtuous man was to be? Indeed, what was the ideal for all of education in the Renaissance? Virtue was a very big word in that educational scheme. I would like to cultivate, and to see, in my students some alertness to other people—some quick and thoughtful courtesy that is finely tuned to people who need help, whether it is simply a matter of quickly and unobtrusively offering a chair to a lady who comes into the room, or giving someone a hand with a bag of groceries, or sitting up for hours with someone who is going through some dark night of the soul. And, it may be another index of how difficult a task this is going to be for you and me when we hear shrill and angry voices telling us now that that old business of offering a chair to a lady—indeed, that the word "lady" itself—is an insult to modern womanhood because it implies that women are the weaker sex and are therefore to be coddled. Alas. What on earth does that fierce, political frame of mind know about the ancient business of offering honor to something that is honorable? What do they know of the grave and joyous courtesies exchanged between our great lord and father Adam and our great lady and mother Eve? Do we think *they* scrabbled at each other for equal time, and droned away at committee tables making sure no gesture or phrase implied any inequality? Politics, and justice in the public domain, may have to grind away at that gritty business, but love, and hence grace and courtesy, know nothing of that calculating and squinting approach.

An Institute for Christian Studies will have as at least part of its mandate the rooting of this vision of things in a soil deeper than what we might find in the nineteenth-century finishing school. Courtesy reaches further than the parlor: it is, eventually, theological, and there is a massive tradition that has been set on one side in the curricular planning at most institutions of higher learning in our own epoch. It remains to be seen whether in thus setting that tradition aside, our epoch has not set aside the building blocks on which the entire edifice of civilization as we know it rests. I would like my students, and my children, to know of the tradition that honors the exquisite and noble mystery of other selves—something that they will not encounter under the disciplines of the modern behavioral sciences—so that they will abhor all the forms of rudeness and discourtesy and self-interest by which we brutalize each other these days—all the forms, I say, from the lechery that calls itself free love and that has long since forgotten the mystery of the other self in its hot pursuit of bliss, to the slogans that reduce us all to frightened and angry pawns in a wearying game of egalitarian chess.

Third, I would like to keep alive in my students and in my children the capacity for contentment—nay, for delight in the utterly ordinary. This is not going to be easy. It is the sort of thing one might encounter in such non-bestselling writers as Saint Benedict and Brother Lawrence. It is going to be difficult because we and our students and our children are told, in a thousand talk shows and a thousand books, and in every journal and seminar, and in every magazine and advertisement, that what we want is something *else*. If you drive a Pinto, what you want is a BMW; if you drive a BMW, what you want is a Mercedes. If you shop at KMart, you need to move up to Neiman Marcus. If you go to Aspen for your holiday, you ought to try Saint Moritz. If you are a mother, you ought to be an investment banker. If you work from nine to five, that is a drag and only dull people do that. If you are middle class, you need to get emancipated. Upward mobility. Self-actualization. Self-assertion. Self-discovery. Self-realization. Aggression. Kicks. Travel. Diversion. The Beautiful People. Radical chic. Anywhere but where we are; nothing could be as dull as this.

How shall we preserve the capacity for contentment and delight in sheer, unvarnished ordinariness and routine, when this is the mythology coming at us so dazzlingly? To have caviar and smoked salmon dangled in front of my nose all the time has the effect of making me sooner or later think that the brown bread and butter on my plate is a bore, and that to be happy I must somehow get hold of caviar and smoked salmon for my daily fare. But caviar and smoked salmon are not the staff of life. They are wonderful garnishings, but precious few of us mortal creatures get them very often. The Caribbean is there, heaven knows, and it is beautiful. But have the advertisements for the Caribbean, with willowy women and lithe men draped languidly on the deck of somebody's 90-foot ketch with tall glasses of rum punch, blunted my taste for walking through the woods to the local pond? Madison Avenue is doing what it can to bring this off, and they know how to administer very effective doses of their magic.

Somehow the education we offer has got to have the effect of keeping students in touch with simplicity. What are our demands from life? Is daily routine a form of joy for us, because it gives us the thing that all exiles and prisoners and dying people would give the universe to get back, namely, the chance to go about the plain tasks of the day? Or is it a bondage? I must say, when I say good-night to my children I think to myself, "Well, I have been given a gift of inexpressible worth here, namely, one more utterly ordinary day, unmarked by tragedy or sickness or accident." God forbid that I should neglect to offer up the sacrifice of thanksgiving for this. I don't want to wait until it is taken away before I look at it and assess its value.

I myself am glad that I grew up at the end of the Depression and during the Second World War. Luxuries were just not around then. Or rather, they were, but they were very, very small, and I think that this did something good for us. I can remember my father taking his pocket penknife and ever so carefully cutting a Milky Way candy bar into about five pieces for some of us children, and passing the little bits out. This was a great treat. We loved it. We did not feel deprived. The idea of eating an entire candy bar was something I never heard of until I was an adult. My children have more than one piece of Milky Way. So do I. So do you. Have we still got the capacity to delight in one piece of Milky Way? If not, where are we? How much do we want? If you think I have strayed once more from the topic at hand, you may recall that the vision of life unfurled for us in the two thousand years of Christian writing, history, liturgy, and art celebrates some such set of values as this. It is hard to find it in contemporary curricula.

Fourth, I would wish to keep alive in my students and my children the capacity for sheer merriment and joy. Plain laughter. Now that sounds like an obvious thing. But it is a rare capacity nowadays. Real, wholesome merriment lies somewhere in the precincts of sanctity, for it presupposes humility. Pompous people cannot really laugh. Merriment has something to do as well with simplicity—sophisticated people can offer only tinkling, silvery mockery. And it has something to do with purity of heart: lechers and gluttons can only leer. And it has something to do with grace— clods and oafs can only grunt. And it has something to do with charity: egotists are seldom amused. The saints seem to be full of merriment. Perhaps the martyrology ought to be part of the curriculum, not in the interest of self-flagellation, but in the interest of learning sheer good health of the soul.

Fifth, and last, I would like my students and children to know something about what a capacity for suffering means.

Now this sounds morbid—sadistic even. What shall I do? Shall I thrash them over their Latin paradigms, or make them sleep on the floor, or feed them on hardtack and water in order to steel them against adversity? No. No, no, no. But somewhere in there I want to be giving them whatever it is that will make them strong and good and will supply them with the sort of resources that can be drawn on when adversity comes. Surely this, too, has something to do with charity—with one's focus being on something other than oneself. If my whole approach to life is to have my own self affirmed, and to indulge my own preferences and whims and inclinations, then when something (sickness, or grief, or trouble) comes at me, where am I going to be? Whereas if I have been learning the disciplines of life—learning what vigil means, and fasting perhaps, and renunciation—then somehow the sinews of my soul will have been toughened. Not, again, that I intend to try making my children kneel on a stone floor somewhere all night in order to teach them what vigil is all about. But can I, somehow, instill in them the habit of watchfulness, and of self-discipline, and of a keen interest in the welfare of others, so that there is hardier material making up the citadel of their souls than the soft mud of indulgence and egocentrism, which will surely be swept away at the first wave of trouble? I used to know an old woman who had everything against her: she was a widow, and she was poor, and she had to work. She had an ungrateful wretch of a son. She was stone deaf. And she had all sorts of arthritis and rheumatism. But that woman was and remains (she is long since in paradise) for me and my whole family probably the most glittering example of sheer, simple joy and contentedness than any of us has ever seen. Again, five or six years ago I visited a church in Connecticut. In the middle of the Eucharistic Liturgy, when the whole congregation was kneeling and singing the

"Alleluia", I saw a woman near me with her hands lifted in praise. The thing was, those hands were terribly twisted and gnarled, and she had a pair of crutches near her. "Dear Christ," I thought, "what makes Christians sing 'Alleluia'?" Clearly there was something besides self-interest welling up from that woman in that act of praise.

By this time it will have appeared that I have taken leave of my topic altogether and sailed off into a homily on the spiritual life. But I would like to protest that when we think of an Institute for Christian Studies and of all that this implies—of rigorous study in the Fathers, and in the Doctors of the Church, and in Church history with all of its thousand faces, from the court of the Borgia popes to little Muggletonian conventicles meeting in thickets, and from huge Athanasian controversies in the fourth century to Christian attitudes toward the pill and abortion now—what does it all come to? Why is it important? Surely every question that arises finds its source in the basic questions of good and evil. What is good? What is evil? How can you know which is which? What is fixed and what is transitory? Does Christianity judge the age, or does the age judge the ancient Faith? *Securus judicat orbis terrarum*, said Saint Augustine, and Cardinal Newman quoted him. It is to be hoped that the scholars who find themselves in the halls of this institute will find themselves at the fountainhead of real wisdom— the wisdom that Solomon said was worth selling all a man has in order to gain.

BEING FORGOTTEN

I awoke this morning, that is to say, forty-five minutes ago, from a dream. Scarcely a Bunyanesque dream, let us hurry to assure everyone. I was at the Hicksite Quaker Meeting at Friends' School in Moorestown, New Jersey, where I had grown up and gone to school. The time was the present, and I had been gone for fifty years (I left home for boarding school in 1950).

The meeting had been updated, however—like these churches that use movie screens instead of hymnals. There was a brisk conviviality in the ethos not traditional at Quaker Meetings. People nattered away the whole time, even when someone stood up to speak. George Fox, readers will remember, had had the idea that the paradigm for church order, and for the order of public gatherings, was best found by leaving everyone free, upon being "moved by the Spirit", to stand up and share something. It is to be noted here that "share" was not a seventeenth-century word.

Actually, by Samuel Hicks' time, the Holy Ghost had himself been jettisoned and this "spirit" might be any impulse in my bosom that prompted me to stand up and descant upon some improving sentiments (what Flannery O'Connor called "uplift"). The sentiments need not imply any theism, God help us all (this is why the orthodox Quakers had

Originally published in a slightly different form in *Touchstone* (June 2003).

split in the nineteenth century from the Hicksites: it looked as though the latter were heading pell-mell toward *Modernism*).

But my dream. We sang (the Hicksites do not sing) "For the Beauty of the Earth", which is safely non-Christological, and "I Love to Tell the Story", which would be as likely to be sung in a Quaker Meeting as "Rule, Britannia", and "Ubi Caritas", which again, deriving as it does from one of the Church Fathers (Augustine? Hilary? Theodore of Mopsuestia? I can't remember), forsooth would not be to Hicksite taste at *all*.

I noticed that a man several pews in front of me had a copy of the first edition of a book I once wrote. It had (in real life, and in the dream) a canary yellow cover with great craggy lettering dominating the entire dust jacket. "Aha!" thinks I. "They remember me, and I shall be introduced." And presently the man stood up. I preened myself surreptitiously, ready to respond graciously to the oohs and ahs of the congregation finding their eminent townsman back amongst them.

This part of the dream was a bit skewed: the only common denominator between me and these folks was Moorestown. I had grown up in a Fundamentalist conventicle a mile along Main Street from the meeting house at the school, so they would scarcely have felt flattered by this Rip Van Winkle in their midst, even though I had indeed been a small schoolboy in their school.

But the man turned out to have something else to say, and that was the end of that.

At this point I woke up. The Quakers had no notion as to who I might be, nor much interest in finding out. Which brings us to the topic of the essay: What about oblivion?

This is a question that has more bite in it for a man than for most women. Oh, to be sure, both sexes struggle with various forms of vanity. God knows there are a thousand such forms, ranging from Mme. Pompadour at her *toilette* to Napoleon and other popinjays strutting the battlements— not to mention the thousandfold daily mutterings of my own heart, e.g., wishing to be frosty to this person or nursing umbrage over not having been placed at the rear of the line at Baccalaureate with the tenured full professors, which they jolly well ought to know I *am*.

That latter case would be, I think, archetypical for us men. We hunt among footnotes and indices to see if our work appears there, and if not? Umbrage. We snap up journals to see if our article has elicited any letters. If not? Umbrage. (I finally gave up writing a column for the *New Oxford Review* many decades ago, since nothing I wrote ever moved a single reader to write *in*.) They float a symposium on C. S. Lewis and don't ask me to speak. Great Scott! What's the matter with them? Don't they know? ...

Or (this one really stung) they organize an Olympian colloquy on Roman Catholicism and Evangelicalism and pay each major speaker $10,000 (this is true), and who doesn't get asked to give a major paper? A pox on the lot of them. Nobody in Christendom knows as much about the topic as old Uncle here. Are they snubbing me? Well then, to h—— ...

What is to be done (to pick up a most apposite question from Lenin)? The trouble is that a Christian, who is supposed to be en route to sanctity, cannot quite settle for this sort of thing. No doubt many people go to their graves blithely practicing all sorts of refinements on the theme of vanity, but Christians don't have that luxury. If we do not grow up to "the measure of the stature of the fullness of Christ" (I did my Scripture memory work from the King James), then we are in the greatest peril.

Will "I never knew you" be spoken over my case when it comes up at the Last Trump? It is a somberly possible turn of events, if we are to credit the Gospels. We are supposed to be altogether and blissfully happy to be anonymous, obscure, uncelebrated, unrecognized, unimportant. The *caritas* of I Corinthians 13 would seem to disbar all of our busy efforts to keep our names *somehow* in the sweepstakes ("seeketh not her own").

Not to mention the Beatitudes ("Blessed are the poor in spirit") and a hundred other texts. The Psalms also, in which I as a Catholic am obliged to immerse myself daily, adjure us all to be content solely with being known by the Most High and "to inquire in his temple". *Quemadmodum cervus*, says Psalm 42. Where is my febrile campaign for recognition in these precincts?

Where is the man among us who finds this set of marching orders easy? One's ego seems indestructible, and one's cunning in looking after the interests thereof unremitting.

But, not to put it too baldly, it is all satanic. What was Lucifer's sin? What Adam's? What (in this day of Tolkien) Sauron's? Pride. Vanity. Ego. All of which thrashes us unmercifully along into the precincts of hell.

I do not wish to be found among the fire-eaters and thunderers. There are grave sins that put our souls in danger (see I Jn 5:16, 17), and there are the sins with which our fallen natures seem tinctured. I think I am speaking in this essay of the latter. We do battle with vanity daily, or at least men like me do. What is the price to be paid in renunciation, penitentiality, discipline, prayer, vigil, and denouncing in oneself all of this stubborn vaingloriousness? It is very high for most of us.

Many years ago I wrote a book that made a brief splash in the Evangelical wing of Protestantism. Aha! I thought: I'm an *author!* And maybe I'll be a *speaker!* Travel! Royalties! Honoraria! Adulation! Thousands of letters! VIP treatment!

But somehow it didn't happen. Nobody *big* (Wheaton, Fuller, Trinity, Dallas, Gordon-Conwell) asked me to speak. Somehow the Booksellers' yearly bash had other business. No conventions. Even though I had been on the InterVarsity staff, and a brother of mine was a figure of immeasurable dignity in that *métier*, somehow Urbana never wanted me. No name in lights. I found myself trekking about the country giving speeches at East Cupcake Tech, and North Overshoe Bible Institute and South Bandaid Junior College. I was on the list of an outfit called The Staley Lectureship, but that never came to much. My royalties? Oh, we could have a few fancy dinners out in New York. My honoraria? $100 a shot.

In this connection I have a theory I could illustrate by putting forward a great number of highly specific names whom all readers would recognize, that *if you bill yourself as a celebrity, everyone will go along with the enterprise.* A good friend of mine wrote one book, and she now lives a splendid, high-rolling life. Her feet never touch any material other than red carpeting. Klieg lights. Glamor. (Her book was jolly good, by the way: I can't carp here.) Her status has endured for, I think, thirty-some years now.

I have found myself obliged, if I weren't to run the risk of being damned for jealousy, to pray for five specific men of my age, or younger, who, on the strength of one starter-book, found themselves able to move into Rock Creek Park,

Bryn Mawr, or Greenwich. (I will let readers amuse themselves by guessing. You know them all.)

But why do I pray for them? Because otherwise I'd be sulking and pouting and muttering between my teeth about how unfair life is. These men (and the woman I mentioned) were able to start out with $1,000 honoraria when that was worth something, and now I would guess that the figure must be $20,000 per lecture. Some of them will agree to speak to no audience smaller than five thousand.

This *is* sounding querulous. But on the other side of the ledger I would urge, first, that every single one of these people is my ally in the Faith (they are Evangelical, but as an orthodox Catholic, I share the biggest things with them). Second, it just *might* be that my stuff wasn't worth very much and theirs *was*. What makes me think that some baleful Fate has given me—I who am ever so important—the back of its hand? And third, God probably knows what each of us can cope with, and my strong guess is that I'd be well on the way to hell if I were buzzing about to the big spas of religion.

I have written eleven or twelve books, I think—I can't keep track—and I am offering $100,000 (Monopoly money) to any reader who can name a single title other than the first of my books. I threw in the sponge on writing books many years ago, not solely in a fit of pique, but also because I realized I had nothing more to say, and, further, that there is no rubric that says that if you have written *a* book you are thereby an author and must keep writing until you die.

Shall I follow the lead of all the wretched momentary Hollywood stars who must make shift somehow to prolong, at least in their sad reveries, their celebrity, what with face-lifts, walls covered with black-and-white framed photos of themselves in the days of their glamor, and

resentment at life gnawing their viscera away? Alas. All failures have some stark options. Shrivel up like Gollum, hiss-
ing away about "My Preciousss!" (read here, "The renown
that was due me, and that was denied me") *or* grip oneself
by the jugular, gird up one's loins, and embrace with songs
of thanksgiving the life of ordinary, anonymous, meat-and-
potatoes reality that 99.9 percent of the race must live with.

Two parting remarks: first, I work in the E.R. at Massachusetts General Hospital. The scene is bleak, quite apart
from the hair-raising suffering and daily death that hails one.
By that I mean that the mortals who come in, either on
stretchers, or those who must wait in silence in the waiting
room, seem, almost to a man, to be those whom life has
passed by altogether. They are sad, blank, poor, and patient.
What about them? Do I suppose that there is some elegant
exemption from all of this which is due me? *Kyrie, eleison!*

Second, to my chagrin, I have to admit (*sotto voce*, to be
sure) that God has vouchsafed me a life that, if I were given
my druthers, I would choose, alas; so I can't pretend that
there is much virtue at work here. To me, airports are hell,
or Purgatory at best, and the sardine-can scene in the "equipment" (why don't they call airplanes airplanes?) is worse.
Delays are worse yet; and being diverted to Wheeling or
Dubuque or Pierre the worst of all.

I have enough money for groceries. What would I do
with all the lovely royalties? Well, let us start with a Bent-
ley, then a flat in Mayfair, and take it from there—all of
which, of course, would obstruct most inconveniently my
efforts to climb the heavenly steeps.

$$\frac{\frac{1}{2} \text{ pie}}{\frac{1}{2}} = \frac{1}{4}$$

$$\frac{\frac{4}{8}}{\frac{1}{2}} = \frac{4}{16} = \frac{1}{4}$$

$$\frac{1}{2} \times \frac{1}{3} = \frac{1}{6}$$

$$\frac{6}{2} \times \frac{1}{3} = \frac{6}{6} = 1$$